An Introduction to
Stylistics

URSZULA CLARK

Investigating English Language

STANLEY THORNES (PUBLISHERS) LTD

First published in 1996 by:
Stanley Thornes (Publishers) Ltd
Delta Place
27 Bath Road
Cheltenham GL53 7TH
United Kingdom

01 02 03 04 / 10 9 8 7 6

A catalogue record for this book is available from the British Library.

ISBN 0–7487–2579–2

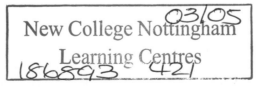
Typeset by Tech-Set, Gateshead, Tyne and Wear
Printed and bound in Great Britain by The Bath Press, Bath

CONTENTS

PART TWO:
RE-REPRESENTING TEXTS

Acknowledgements

I should like to thank the staff who teach English Language at A level at The Trinity School, Leamington Spa, and The Joseph Rowntree School, York.

The author and publishers wish to thank the following for permission to use copyright material:

Ronald Carter for an extract from Ronald Carter and Mike McCarthy, *Language as Discourse*, 1975. Copyright © FDA Consumer; The 'text frame' idea employed in Unit 8 pp 131–137 comes from Ronald Carter and Mike McCarthy, *Language as Discourse*, (Longman, 1994); Casarotto Ramsay Ltd on behalf of the author for material from Willy Russell, *Terraces*. Copyright © 1973 Willy Russell. All rights whatsoever in this play are strictly reserved and application for performance etc., must be made before rehearsal to Casarotto Ramsay Ltd., National House, 60–66 Wardour Street, London W1V 4ND. No performance may be given unless a licence has been obtained; CompuServe Magazine for material from Cathryn Conroy, *Getting the Idea Across to a Boss*, *CompuServe Magazine*, Feb. 1995; Gîtes de France for material from their holiday brochure; Faber and Faber Ltd for Ted Hughes, 'Snowdrop' from *Lupercal*; Gareth Grundy for material from his interview with Irvine Welsh, *Select Magazine*, Feb. 1996; Greek National Tourist Organisation for their advertisement; Prentice Hall Inc. for material from A. C. Bough and T. Cable, *A History of the English Language*, 3rd ed., 1978; HarperCollins Publishers for material from Shirley Price, *Practical Aromatherapy*, pp. 11–15, Thorsons Publishers, 1983; David Higham Associates Ltd on behalf of the author for Louis MacNeice, 'To Hedli' from *Collected Poems*; The Independent for material from Danny Penman and James Cusick, 'Police get tough in the battle of Brightlingsea', *The Independent*, 19.4.95; Lancaster University for material from their Postgraduate Prospectus 1994–95; Land Rover and Bates Dorland for material from a Land Rover advertisement; London Management on behalf of the author for material from Peter Shaffer, *Equus*; Macmillan General Books for material from Thomas Hardy, *Tess of the D'Urbervilles*; The National Magazine Company Ltd for Penny Rich, 'Personal Guide to Aromatherapy', *Good Housekeeping Magazine*, Aug. 1994. Copyright National Magazine Company; Oxford University Press for Anne Stevenson, 'Resurrection' from *Selected Poems 1956–1986*, 1987. Copyright © Anne Stevenson 1987; Pentel Stationery Ltd for material from an advertisement; Peters Fraser & Dunlop Group Ltd on behalf of the author for material from Ruth Inglis, *The Children's War*, HarperCollins, 1989; The Post Office for material from their Customer Charter; Random Century UK Ltd for material from Gill Martin, *Aromatherapy*, Vermilion, 1989, Arnold Wesker, *Roots* from *The Plays of Arnold Wesker* Vol. I, Jonathan Cape, and Mark Thompson, *A Paper House*, Hutchinson Radius, 1992; Reed Books for material from Angus Wilson, *Anglo-Saxon Attitudes*; Royal Academy of Arts for teachers' material from their *Monet in the '90s* information pack; Royal Society for the Prevention of Cruelty to Animals for material from an RSPCA leaflet; George T. Sassoon for Siegfried Sassoon, 'The Kiss'; The Society of Authors on behalf of the Estate of E. M. Forster and King's College, Cambridge for material from E. M. Forster, *A Passage to India*; Solo Syndication for material from a horoscope by Jonathan Cainer, *Daily Mail*, 16.12.95, and Chris Tarrant, 'Floating safari to the lake full of monsters', *The Mail on Sunday*, 2.4.95; Times Newspapers Ltd for material from Geordie Greig, 'President Clinton to be sued for sexual harassment', *The Sunday Times*, 1.5.94. Copyright © Times Newspapers Limited 1994; Slendertone Ltd for an Ultratone advertisement included in *Cosmopolitan*, Oct. 1995.

Hulton Deutsch Collection, for the photograph on page 142. John Feltwell/Garden & Wildlife Matters Photo Library, for the photographs on pages 151 and 152. Wigmore Publications for permission to reproduce artwork on page 166.

The cover picture is *Various Activities No. 1* by Jack Smith (b. 1928). Courtesy Bonhams, London/Bridgeman Art Library, London. Reproduced with permission of the artist.

Every effort has been made to trace all the copyright holders but if any have been inadvertently overlooked the publishers will be pleased to make the necessary arrangements at the first opportunity.

Introduction

This book is intended to introduce students to the linguistic analysis of written texts. As such, it presupposes little prior knowledge of either grammatical or linguistic terminology, or of their application to written text analysis. It is designed as a practical and accessible introduction to the various areas of linguistic analysis needed to produce a stylistic description of written language.

The book is not intended as either an introduction to linguistic theory or a grammar of the English language. An introduction to linguistic theory can be found in the accompanying volume to this book, *The Nature and Functions of Language* by Howard Jackson and Peter Stockwell. However, since many students studying language and linguistics will have little or no knowledge of basic grammatical concepts and their accompanying terminology, these are explained whenever they are used in this book. In other words, as much grammar is introduced and described as is needed by students studying English at an advanced level in order to undertake an analysis of written texts.

A further underlying principle of the book is that a textual rather than a grammatical approach to the analysis of written language is adopted throughout. Grammatical analysis tends to concentrate on describing and analysing units of language up to the level of a sentence, whereas textual analysis includes the description and analysis of units of language larger than a sentence which make up a text. It is this further analysis of text, as well as of sentences and words, that characterises stylistic analysis.

Each unit illustrates the points it makes with examples taken from actual, rather than invented, written texts and includes practice activities for students to do themselves. The texts used in both the examples and the practice activities are taken from a wide range of written material. This material is not divided into categories, such as those traditionally described as literary and non-literary. Accompanying explanations of linguistic features are similarly applied to a variety of types of text, rather than associating particular kinds of language with a particular type of text.

The book is not primarily designed to be read on its own, unit by unit, although it is possible to use it as such. It is intended as a resource for teachers and students alike, which can be used at various times during a course either as set course reading or as the need arises. Most of the units which make up Part 1 of the book can be worked through independently. Part 2 of the book can be used as a self-contained unit at any time, although references are made in the units within it to the points covered in Part 1.

Part 1 deals specifically with the description and analysis of written language, within a textual framework. It takes a stylistic approach to the study of written texts: that is, it looks at texts from the perspective of their style and at the relationship between style, content and form. After the introductory unit, two units cover the terms associated with sentence grammar. Unit 4 considers aspects of description and analysis at text level, while the two subsequent units consider different styles of writing. The final unit of Part 1, Unit 7, considers aspects of language change in writing and introduces a framework for analysing texts written in earlier times. The examples used in all the units to illustrate the points made are taken from actual written texts and each unit contains activities for students to undertake in groups or on their own.

Part 2 concentrates on developing students' ability to write their own texts, specifically those based on a range of pre-selected material and written for a specific audience and purpose. It focuses on the processes and skills required to transform a variety of texts, derived from various sources, into a new, coherent text. Unit 8 looks at ways in which writing on a particular topic can be changed into a different format and style for a specific target audience. The final unit, Unit 9, consists entirely of practice activities.

Appendix 1 at the end of the book provides answers to selected activities in Part 1 of the book, while Appendix 3 contains examples of marked answers written for part of the stylistics section in an NEAB English Language examination paper.

Principles and Practice of Textual Analysis

1 Categorising written language

1.0 Introduction
1.1 Categorising written language: where to start?
1.2 Analysing and describing individual texts
1.3 Register

1.0 Introduction

We are used to reading different types of written text every day, so much so that we probably take many of the forms of writing we encounter for granted. Over the years, you will have learnt to recognise the many and varied ways a text has of signalling what *kind* of text it is – for example, a novel, a newspaper or a magazine – often before you have read a single word of it. Each of these different kinds of text may also contain further varieties of text within it: a novel may include poems and letters, a newspaper may have comic strips, cartoons, adverts and poems as well as news items, and a magazine may contain letters, poems, adverts and problem pages as well as feature articles. Each of these different kinds of text has its own distinguishing features, which help us to identify it as a particular type or kind.

Studying the ways in which language is used in different types of writing means just that: looking at the very things we have learnt to take for granted. It involves considering how language is patterned and structured within written texts and the relationship between that structure, its content and its purpose in conveying its message.

Anything that is written takes the form of a **text** of some kind, written with a particular **purpose** in mind and within a particular **context.** Shopping lists, notes passed round the classroom, diary entries and letters to friends are all examples of texts, as are published novels, poems and newspaper items. The writer of each one will have been motivated by a different purpose, be it to entertain, inform, instruct or persuade. The degree of shared knowledge of the context between the writer and the intended audience will also have some bearing on what is written. In a note passed between two friends, certain information will probably be taken for granted and will not need to be explained, whereas in a text where the distance between writer and audience is greater, as in a novel, there will probably be a greater degree of explanation. The context will also determine the degree of formality or the language register (see 1.3 below) in which the text is written. Certain ideas will also be taken for granted and so not fully explained in virtually any text, especially those ideas which relate to the cultural and social background against which the writing takes place.

Approaching the study and analysis of the stylistic elements of written language involves bringing together the grammatical structures of language and the meanings of words within a textual framework. However, language study has not always been approached in this way. In the past, the study of the written structures of the English language developed separately from the study of words and their meanings, as well as ignoring the social dimensions of writing. In recent years, the study of language has begun to bring these different dimensions together.

The study of language structures and patterns has traditionally been called **grammar**. The study of grammar was divided into two categories: **syntax** and **morphology**. Syntax explained how words combined to make a sentence: it is mainly with this particular area of study that the word 'grammar' is associated. Morphology explained how parts of words combined with one another, using units known as **morphemes** (e.g. adding an 's' to form a plural: see 1.2.3 below). Grammar books generally dealt with explaining 'rules' of syntax and morphology, without paying much attention to the meaning of the words and sentences themselves.

The study of vocabulary was divided into two categories, **lexis** and **semantics**. Lexis is the Greek for 'word', and describes all the individual words in a particular language, sometimes called **lexical items**. Semantics explains the meaning or meanings of words themselves. Dictionaries generally form a collection of lexis or lexical items and their associated meanings. The following diagram represents the traditional relationship between these different aspects of language study and the texts which describe them.

More recently, linguists have become much more concerned with how the grammatical forms of syntax and morphology connect with lexis and semantics, so that the term **grammar** describes not only how words link together to form sentences, but also the meanings of the words themselves. In modern grammar systems, grammar covers both syntax and morphology as before, but also incorporates the study of semantics alongside syntax, so that:

grammar = syntax + semantics (including morphology and lexis)

Modern linguistics has shown that, far from being a transparent medium through which information is given, language itself forms an important part of the message being conveyed. Studying the grammar of a written text in this way involves not only identifying patterns of words in sentences, but also examining how these patterns and the meanings of the words within them combine to convey a message: in other words, to 'see through' the language to discover its actual meaning, which may or may not be the same as its surface or intended meaning. This sort of grammar is called **functional grammar**, since it aims to describe how language is actually used, rather than making language fit 'rules'. This is what traditional, prescriptive grammar aimed to do, with all sorts of regulations about what you could and could not do with language.

Another difference with such an approach is that whereas the traditional units of grammar were words and sentences, modern, functional grammar extends beyond the sentence to the text itself. Thus, it describes not only the grammar of words and sentences, but also that of texts. All the units in this book adopt a functional approach to describing and analysing written language, aiming to describe the interrelationship between words, sentences and text to discover how they construct their message.

1.1 Categorising written language: where to start?

You have a piece of writing in front of you. How can you tell what *kind* of writing it is? Take stories, for example. We are probably more familiar with stories than with any other type of writing, and you can probably easily recognise a story when you see one, but *how* do you do this? Is it simply a matter of layout: that is, how it is printed on the page? What is it about the text that tells us that it is a story? Are all novels and short stories examples of stories? In which case, is it true that if a piece of writing tells a story it has to be either a short story or a novel and nothing else?

The following activity invites you to consider the answers to these questions.

ACTIVITY 1.1

1 Individually or in pairs, compile two lists of texts. In the first, list texts which you think contain a story, and in the second list texts which you think do not. You could do this as a table. Two examples are given below to start you off.

Texts which contain a story	Texts which do not contain a story
a novel, e.g. *Gone with the Wind*	a driving licence

2 **a** Compare your lists with those of your partner or another pair. Are the lists the same, or different?

 b How do you account for any differences?

3 In pairs or as a group, compile lists of features that helped you to decide which column to put each type of text into. The lists have been started for you below.

Texts that tell a story
- Describe events or happenings
- These happen in a sequence

Texts that do not tell a story
- Describe facts or states
- Facts can be given in a particular order rather than sequence

Doing this activity should make you aware that different types of writing usually have distinctive features, but that very different kinds of writing can share common characteristics. Because of this, it is very difficult – some would say impossible – to list the definitive features of a particular kind of text. For example, you could say that novels are texts that tell a story. Does that mean, then, that newspaper and magazine articles that tell stories are also examples of novels? Or that if a novel contains a letter or poem it is no longer a novel? Clearly not. It is evident that whilst a particular form of writing, such as a poem, has certain distinctive characteristics, any of these may also be used in different forms of writing in a different combination. Rather than concentrating on defining the characteristics of particular kinds of text, therefore, this book considers the ways in which different texts *use* particular features and their effect.

Another way of identifying the type of text you are reading could be by the conventions of its visual layout: for example, a novel is usually a certain size and thickness, with a front and back cover, and with the text within it running from left to right across each page with indentations for paragraphs and speech. An application form usually has blank spaces for you to fill in; a newspaper comes written in columns broken up by photographs, headlines and adverts. The page layout by itself, however, doesn't produce meaning, since you could in theory take one type of text, such as a poem, and write it out again as a piece of prose or an insurance policy, or package it as a novel. Nevertheless, although it is quite clear that conventions can be altered or changed, texts generally conform to the layout normally associated with their particular type, unless they wish to make some special effect.

Everything else being equal, closer reading of a text will usually confirm your initial response as to the particular type of writing you are reading. This closer reading will usually include taking in such things as the content, the vocabulary, the sentence structure and the ways in which words are used in sentences. Knowing what kind of text you are reading involves you in picking up a whole variety of signals with which you have become familiar. Even though it may be difficult or impossible to list a set of characteristics which appear only in a particular type of text, a given text type will generally have enough defining features, both of visual layout and of style, to make it possible to recognise it as a poem, a leaflet, a textbook, a magazine or whatever.

To go back to the example in Activity 1.1, it is clear that working out what counts as a story and what type of text is associated with telling a story is not as straightforward as you might have thought at first. The first list you made for question 3 probably looked something like this:

A story usually has:

happenings or *events*
a *sequence* of events

a relationship of *cause* and *effect* between the events
characters (usually human)
patterning between characters and events
a particular *point of view* (or several), from which the events are told
a *narrative voice*
an *opening*, where something happens which starts off a sequence of
connected events
a *closure*, where something happens to bring the sequence of events to a close,
often bringing with it a restoration of order.

Does this mean, then, that for a text to count as a story it has to have all of these features? The following activity asks you to consider the idea of a story further.

ACTIVITY 1.2

1 Individually or in pairs, take each text you have listed in the table for Activity 1.1, and note which of the features above are present within it. Make a note of what leads to your decisions (e.g. why you think *Gone with the Wind* has an opening, etc.). Also record any problems you encounter in deciding whether any text has a particular feature.

2 a Do all the texts you intuitively classified as telling stories include all the elements of the definition listed above?

   b Do all the texts you intuitively classified as not telling stories have none of the elements of the definition?

From this activity, you should see that it is not as easy as you might first have thought to decide what kind of writing a particular text is. For example, there is a 'story' in a driving licence, especially if it has penalty points, or in a passport, particularly if it is covered with entrance and exit visas. With texts such as these, though, you have to use inference – guesswork – to discover the story.

Although we can generalise about patterns of language and their characteristics, and write abstract sets of lists or principles about particular kinds of texts, these can never be completely fixed. Features of different kinds of writing may overlap, as in the concept of a story, or patterns may be broken and new ones formed. Even a single identifiable kind of writing, such as fiction, usually associated with novels, may have further distinct variations within it, such as science fiction, detective fiction, thrillers, romance fiction or gothic fiction. Letters form another seemingly distinct category of writing, but within it there is a variety of different kinds of letter, such as business or personal, formal or informal.

However, even though it may not be possible to define every different kind of text, nevertheless the fact that we recognise them as being different points to them having certain distinguishing characteristics. These can provide a broad framework for analysis. They also help us to begin to divide texts into groups with similar characteristics. These categories are as follows:

fiction or *fact*
narrative or *non-narrative*
chronological or *non-chronological*

You may also come across the categories *literary* and *non-literary*.

1.1.1 Fiction and fact

One way of describing texts is to divide them into those which describe imaginary events or happenings, called **fiction**, and those which describe actual events or happenings, called fact, or **non-fiction**. Unlike the term 'literary' (see 1.1.4 below), the term 'fiction' has no associations with 'worth' or being 'good'. Under the category of fiction would come all novels, short stories, poems, stage play scripts, television and radio drama scripts and film scripts. Non-fiction would include texts such as news articles, adverts, letters, documentaries, travel writing and biography.

The categories, though, are not as clear cut as they may first appear to be. Drama–documentaries, for example, imaginatively re-create real events, as may some biographies or autobiographies. Creating fiction out of facts is called **factional** writing. News reports may also select events and quotations which are true but which stress one particular point of view over another, resulting in a biased presentation of actual events (see 5.3 and 6.2).

1.1.2 Narrative and non-narrative

Texts which tell a story, in the traditional sense of recounting a plot with events that happened over a period of time, in space and involving characters, in the way described above, can also be called **narrative**, while any other kind is **non-narrative**. This may seem similar to the distinction between fiction and non-fiction, and in many ways it is, but there are stories in real life as well as in fiction.

Narrative texts usually have a plot with a definite beginning and end. The beginning starts a series of events connected with the plot, which the ending brings to a close. Often this ending sees a return to order. Narrative involves characters, and the story is told from a particular point of view; like fiction, it generally incorporates the elements of a story listed above. Under this definition, films as well as novels can be classified as narratives. Certain kinds of factual writing, such as autobiography or biography and drama–documentary, are also narratives.

Texts traditionally classified as non-narrative, however, may use a narrative form. Adverts are a good example of this. Sometimes, adverts interweave a story containing all the classic elements of a narrative – plot, action and characters – with information about the product. A television advert for a particular brand of coffee did just this, telling a boy-meets-girl story with a plot that continued over a series of adverts.

Non-narrative texts do not have a plot in the same way as narrative writing. They refer to states of things rather than to series of events. Examples might be instructions and legal documents.

1.1.3 Chronological and non-chronological

A further classification of texts can be made on the basis of whether their writing is **chronological** or **non-chronological**. These terms describe different ways of ordering content within texts.

Chronological writing, as the term implies, is to do with time, and describes writing whose order and sequence is dependent on time. In chronological writing, events follow one another forwards – or backwards – through time. Time connects the events to one another, so that their sequence depends to a great extent on what has happened before. This in turn determines what is happening now and in the future. Novels, for example, as well as short stories and plays, are usually examples of chronological writing, although not always. Chronological writing is often associated with narrative, since they both share the common feature of being linked to time. Non-narrative texts, however, can also be chronological. Reports of science experiments and cookery recipes, for example, follow a chronological sequence of events, recorded in a particular time-dependent order.

Non-chronological texts are those which are not dependent upon time for the ordering of their content. Instead, a different ordering principle applies, for instance alphabetical order in encyclopaedia entries, telephone books and address lists. How content in non-chronological texts is ordered depends on an entirely different set of conventions, within which various options are available to the writer. Even history books, for example, may be ordered according to the themes of a period: they are not themselves dependent on time, although they are describing events which happened in time. Poems may be either chronological or non-chronological, depending upon what they are about. A ballad, for example, which tells a story, would be classed as chronological, whereas a poem which describes a state, such as Burns' *My Love is like a Red Red Rose*, would be classed as non-chronological.

1.1.4 Literary and non-literary

Literary texts are usually defined as those which have been written for an artistic purpose, to give pleasure or to provoke thought. They tend to deal with thoughts and emotions which make the text 'worthy' in some way, as well as, or instead of, characters and events. Deciding whether a text is literary or non-literary, therefore, is a matter of judgement which relates more closely to the message of a piece of writing than to whether it describes real or imaginary events.

Until fairly recently, the study of literature was mainly concerned with explaining why some texts were more 'worthy' of study than others, and with making sure that their worth was interpreted in a particular way. The texts chosen for study made up what is called a literary 'canon', where those included were deemed worthy of study and by implication those not included were 'unworthy'.

This canon included novels by established writers such as Jane Austen, the Brontë sisters, George Eliot, Charles Dickens and William Thackeray; poems by poets such as Dryden, Shelley, Keats, Wordsworth, Tennyson, Browning and T.S. Eliot; plays by playwrights such as William Shakespeare, Ben Jonson, Sheridan, Oscar Wilde and Arthur Miller. It also included writing which has survived from Old and Middle English, such as *Pearl* and Chaucer's *The Canterbury Tales*, non-fiction such as diaries and letters, including Samuel Pepys' diary, and historical and philosophical writing, such as that of Francis Bacon and Edmund Burke.

The decision as to whether a text merits the label of 'literary' or not is largely a cultural one, and as such is influenced by social changes, which may challenge an established position. For example, feminists have questioned the inclusion of a disproportionate number of male writers, who are generally also white and dead. Similarly, the existence of English-speaking communities outside the British Isles has broadened the range of writing in English: newer works have backgrounds in widely different geographical locations and lifestyles. As literacy has become established amongst sections of society which hitherto did not have access to it, such as males from a working-class background and women from most classes, and as both men and women have become more highly educated, so writing is beginning to reflect the ideas and concerns of a much wider cross-section of society than ever before. All these various changes in modern life have challenged a single concept of 'literariness'. For these reasons, categorising texts as non-literary or literary is not a useful distinction.

Another claim made for 'literary' writing has been that its use of language is somehow special, and that its surface meaning hides a deeper, less obvious meaning. But texts recognised as 'literary' are not the only ones that do this: analysis of a diverse range of texts, such as political speeches, newspaper articles and television reports, not usually recognised for their literariness, can also reveal meanings below the surface. Similarly, the use of devices such as metaphor and simile, most often associated with literature, occurs in every type of text, not just in literary texts.

That 'literary' language is different from other kinds is not really in dispute. It generally displays a particular style of narrative patterning and an interaction between a variety of linguistic levels, producing a more complex message and a more intellectually demanding experience for the reader. Its difference lies, however, in its 'function', rather than its 'worth'. In other words, it should be judged on whether it succeeds in achieving what it set out to do: to give pleasure, to provoke thought or to achieve an artistic effect.

The means of approaching the study of written texts adopted by this book is to think in terms of **text** and **textuality** rather than literature and literariness. Such an approach involves analysing the way a text is constructed from language, including coherence (see 4.2 below), and the degree to which the writer makes language an issue in itself rather than just a tool. Evaluating the quality or worth of a text would then depend on its success in conveying its particular message.

1.1.5 Conclusion

Whether a piece of writing can be classed as narrative or non-narrative, fiction or non-fiction, chronological or non-chronological depends largely upon the way in which an individual text, such as a novel, advert, letter or poem, is written, rather than being a defining characteristic of the form itself. It is true that a novel, for example, is more likely to be fictional, narrative and chronological and an information leaflet non-fiction, non-narrative and non-chronological, but it does not *have* to be.

ACTIVITY 1.3

In pairs, read through the following extracts, then do these activities.

1 Write down the kind of text you think each one is taken from (e.g. extract 1 is an example of a horoscope).

2 Categorise each one according to whether you think it is fiction or non-fiction, narrative or non-narrative, chronological or non-chronological. Remember that each text should end up with three categories (e.g. extract 1 is non-fiction, narrative and chronological).

3 Discuss which particular features of the language led you to make your decisions (e.g. layout, vocabulary, length of sentences).

4 Did every extract conform to your initial expectation of its text type? If not, why not?

1 *Aquarius (Jan 21–Feb 19)*
The planets seem keen to make you an early Christmas present. Expect not so much a material gift as a psychological boost. You are understandably worried about the precarious nature of a certain arrangement. You sorely want to hear or see something that will put your mind at rest about this matter. Soon, you will get, at the very least, the reassurance you seek, and possibly quite a bit more.

Daily Mail, 16 December 1995

2   *To Hedli*

       Because the velvet image,
       Because the lilting measure,
       No more convey my meaning
       I am compelled to use
       Such words as disabuse
       My mind of casual pleasure
       And turn it towards a centre –
       A zone which others too
       And you
       May choose to enter.

Louis MacNeice

3 *Handling Ponies*
Understanding of, and sympathy with, a horse's mentality, is essential to success. A horse is very much a creature of habit and favours the same thing being done in the same way every day. Picking out feet, for example, is much more easily accomplished if carried out in the same rotation each time it is done.

The Manual of Horsemanship. British Horse Society, 1961

4 *Dear Madam*
Re: VEHICLE REGISTRATION MARK XXXX XXX
Thank you for your letter concerning the unlicensed use/keeping of the above-numbered vehicle on 7 May 1994. Its contents have been noted.
It is an offence under section 8 of the Vehicles (Excise) Act 1971, which on conviction carries a maximum penalty of £1000.00 or five times the annual rate of duty, whichever is the greater. Payment of the duty after the offence does not absolve you from liability to penalty.
In view of your explanation the Department has decided to offer a reduced penalty of £26.00.

5 *To John Hamilton Reynolds*
Sunday 3 May 1818
…I will return to Wordsworth – whether or no he has an extended vision or a circumscribed grandeur – whether he is an eagle in his nest, or on the wing – And to be more explicit and to show you how tall I stand by the giant, I will put down a simile of human life as far as I now perceive it; that is, to the point to which I say we both have arrived at – Well – I compare life to a large Mansion of Many Apartments…

John Keats

6

"'Save yourselves,' I cried. But no one listened.

Then midnight struck and the virus was unleashed.

People moaned and prayed in every house in the village... but too late.

Without protection,

you're scuppered when a virus sneaks into your hard drive."

IBM's labs have a massive collection of computer viruses, all being dissected under tight lock and key.

This research has led to IBM AntiVirus, one of the most powerful security programs available on the market today.

We're also developing an antidote that simulates the human immune system.

When a virus invades, computers will be able to meet and neutralise the attack.

It may not save lives. It'll definitely save data.

Protect yourself. Call XXXX

Solutions for a small planet

7   *'Hebe,' the old man called.*
    'Yes?'
    'Take these letters to the post for me.' He had sat in his room writing his letters as if
    nothing untoward was happening, filling in his time usefully while waiting for the
    arrival of his elder granddaughters and their husbands. With a flip of his hand he
    indicated the pile of letters. Hebe took them. She did not look up.

                                             Mary Wesley: Harnessing Peacocks

1.2 Analysing and describing individual texts

As pointed out in 1.1. above, the study of a particular language such as English has traditionally worked on the principle of studying a hierarchy of units, where the largest unit is a sentence. These units are:

morpheme
word
phrase
clause
sentence

A modern, functional grammar system includes all these units, but rather than studying each one individually and in isolation it also takes account of how they relate to one another. As a result, a further unit is frequently added to the list, that of **text**.

In modern, functional grammar, the units of language listed above have been replaced by three distinct, though related, levels of language: **text**, **sentence** and **word**. The descriptions of each level, and of sub-sections within them, are based on considerations of how language itself is actually used. To a certain extent, how we use language is determined by convention rather than by strict rules. This allows for flexibility and change within each category and between categories, as well as uniformity. Categorising language in this way has been likened to biological classification, which describes broad, flexible categories whilst recognising that there may be both exceptions to them and the possibility of crossover between categories.

1.2.1 Text

One important way in which functional grammar differs from more traditional grammar is in its recognition that texts, as well as sentences and words, have distinct, recognisable patterns or features. Furthermore, these patterns interrelate with the content and vocabulary of the sentences that make up the text.

Visual Layout

What a text looks like on the page can provide us with a lot of information about what sort of text we are looking at, before we have read any of its words. How a text is laid out, or its design, is usually closely connected with its purpose and its intended audience. A comic strip, for example, is instantly recognisable by its distinctive layout, as is a newspaper article; there is a limited number of texts where we would expect such a layout to appear. The size of the print, together with other considerations such as use of colour, will generally depend upon who the writing is intended for. Comic strips intended for young children are made much larger than those intended for adults, quite apart from the choice of vocabulary and subject matter.

Other aspects of layout include the use of conventions such as headings or headlines, sub-headings and numbered points. We expect certain kinds of writing, such as textbooks and magazine articles, to make use of such conventions in displaying their content, and others, such as novels and plays, not to use them.

Similarly, we expect some texts to use diagrams, tables, photographs, graphs and maps. Texts such as atlases, instructions and art or cookery books would be likely to do so, whereas poems and letters might not.

Thematic structure

The primary intention of any text is first and foremost to communicate something, though the complexity of what is being communicated will vary a great deal. A shopping list, for example, is a straightforward list designed to jog the memory, whilst the report of a scientific research project may be extremely complex. Nevertheless, however simple or complicated, the content of a text must be organised in such a way that its main message is conveyed clearly and coherently if it is to succeed in putting this message across.

This organisation usually relates to the overall **metatheme** of the writing, that is, what it is about, which provides a **thematic structure** enabling the writer to pursue different directions without losing the reader. For example, a shopping list may refer to items that need to be purchased at different shops grouped by shop rather than alphabetically or as they occurred to you when writing them down, whilst a scientific research report would be organised into different related sections and sub-sections.

In a narrative, this framework can be used to create tension and interest within the plot and between the theme or themes.

Paragraphs

Visually, the division of a text into paragraphs is part of the text's layout, with markers such as indentation and spaces between one paragraph and the next, but paragraphs also break up the content of a text into more manageable 'chunks'. However, simply starting a new line is not enough to make a paragraph: a paragraph's content will be part of the overall thematic structure. A new paragraph indicates a change of direction of some kind, usually linked to what has just gone before in the case of an academic essay, or continuing an earlier theme begun in a novel.

There is in theory no limit to how long a paragraph can be, and it can be as short as a sentence or one word. What determines where one paragraph ends and another starts is the direction that the content of the text is taking.

ACTIVITY 1.4

Read the two extracts below. For each one answer these questions.

1 Re-write the text into paragraphs, or indicate where it would break into paragraphs.

2 Compare your suggestions with one another.

3 For each break you suggest, say why you made it where you did.

4 **a** What is each extract's metatheme?

   b Can you draw a diagram of the text's thematic structure?

5 What kind of texts are the extracts taken from? Which particular features of the writing led you to your answer?

---

1 *The biggest hurdle you're likely to face as a telecommuter is persuading your boss to let you try it. 'Even managers who are supportive of the concept in their heads have butterflies in their stomachs,' quips Gil Gordon, a telecommuting consultant with Gil Gordon Associates in Monmouth, New Jersey. Gordon and Nick Sullivan, the telecommuting senior editor of Home Office Computing magazine, offer these tips to telecommuting wannabes when negotiating with the boss: Look at telecommuting from your boss's perspective. How will a telecommuting schedule help your company and your supervisor? Perhaps telecommuting will help you to do better-quality work, shift your hours to provide improved service for your company's customers, or help you stay in a job you might otherwise have to leave. Sell your boss on quantity and quality. You'll get more and better work accomplished from home. Define your goals. Write a formal proposal that includes detailed information on your telecommuting schedule, how you will accomplish the work, and anticipated expenses. Devise a foolproof way to stay in touch with the office. Send daily e-mail and fax messages to keep the office updated on your work progress. Encourage your colleagues to call you at home, and be available to them when they do. Begin telecommuting with a modest request, such as working from home one day a week for a month. That's a trial period of just four days with minimal risk. Or, suggest an initial telecommuting period in order to complete a special project or report. Once the trial is successful, gradually expand the time you telecommute. The boss may counter all your good arguments with: 'If you telecommute, everyone will want to. And we can't have that.' The fact is, not everyone will want to telecommute, not everyone's job is suited to it, and not everyone has the self-discipline and independence to work from home.*

Getting the Idea Across to a Boss. Compuserve Magazine, February 1995

---

2 *I had scarcely crossed the hall and gained the corridor, when Mdlle Reuter came again upon me. 'Step in here a moment,' said she, and she held open the door of the side-room from whence she had issued on my arrival; it was a* salle-à-manger, *as appeared from the* buffet *and the* armoire vitrée, *filled with glass and china, which formed part of its furniture. Ere she had closed the door on me and herself, the corridor was already filled with day-pupils, tearing down their cloaks, bonnets and cabas from the wooden pegs on which they were suspended; the shrill voice of a* maitresse *was heard at intervals vainly endeavouring to enforce some kind of order; vainly, I say: discipline there was none in these rough ranks, and yet it was considered one of the best-conducted schools in Brussels. 'Well, you have given your first lesson,' began Mdlle Reuter in the most calm, equable voice, as though quite unconscious of the chaos from which we were separated only by a single wall. 'Were you satisfied with your pupils, or did any*

circumstance in their conduct give you cause for complaint? Conceal nothing from me, repose in me entire confidence.'

Charlotte Brontë: The Professor. Penguin

Cohesion and coherence

Essentially, these terms describe ways in which writers link their subject matter within and between sentences in a text to make it coherent. Sections 4.1 and 4.2 below explain in more detail ways in which this is done.

1.2.2 Sentence

All texts are made up of sentences. A text can be as short as one sentence, as in an advertising slogan on a street hoarding ('Go to work on an egg', 'Beanz meanz Heinz'), or may consist of thousands of sentences, such as the Bible or the *Encyclopaedia Britannica*. Similarly, there is no limit to the number of words there may be in a sentence, as long as its sense is maintained. A sentence can have as few as one word (*Shoot! Stop!*), or it may have tens and hundreds, as in legal documents or a novel such as James Joyce's *Ulysses*.

In a language such as English, word order is very important for a group of words to make sense as a sentence. For example, the words

saw round bridge corner the a I

do not make sense when placed in this particular order. Placed in a different order, they do:

I saw a bridge round the corner

If we take each word individually, it becomes clear that some of the words may have different meanings, depending on the context in which they are used. For example, the word 'saw' by itself could mean either the past tense of the verb *see*, or the noun used to describe a tool used for cutting. 'Bridge' could mean a structure for crossing a road, river or railway, or a game of cards, again depending on the context in which it was used, or it could be part of the verb *to bridge*. With the words *I*, *a* and *the*, there is not the same problem with meaning, but we would usually expect these words to accompany at least one other word, and would not expect to find them used on their own.

The ways in which words are organised into sentences and the terminology associated with the description of sentences occupy most of Units 2 and 3 of this book.

1.2.3 Word

Graphology

The marks on a page which we read as words, punctuation, tables, graphs, maps and so on are called **graphic** elements. They make up different aspects of **graphology**, just as the raw materials of speech are known as phonemes and the study of the speech of a particular language is phonology. The graphology of a text includes the use of punctuation markers such as full stops, commas, capital letters and speech marks, as well as other visual aspects of the text. Punctuation marks the divisions between parts of sentences and between sentences themselves. These divisions are linked to the organisation of the sentence. Just as a sentence isn't just a string of words in any order, so, too, a capital letter and full stop do not by themselves demarcate a sentence, but are linked to the syntax of the sentence.

The visual appearance of the words themselves is known as **typography**. Features of typography include the print size, the font or typeface used, and the use of columns, dashes, underlining and bold or italic type.

Morphology

Words are made up of segments called **morphemes**. Some words are composed of a single morpheme, such as *single, word, marry, eat, gone*. Many words, though, are made up of more than one morpheme, or have morphemes added according to how they are used in syntax. Many nouns, for example, may have more than one morpheme, whilst verbs will change their shape according to how they are used.

For example, in English we usually turn a single word into a plural by adding an 's': e.g. *table, tables; son, sons; daughter, daughters*.

However, because of the different influences that have gone into making the English we use today, this rule doesn't always apply and there are other variations. For example, words which end in a 'y' usually replace the 'y' with *-ies*: e.g. *baby, babies; country, countries*.

Another reason for variations is that the English spelling system is not a phonetic one; that is, words are not always spelt as they sound, as they are in other European languages, such as Italian or German. English is semi-phonetic, with some words spelt as they sound and others not. The reasons for this are varied, and relate to the way in which English has developed historically.

Morphemes can be added after words, where they are known as **suffixes**, and before words, where they are known as **prefixes**, with some words having both:

> *im-possible   possib-ility   im-possib-ility*

Common prefixes are *un-, im-* and *re-*, as in *un-repentant, im-polite* and *re-turn*. Common suffixes are *-able, -ing* and *-ly*, as in *love-able, rain-ing* and *loud-ly*.

Tense and participle   These particular aspects of words are to do with verbs, and are explained in Units 2 and 3.

Very briefly, **verbs** describe an action. They have what is called a root, stem or infinitive, which alters according to the **tense** in which the verb is used. There are two main tenses in English, the present and the past, and the form the verb takes will be different in each case. For example, the present tense of the verb *to walk*, using the first person, would be *I walk*.

In the past tense, *walk* would have the morpheme *-ed* added to it to make *I walked*. *Walking* is called the **present participle**, and *walked* the **past participle**.

The different ways in which verbs are altered to create tenses is probably one of the most complex areas of English grammar. While this book aims to provide you with enough information to be able to describe their use and effect within most kinds of writing, it is by no means exhaustive.

Semantics

The grammatical ordering of words and sentences does not by itself produce meaning: the words combine to make semantic as well as grammatical sense. Unit 4, particularly Section 4.1, looks at the semantic properties of words in more detail, with especial regard to collocation and figures of speech.

1.3 Register

Finally, an important point to make is that, just as in speech there is a spectrum of speech styles ranging from formal to informal, so there is a range of different kinds of **register** in writing.

As a means of communication, the English printed writing system has a much shorter history (about 500 years) than speech itself (perhaps a million). The codification of speech into a written system has had a standardising effect on the written form, particularly its spelling and syntax. Although there are many dialect variations in spoken English, there is nothing like the same degree of variation within writing. Written standard English originates, for historical reasons, from the spoken dialect known as the East Midlands dialect, which has become known more widely as spoken standard English. Written standard English is generally characterised by the vocabulary to be found in dictionaries such as the Oxford English Dictionary (OED), and its grammar is the one that is described in grammar books and generally taught to non-native speakers of English.

Nevertheless, varying degrees of formality exist in writing as well as in speech. Contrary to a widely held belief, the grammar of written English operates in distinctly different as well as similar ways to that of speech, and writing is not just speech written down. Written standard English is not at all the same thing as spoken standard English.

Writing that is very formal tends to be that which is not meant to imitate natural spoken conversation in any way, such as an academic essay or a legal contract. These also require a fair degree of clarity and are less dependent on context than other forms. Less formal writing tends to imitate spoken natural speech more closely: examples would be articles in tabloid newspapers, plays, prose and adverts. Terms that are often used to describe informality in written language are **colloquial**, **non-standard** and **dialect**. However, they mean very different things.

1.3.1 Colloquial language

If you really want to hear all about it, the first thing you'll probably want to know is where I was born, and what my lousy childhood was like, and how my parents were occupied and all before they had me, and all that David Copperfield kind of crap, but I don't feel like going into it, if you want to know the truth.

In this opening sentence of J.D. Salinger's novel *The Catcher in the Rye*, the character Holden Caulfield 'speaks' without any regional or non-standard forms. However, the language is very casual and informal, and it is this casualness that identifies the speech as colloquial. Its use of contractions ('you'll for 'you will'), its string of loosely connected clauses, the interjection of personal evaluation such as 'lousy' and 'if you want to know the truth' and the use of a swear word, 'crap', with its social insult, all contribute to the character's rejection of the reader and his or her expectations. Its language is still within the forms of standard English, but its register is informal and casual.

1.3.2 Non-standard language

You don't know about me, without you have read a book by the name of 'The Adventures of Tom Sawyer' but that ain't no matter. That book was made by Mr. Mark Twain, and he told the truth, mainly. There was things which he stretched, but mainly he told the truth. That is nothing, I never seen anybody but lied, one time or another, without it was Aunt Polly, or the widow, or maybe Mary.

This extract, taken from *The Adventures of Huckleberry Finn* by Mark Twain, uses the same kind of colloquial features, for example contractions, as the character Holden Caulfield in *The Catcher in the Rye*. Huckleberry Finn, however, also uses common non-standard features of language, such as double negatives – 'that ain't no matter' – and a plural subject with a singular verb – 'There was things'. Even so, there is nothing distinctly regional to link Huck to a particular dialect, since the features which appear here are syntactic ones that are common to many dialects rather than belonging to any particular one.

1.3.3 Dialect

Well, they sure got a whole lotta coloured faces into that promo. He and Patricia ended up passin out one-dollar bills left and right to keep some of the brothers and sisters from clutterin up the set and ruinin everything.
'Yall gon play this flick over television?' one particularly obstreperous teenager come askin Crews just when we bout to do a take.
'That's correct,' Patricia answer, runin interference.
'I wasn't talkin to you, sister,' the little dude say, 'I was askin this white man that's actin like he is in charge.'
'I am in charge here,' Crews say. 'What can I do for you?'
'Yall comin down in the community, exploitin us to make this picture and we wanna know what's in it for us?'

This extract is taken from a novel by Al Young called *Their Eyes Were Sitting Pretty Watching God*. It has features of colloquialism such as contractions, as in the extract from *The Catcher in the Rye*, as well as non-standard features such as dropping 'g's from the ends of words. In addition to these syntactic differences, the extract uses lexis that is not part of standard English, which characterises it as a dialect, in this case Black English. The contraction of two words to make one ('Yall' for the colloquial 'you all') and the use of words such as 'dude' for a person and 'brothers and sisters' are all identifiable features of Black English.

It has been within literature – plays, poems and novels – that written non-standard forms have been most commonly used. Although writers of prose have long represented characters' actual speech in dialect – for example Emily Brontë in *Wuthering Heights* and Thomas Hardy in his Wessex novels – the narrative itself has generally followed the conventions of written standard English. Writing such as Al Young's and more recently Alice Walker's breaks the norms of standard written English in narrative as well as in represented speech. Indeed, changing attitudes towards literary writing have resulted in greater attention being paid to the use of non-standard forms such as Black English, which, it is thought, may eventually establish new norms of writing in their turn.

Whether or not this in fact happens, it is important to remember that 'getting the message right' in any text is more than simply using vocabulary and grammar in an appropriate way. It is also a question of writing in an appropriate style or register that best conveys the intended meaning. The reasons why particular conventions have come to be associated with particular kinds of writing are often more to do with reasons of history, as Unit 7 explores, than with fixed 'rules'.

ACTIVITY 1.5

1 In pairs, go back over each of the extracts in Activity 1.3.

2 For each extract, decide whether its register is formal, colloquial, non-standard or dialect, and list the reasons that led you to make your choice. For example, there may be differences in vocabulary and the length of sentences, and direct or impersonal address may be used.

3 Decide the audience for which each extract was primarily intended and try to relate it to the language style of the extract. Can you make any connections between them?

4 Compare your answers with those of other pairs.

Units 2 and 3 take a closer look at the patterns of standard English words and sentences, before we return to broader considerations of language in and across whole texts.

2 | What's in a sentence?

2.0 Introduction

This unit, together with Unit 3, moves further into the text to consider different sentence patterns. They look at the terminology associated with the syntactic analysis of sentences: the units which you may have heard called **parts of speech** but which in modern grammar tend to be called **word classes**. This unit considers combinations of words known as phrases and clauses, as well as sentences, while particular word classes are described in more detail in Unit 3. These two units are intended to provide a sufficiently full introduction to the main word classes to enable you to undertake your own stylistic analysis of the written text extracts in the first part of this book.

2.1 Word classes

A word class or part of speech is a collection of words which have certain characteristics in common. Where a word appears in a sentence determines how it functions grammatically and so which word class it belongs to. Words generally conform to particular word orders if they are to make sense as a sentence. As was discussed in 1.2.2, a string of randomly selected words may not make sense, whereas in a different order they may. But to make sense the words have to be re-ordered in such a way that they make grammatical (that is, semantic as well as syntactic and morphological) sense, as the following activity shows.

ACTIVITY 2.1
1 Divide into groups of four or five. Ask each member of the group to say a word, and write it down.
2 Do these words make a sentence? Why not?
3 Can they be re-ordered to make a sentence? Why or why not?

4 Can the following words be re-ordered to make sense?
   a goes bought town maybe I to and hospital now
   b justification experience arguments the from of
   c Hamlet information the and long interaction opening of short is on on
   d Manchester at the on north road be city and countryside
   e journey the catch car people in sometimes under grass

It is worth remembering that it is not the number of words used that makes a sentence. A single word, such as 'Fire!', is a sentence, consisting of one clause made up of one phrase made up of one word. Although most sentences contain several words, usually grouped into smaller units of clauses, phrases and words, it is the way in which the words are used that makes them into a sentence, not their number.

Each word that is used in a sentence can be classified according to the word class to which it belongs. The most common **word classes** are:

noun
adjective
verb
adverb
determiner
pronoun
preposition
conjunction

2.1.1 Nouns

Words which tell us which people or things are being talked or written about are called **nouns**. Nouns are sometimes defined as 'naming words'. They are a very large class of words which can be divided into different categories. (See 2.2 below and Unit 3 for more on nouns.)

Some examples of nouns are: *eggs, woman, boy, girls, horse, Lucy, Warwick, Woolworths, shops,* etc.

Nouns can be compound, with two words functioning as one noun, e.g. *handbag, textbook, hod-carrier.*

2.1.2 Adjectives

Words which give more information about something or someone than is already given by the noun are called **adjectives**. They usually appear before the noun they are describing. Like nouns, adjectives are a large class of words.

Some examples of adjectives are: *large, small, funny, anxious, green, big, little,* etc.

Adjectives, like nouns, can be compound, that is two adjectives which together function as one, e.g. *bright blue,* or complex, that is made up of an adverb followed by an adjective, e.g. *well known.*

Present and past participles of verbs (see 1.2.3 and 3.3) can also be used in an adjectival position: e.g. *screaming voice, glistening gold, broken ankle, fitted kitchen.*

As the last two examples show, adjectives usually give us more information about a noun; that is, they **modify** nouns, e.g. *cold water; dark, clear night.*

2.1.3 Verbs

Words which tell you what sort of action, event or state is being talked or written about are called **verbs**. You might also have heard these described as 'doing words'. Like nouns and adjectives, they are a very large class of words, which can be further sub-divided.

Some examples of verbs are: *go, see, sleep, feel, be, grow, walk, shine.*

Verbs have a base form, or **infinitive**, from which other forms are derived. For example, the infinitive *to run* becomes *I run, I am running, I ran, I will run.*

(See 2.4.1 below and Unit 3 for more about verbs.)

2.1.4 Adverbs

Words which give more information about a verb, in the same way as adjectives give more information about nouns, are called **adverbs**. It would be very unusual to see an adverb being used without a verb, whereas verbs can be used without adverbs.

An adverb may appear either after the verb or before it, where it may be separated from the verb by other words and where the emphasis is placed on the motion or action of the adverb, rather than that of the verb: e.g. she ran *quickly; slowly* he walked up the stairs; Linda said that she felt *better* today than she had done yesterday.

2.1.5 Determiners

Nouns are usually accompanied by a **determiner**, which tells you whether the noun is something specific or something more general; that is, a determiner **modifies** a noun.

A sub-category of determiners is known as the **article**. The word 'the', as in *the road* (that is, a particular road) is known as the **definite article**, whereas the word *a*, as in *a road* (that is, any road) is known as the **indefinite article**.

The articles *a* and *an* are the most common determiners. Whether *a* or *an* is used depends upon the spelling of the noun it accompanies. The difference between *a* as in *a ball* and *an* as in *an antelope* is that *antelope* begins with a vowel letter (a, e, i, o, u) and *ball* with a consonant (every other letter of the alphabet). An 'n' is put after the 'a' to avoid having two consecutive vowel sounds. Note that the vowel 'u' has moved to become associated with the consonant group of letters, and many words beginning with 'u' take the article *a*, as in *a unicorn*.

Other determiners are: *all, some, any, no; every, each, either, neither; one, several, enough, such; many, much, more, most.*

2.1.6 Pronouns

Words which stand in place of a noun instead of the noun being repeated are called **pronouns**. They too can be divided into different categories, although they are not such a large class of words as nouns (see Unit 3 for more information about this).

Some examples of pronouns are: *I, me, mine; we, us, ourselves, ours; you, yourself, yours; he, him, his; she, her, hers; it, its.*

2.1.7 Prepositions

Prepositions are relational words; that is, they are usually to do with time, sequence or the position of something.

Some examples of prepositions are: *up, on, in, through, after, of, since, despite*. (See 2.2 below for more about prepositions.)

2.1.8 Conjunctions

Words which join together clauses within a sentence are known as **conjunctions**, sometimes called connectives.

Some examples of conjunctions are: *and, because, although*. (See 2.3.2 below for more about conjunctions.)

2.1.9 Open and closed word classes

These eight main word classes can be further divided into two categories: **open** and **closed** word classes. The first four, noun, adjective, verb and adverb, are open word classes. This means that the number of words belonging to each class is not limited: words are constantly being added to each one and falling out of use. It is also possible for a word to belong to more than one of these four classes, e.g. I went for a *walk* (noun); She *walked* to college (verb); The sun *blazed* (verb); the *blazing* fire (adjective). Together, they form the largest part by far of the English lexicon, vastly outnumbering those belonging to the closed word classes. Note that although the majority of verbs are open-class words, a small number, called auxiliary verbs (see 3.3.1), form a closed class.

Determiner, pronoun, preposition and conjunction are closed word classes. This means that a limited number of words belong to each class, and it is not possible to add to them. They are used a great deal in the basic syntactic structures of sentences. It is not possible for a word belonging to one closed class to belong to another.

Open word classes	**Closed word classes**
adjective	determiner
noun	pronoun
verb	auxiliary verb
adverb	preposition
	conjunction

ACTIVITY 2.2

Each of the poems below has words missing from it.

1 The first poem is missing most of its determiners and prepositions. Copy the poem, filling in the missing words, and categorise each one according to its word class.

2 The second poem is missing its verbs. Copy the poem and fill them in.

3 Compare your work with that of the originals (Appendix 1). Are your versions very different from the originals? Which one is the closest? Why do you think this is?

4 Which of the two exercises was easier to do? Why? Did your choice of words alter the meaning of either poem in any way?

1   *The Garden of Love*

                            I went — — Garden — Love,
                            And saw what I had never seen:
                            — Chapel was built — — midst,
                            Where I used to play — — green.

                            And — gates — — Chapel were shut,
                            And 'Thou shalt not' writ — — door;
                            So I turned — — Garden — Love
                            That so many sweet flowers bore;

                            And I saw it was filled — graves,
                            And tomb-stones — flowers should be;
                            And Priests — black gowns were walking their rounds,
                            And binding — briers my joys and desires.
                                                   William Blake

2   *Snowdrop*

                          Now is the globe — tight
                          Round the mouse's — wintering heart.
                          Weasel and crow, as if — in brass,
                          — through an outer darkness
                          Not in their right minds,
                          With the other deaths. She, too, — her ends,
                          brutal as the stars of this month,
                          Her pale head heavy as metal.
                                                   Ted Hughes

2.1.10 The functions of words

You have seen that every word in a sentence can be categorised according to the word class to which it belongs. Usually, though, we tend to group words into larger units, known as **phrases**, and these larger units into what are known as **clauses**. Sentences can then be made up of any combination of phrases and clauses.

The fact that sentence patterns and structures follow conventions rather than strict rules is illustrated by the way in which newspapers in particular structure their headlines, using words in an unconventional way. The main purpose of a headline is to grasp a reader's attention, so that he or she will continue to read the article. Because of this, headlines tend to be pared down to the minimum number of words that can be used in a sentence and yet still make sense, leaving out closed word classes such as determiners and prepositions much in the same way as telegrams used to do. Headlines are usually no more than one sentence long, and to get all the information in writers of headlines may alter the grammatical functions of words. For example, they may reverse the normal word order, or change words commonly used as nouns into adjectives and vice versa. For example, take the following headline:

TEACHERS RISK SEX LESSON PROSECUTIONS

The way in which these words are organised does not conform to conventional sentence patterns (see 2.4 below). Their particular patterning, as well as their graphology, leads us to recognise that the clause is a newspaper headline.

As an ordinary sentence, it might be written as: 'Teachers risk prosecution if they give sex lessons to pupils.' There are no such things as 'sex lesson prosecutions'. The writer of the headline uses the compound noun 'sex lesson' (see 3.4 below) and puts it in an adjectival position to describe another noun, 'prosecution'. Forming a compound adjective like this is not in itself unusual, but this particular combination is not generally used in this way.

'Teachers risk prosecution' is not such an exciting headline as 'Teachers risk sex lesson prosecutions' or even 'Prostitutes risk sex lesson prosecutions', since teachers are not normally associated with activities that lead them to break the law as part of their job. The mention of sex adds a *risqué* element to the story, and we understand the phrase 'sex lesson' when it is used in this way.

Newspaper headlines have a syntax of their own, which we have come to accept, even though it works by 'breaking' more conventional syntactic patterns to form alternative ones.

Whatever a writer writes is drawn from an infinite range and variety of possibilities to do with the choice of word, the patterning of words into sentences and the arrangement of sentences into texts to create a particular meaning for a reader to share. Usually, what is written will also be influenced by the overall style of a particular text type, but even so any writer has a vast range of language upon which he or she can draw to achieve particular effects, which usually exploit our shared understanding of the world within which we live.

The following activity explores this further.

ACTIVITY 2.3

1 In pairs, discuss the text type you would expect the following heading to be taken from: 'M.P. involved in cover up.'

2 What would you expect the writing to be about?

3 Now read the text.

4 **a** Compare your reaction to the text with the one you anticipated above.
   b Which particular features of the headline are exploited in the text?

5 What comments can you make about the use of words in this text (e.g. the use of the word *you*)?

6 Share your ideas with the rest of the class.

7 Playing with words, as this text does, by exploiting the different contexts in which a word may be used is known as a **pun**. What is the point of using a pun in this advert?

If you want to be sure
of an effective cover up
our MICRO CORRECT
POCKET pen gets
the vote.
You can issue your
manifesto confident
that any blunders are
masked beneath an

*even film of opaque
white fluid – rather than
a thin film of
gobbledygook. There's
no mess or waste and
its advanced tip
design ensures the
fluid gets to the point
without drying up.
And how many MP's
can you say that about?*
PENTEL

2.2 Phrases

Phrase is the term used for a word or group of words, based on a particular word class, which are ordered in a certain way. Just as every word in a sentence can be described according to its word class, so too can a sentence be divided into different kinds of phrase.

They can be classified into three main kinds:

noun phrase
verb phrase
adverbial phrase

2.2.1 Noun phrases

Phrases that are built around a noun are known as **noun phrases**. A noun phrase is a word or group of words which functions as a noun. It can do all the things a noun can do. The general pattern for a noun phrase is to have a determiner followed by a noun, or a determiner followed by an adjective (or adjectives) describing the noun, followed by the noun itself. For example:

a ball   a green ball   the dirty, green ball   some fruit

Semantically, the noun phrase gives us the **participants** involved in the process given by the verb phrase (see 2.2.2 below); that is, who or what is involved in what is happening. This can be an event, state or object, as well as a person.

ACTIVITY 2.4
Copy and complete the table below to make eight examples of phrases with a determiner, adjective or adjectives and noun. You may find that some phrases have more than one adjective or lack a determiner, but that otherwise they will conform to the overall pattern. Use a class text or other source of written material to do this. The first example is done for you.

article	adjective(s)	noun
the	broken	window

2.2.2 Verb phrases

A **verb phrase** is a word or group of words which functions as the verb. It includes the main verb plus any other words related to it, called **auxiliaries**; that is, other words that form part of the verb form, such as *be, do, will, may*, etc. For example:

> The bull *was charging* at the people in the field.
> They *had been shaken* by the noise.

A verb phrase usually comes after a noun phrase, or in between two noun phrases, the first of which forms the **subject** of the verb (see 2.4 below). The two noun phrases will relate to one another semantically (e.g. as subject and object of the same verb). The verb phrase gives us the process; that is, what is happening.
  (See Section 3.3 for more about verbs.)

2.2.3 Adverbial phrases

Syntactically, for a sentence to make sense, it usually has to have at least one noun phrase and one verb phrase. An adverbial is an optional or extra bit: it is not necessary in a sentence in the same way as noun and verb phrases.
  Most commonly, adverbials provide information relating to the following elements:

> *place*   where something happened, e.g. Andrew left his coat *in the restaurant.*
> *time*   when something happened, e.g. She went to the cinema *yesterday.*
> *manner*   how something happened, e.g. He dived into the pool *gracefully.*
> *frequency*   how often something happened, e.g. Lucy drove to town *twice.*

Sentences can have more than one adverbial, e.g. Lucy drove to town *twice yesterday.*
  Often, adverbials take the form of a **prepositional phrase**. A prepositional phrase is a noun phrase with a preposition coming before it: *on, after, under, before.* For example:

> *on* the table   *after* the prolonged rainburst   *before* my homework

Semantically, adverbials and prepositional phrases give us the circumstances associated with the process; that is, how the process given in the verb phrase is taking place.

ACTIVITY 2.5

1 Read the sentences below. The first set is taken from a short story by Graham Greene called *The Innocent* and the second set from Jane Austen's novel *Mansfield Park.*

2 Divide each one into phrases using the syntactic categories given above, namely noun phrase, verb phrase and the different kinds of adverbials. The first one is done for you as an illustration.

3 Can you make any observations about the language style of each set of sentences from such an analysis?

1 **a** *The first men were miners.*

noun phrase	verb phrase	noun phrase
The first men	were	miners

b *I could hear the piano.*

c *It was the smell of innocence.*

d *The little girl performed her long journey in safety.*

2 **e** *The first event of any importance in the family was the death of Mr. Norris.*

f *The Miss Bertrams were now fully established among the belles of the neighbourhood.*

g *Fanny had no share in the festivities of the season.*

2.3 Clauses

The main syntactic difference between a phrase and a clause is that a clause contains both a verb phrase and other types of phrases. Generally speaking, the longer a sentence is, the more clauses it is bound to contain.

There are four different types of clause:

> *single* or *independent clause*
> *coordinate clause*
> *main clause*
> *subordinate* or *dependent clause*

2.3.1 Single or independent clause

A **single or independent clause** is a phrase or group of phrases which forms a sentence by itself and makes sense on its own. For example:

> I (*noun phrase*) lingered (*verb phrase*) at the bottom of the road (*prepositional phrase*).
> Next morning (*adverbial noun phrase*) the serious destruction (*noun phrase*) started (*verb phrase*).
> Place (*verb phrase*) the screw (*noun phrase*) in the hole (*prepositional phrase*).

2.3.2 Coordinate clause

Coordinate clauses are two clauses of equal status joined by a conjunction such as *and, or* or *but*, as in the following examples:

> I shivered there in the mist *and* turned my collar up.
> I used to go to her birthday parties *and* she used to come to mine.
> We had several drinks at the bar, *but* there were several hours to go before dinner.

Although syntactically the status of the two coordinate clauses is equal, we tend to think of the first one as describing the more important aspect, so that the first coordinate clause is often 'read' as being more important than the second.

2.3.3 Main clause

A main clause is a phrase or group of phrases which, like a single clause, could form a sentence by itself, but which has a subordinate clause added to it.

2.3.4 Subordinate clause

As its name suggests, a **subordinate clause** is one that is in some way dependent on the main clause for its meaning. Hence they are sometimes called dependent clauses. In theory, there is no limit to how many subordinate clauses may be linked to a main clause. Generally speaking, the longer a sentence is, the more likely it is to contain subordinate clauses. The subordinate clause can come either before or after the main clause.

A single clause can stand on its own as a sentence, and the two parts of a coordinate clause can stand on their own as sentences, but a subordinate clause cannot, whereas its main clause usually can. A rough-and-ready way of working out whether a sentence contains subordinate clauses is to identify the part (or parts) that could stand alone as a sentence, then see what is left. In the case of relative and comparative clauses (see below), the subordinate clause is one which begins with a relative pronoun or with *than*.

The three most common kinds of subordinate clause are:

adverbial clause
adjectival or relative clause
comparative clause

Adverbial clause

Like adverbial phrases, adverbial clauses often begin with a preposition (see 2.2) and can be identified according to the questions they answer:

Adverbial clause of manner   This answers the question *How?* For example:

As I did every morning, (*adverbial clause*) I looked up at the sky (*main clause*).

Adverbial clause of time   This answers the question *When?* For example:

When the weather improves, (*adverbial clause*) we are going on holiday (*main clause*).

Adverbial clause of place   This answers the question *Where?* For example:

They went (*main clause*) wherever they could get work (*adverbial clause*).

Adverbial clause of purpose or reason   This answers the question *Why?* and often begins with the conjunction *because* (see 2.1.8 and 4.1.1 page 60). For example:

I lent her my savings (*main clause*) because she was short of money (*adverbial clause*).

Relative clause

A relative clause usually begins with one of the pronouns *who, which* or *that*. The pronoun relates (hence its name) the clause to the noun in the main clause. It can also 'interrupt' the main clause, and be put in the middle of it – that is, be **embedded** in it – as in the second example:

> Fanny was the only one of the party (*main clause*) who found anything to dislike (*relative clause*).
> The old coachman, (*start of main clause*) who had been waiting about with his own horse, (*relative clause*) now joined them (*end of main clause*).

See also Section 3.2.5 on relative pronouns below.

Comparative clause

A comparative clause, as its name suggests, compares aspects of the main clause with something else. It follows a comparative word such as *more, less* or *bigger,* and is introduced by the conjunction *than:*

> In this country, we eat more food (*main clause*) than we can grow (*comparative clause*).
> His hands were bigger (*main clause*) than she remembered them to be (*comparative clause*).

2.3.5 Conclusion

There are many other sub-categories of clauses, about which any modern grammar book will give you more information. The ones described here are the main categories, and no claim is made for them as an exhaustive list.

When you are analysing a text, one of the things you can do is to see what types of clause are used, and to discover whether any pattern emerges. This will help you decide whether particular text types use particular clause structures and why. For example, legal documents, such as hire purchase agreements and insurance policies, tend to use multi-clause sentences. This is because they have to make certain that absolutely everything covered by the terms of the agreement is explained; otherwise, legal action could be taken against the companies issuing them. Advertising slogans, newspaper headlines and book titles, on the other hand, tend to use short single-clause sentences to attract the reader's or listener's immediate attention.

The following activity asks you to identify clauses in a variety of extracts and to comment on the effect they have on the writing style.

ACTIVITY 2.6

1 The following five sentences all contain more than one clause. For each one, analyse it into its constituent clauses.

2 What is the effect of any coordinate or subordinate clauses? The first one is done for you as an example.

---

1 *The afternoon was fine, and Yeobright walked on the heath for an hour.*

> The afternoon was fine (*coordinate clause*) and (*conjunction*) Yeobright walked on the heath for an hour (*coordinate clause*).

Effect: although the two clauses are syntactically equal, the fact that Yeobright is outside seems to depend on the fact that the weather was good, because the description of the weather comes before his action.

2 *He had often come up here without stating his purpose to his mother.*

3 *Mushrooms and toadstools are names given to a large group of gill-bearing, fleshy fungi, which are collectively given the scientific name of 'agarics'.*

4 *When going for country walks, one often comes across a railway line, and it is tempting to walk along either beside the rails or stepping on the sleepers between the rails.*

5 *Stella Artois Dry has linked up with one of the UK's top street fashion labels, Dr Martens, and will be bringing their gear direct to your local watering-hole.*

The sentences given in the activity all have two or more clauses. You probably found them straightforward to read and understand. Sometimes, though, writers construct sentences that contain lots of clauses, which makes it difficult for us to retain the link between the main clause and its subordinate clauses. In addition, the main clause might not appear at the beginning of the sentence, or it might have a subordinate clause embedded within it, making it even more difficult for us to work out how all the parts of the sentence relate to one another.

The following activity asks you to analyse extracts with multi-clause sentences.

ACTIVITY 2.7

1 Read the two extracts below.
2 Summarise each text in one sentence.
3 What is the effect of the texts on you? Were they easy or difficult to read? Why?
4 Are the sentences written in a straightforward way?
5 Write down the first and last word of each sentence in both texts.
6 Write out the first main clause in each sentence.
7 Try to explain why each writer wrote in this way. Were there any other options?

1 *Mr Pickwick and his three companions stationed themselves in the front rank of the crowd, and patiently awaited the commencement of the proceedings. The throng was increasing every moment, and the efforts they were compelled to make, to retain the position they had gained, sufficiently occupied their attention during the two hours that ensued. At one time there was a sudden pressure from behind, and then Mr Pickwick was jerked forward for several yards, with a degree of elasticity highly inconsistent with the general gravity of his demeanour; at another moment there was a request to 'keep back' from the front, and then the butt-end of a musket was either dropped upon Mr Pickwick's toe, to remind him of the demand, or thrust to his chest, to ensure its being complied with. Then some facetious gentleman on the left, after pressing sideways in a body, and squeezing Mr Snodgrass into the very last extreme of human torture, would request to know 'vere he vos a shovin' to', and when Mr Winkle had done expressing his excessive indignation at witnessing this unprovoked assault, some person would knock his hat over his eyes, and beg the favour of his putting his head in his pocket. These, and other practical witticisms, coupled with the unaccountable absence of Mr Tupman (who had suddenly disappeared, and was* *nowhere to be found), rendered their situation upon the whole rather more uncomfortable than pleasing or desirable.*

Charles Dickens: The Pickwick Papers

2 *If at any time during the term of this Policy, but before the Insured attains the age of 55, further life insurance to cover an additional loan becomes necessary, the following Options are available to the Insured without any evidence of health being required. The loan must be used to purchase, or to change or improve, a property to be owned, or already owned, and occupied by the Insured as his/her main residence.*
The Options are limited to making such changes in the terms of this Policy as are compatible with the requirements of Paragraph 3 (3) Schedule 2 Finance Act 1975 for a qualifying policy and any additional Policy effected pursuant to Option B must be a qualifying policy within the terms of the Income and Corporation Taxes Act 1970.

Norwich Union life insurance policy

2.4 A functional analysis of sentences

Every word, phrase or clause used in a sentence can be described according to its grammatical function, as described above. As well as this, however, the elements of a sentence can be analysed according to their function as **subject**, **verb**, **object** or **complement**, and **adjunct**. A phrase may perform different functions in different sentences.

The pattern of sentences usually follows a set order. The **subject (s)**, which is usually a noun phrase, comes first, followed by the **verb** or **predicator (v)**, which is usually a verb phrase, followed by the rest of the sentence, if any, as an **object (o)** or a **complement (c)**, followed by an **adverbial** or **adjunct (a)**.

The subject and object(s) of sentences are usually noun phrases. Complements describe or identify the subject; their structure is usually built around either an adjective or a noun. Adverbials and adjuncts add information about the circumstances of an event or situation.

To function as a sentence, then, a group of words usually has a subject, a verb and an object or a complement, which link the parts semantically as well as syntactically. The use of adverbials or adjuncts is not so frequent.

subject	verb	object
The children *(noun phrase)*	finished *(verb phrase)*	their homework *(noun phrase)*.

2.4.1 Subject and verb

Verbs usually have a subject, and the form of the verb can change according to who the subject is. In English, the subjects of verbs are:

I	first person singular
You	second person singular
He/she/it	third person singular
We	first person plural
You	second person plural
They	third person plural

One way of categorising verbs is by whether their form is **regular** or **irregular**. Regular verbs follow a straightforward pattern, whilst irregular ones do not conform to any particular pattern. For example:

I run	I am
You run	You are
She runs	She is
You run	You are
We run	We are
They run	They are

2.4.2 Object

Verbs usually have objects as well as subjects, and these are of two kinds: **direct** and **indirect**.

As its name implies, a direct object relates directly to the action of the verb. Examples are: I like *ice cream*; He stroked *the cat*.

An indirect object relates to the action of the verb, but, rather than being directly related, it is distanced from the verb.

For example, in the sentence *The nurses gave her ice cream*, 'The nurses' is the subject, 'gave' is the verb, 'her' is an indirect object and 'ice cream' the direct object.

Subject	verb	indirect object	direct object
The nurses	gave	her	ice cream.
The children	ran	to the shops.	

A good way of deciding whether a sentence has an indirect object or not is to see whether you can put the preposition *to* before the noun:

The nurses gave ice cream *to* the children.

2.4.3 Transitivity and intransitivity

Transitivity and intransitivity are terms which describe the verbs used in sentences where the action involves one or more participants. **Transitive verbs** are those which need an object to complete their sense, whilst **intransitive verbs** do not. Whether a specific verb is transitive or not often depends upon the semantics of the clause. For example:

Pat smokes those awful cigarettes.

Smoke here is transitive, because the act of smoking is directly related to the cigarettes. But in the sentences *Pat smokes*, or *Pat smokes to keep calm*, the relationship of *smoke* to the sentence changes, so that no object at all is needed. Analysing whether verbs are used transitively or intransitively in a text can reveal a great deal about whether actions occur in a vacuum or whether they are directed at a particular object.

ACTIVITY 2.8

1 Add phrases which involve another participant (person, thing) to the following intransitive constructions to make them transitive:

the river flows
children play
planes drone
apples fall
the sky reddens

2 How do your sentences compare with the original sentences?

3 What is the effect of the change from intransitivity to transitivity?

2.4.4 Complement

Instead of an object, verbs may take a complement; that is, something that adds more information about the subject. A complement usually follows the verbs *be* or *become*. For example:

My clothes are *fashionable*.
Awkward adolescents become *sophisticated adults*.

A complement may also give more information about the object, especially after the verbs *consider* and *regard*.

2.4.5 Adverbials or adjuncts

These add more information about the action of the verb, and perform much the same role as adverbs and adverbial phrases, as described in 2.1.4 and 2.2.3. They generally come at the end of the sentence, although sometimes they appear at the start. For example:

Lucy slept *soundly*.
Uncle Tom has seemed rather preoccupied *lately*.

ACTIVITY 2.9

1 Analyse the following sentences according to both their grammatical function (see Sections 2.2 and 2.3) and their semantic functions (see Section 2.4).

2 What comments can you make on the effect each particular structure has on the meaning communicated?

a *The year began with lunch.*

b *The proprietor of the restaurant was dressed for the day in a velvet smoking jacket and bow tie.*

c *He beamed.*

d *Henriette was a brown, pretty woman with a permanent smile and a spinster's enthusiasm for reaching the finishing line of each sentence in record time.*

e *The cold weather cuisine of Provence is peasant food.*

f *Over the next four or five days, we came to know the chemist well.*

Peter Mayle: A Year in Provence

Generally, the SVO/CA (subject, verb, object/complement, adverbial) pattern of sentences is the one we are most familiar with in prose, especially as it is widely used in published reading schemes that are used to teach children to read. Just as we read from left to right, so we expect sentences to order their information in a particular way from left to right. For example, we expect to find the subject of a sentence at the beginning, or very near to it, with the verb following close after it. When we come across sentences that violate this pattern, such as in poetry or legal contracts, it may take us longer to understand the message being conveyed. Insurance policies, for example, may **embed** the subject of a sentence in the middle or towards the end of a sentence and separate it from the verb by complements, adverbials or both, since they have to be, by nature of their function, highly explicit. Scientific writing tends to use passive constructions (see 3.3.3), which might do away with a subject altogether, in order to focus on the event. Similarly, poetry may alter the SVO/CA pattern to achieve, among other things, a particular rhythm or rhyme.

One of the fascinating things about how language is used in sentences is its ability to contravene or break any rule or convention. Nevertheless, understanding the general principles of language organisation will help you not only to identify where certain forms are used but also to see where there are variations and the effect of this.

2.5 Categorising sentences by function and form

Finally, as well as looking at sentences in the ways outlined above, we can also consider them from a communicative point of view: that is, according to the type of information they are giving. There are four different forms of sentence, sometimes called **moods**, which correspond to four different functions. These are:

form	function
declarative	statement
interrogative	question
imperative	command
exclamatory	exclamation

2.5.1 Declarative sentences

Declarative sentences proclaim a statement about something or someone, and are most likely to follow the SVO/CA pattern described above. Descriptive narrative, textbooks, information articles and leaflets are all likely to use a high proportion of declarative sentences.

2.5.2 Interrogative sentences

Interrogative sentences ask a question. They often begin with the question words *which, who, what, where, when* or *how*. If the question word is the subject, or forms part of the subject, the sentence pattern is the same as for a declarative sentence; otherwise, the position of the subject and verb is reversed, with the subject coming after, instead of before, the first verb in the sentence. For example:

> *Which mattress is* best?
> *What am I* going to do without you?

Interrogative sentences can also be used to issue a command, more usually associated with imperative sentences (see 2.5.3 below). Turning a command into a question is considered a polite way of issuing a command: an answer is not expected. For example, when a teacher or lecturer says, 'Can I see your essay?', he or she does not expect to receive the answer 'No'. Using interrogative sentences as commands is a particular feature of classroom discourse and of conversation generally, both in spoken and written language.

Declarative sentences can be turned into questions by using **tags** or **question tags**. A tag is a short structure added to the end of a statement, which turns it into a question. The whole sentence is then known as a tag question. They are usually used in spoken English or in scripted speech. They consist of forms of the verbs *be* or *do*, using the negative if the main statement is positive (or affirmative) and the affirmative if the main statement is negative. For example:

> It is quite warm, *isn't it?*
> You didn't know I was an artist, *did you?*

Like interrogative sentences, they are often found in speech and in other kinds of text that address the reader or listener directly, such as adverts, political speeches, advice leaflets and articles.

2.5.3 Imperative sentences

Imperative sentences give orders, instructions, advice and warnings. They can begin with the verb: for example, *Put that gun down*.

They can begin with the word 'let': for example, *Let me have a look*.

They can also be made negative by using *don't* or *do not* or *never* in front of the verb: for example, *Do not move out of your home without legal advice; Never leave your car unlocked*.

In writing, such sentences are often found in instruction books, such as a textbook of this kind.

2.5.4 Exclamatory sentences

Exclamatory sentences express something with emphasis, usually in speech or as a form of direct address to a reader. In speech, we do this by our tone of voice, whereas in writing we show it by the use of an exclamation mark: for example, *What a whopper!*

ACTIVITY 2.10

1 **a** Think of an example of each of the four different types of sentence described in Section 2.5 and write it down. You should do this in groups of four, where each one of you writes a sentence of a different kind.

  b For each sentence, discuss the type of writing in which you would expect such a sentence to appear. Discuss your ideas with the rest of the class.

2 **a** In pairs, find two or three examples of each of the four types of sentence in texts that you have in your library or at home.

  b Swap your sentences with another pair, and see if you can determine the type of text from which each sentence came.

  c Work together as a four, telling each other what your answers are.

3 More about words and word classes

3.0 Introduction

The open word classes of nouns, verbs, adverbs and adjectives described in 2.1 are very large, and together they contain the majority of words to be found in any dictionary. As open word classes, their content is not fixed, and it is constantly being added to as, for example, words are borrowed from other languages or compounds are formed (see 3.4 below).

Some words can also belong to more than one word class, depending on how they are used. In the case of verbs or adverbs, their form might also change. For example, in the sentence *I sleep lightly these days*, 'sleep' functions as a verb. In the sentence *I'm going for a sleep*, 'sleep' functions as a noun. It can also function, with morphological additions, as an adverb – *He yawned sleepily* – or as an adjective – *A sleepy toad lay in the long grass*. It is important to remember, therefore, that if you recognise a given word as belonging to a particular open word class in one sentence, you cannot assume the next time you come across it that it will belong to the same one. Which word class a particular word belongs to is determined as much by its syntactic function as by its lexical and morphological form.

Nouns and verbs are two open word classes that can be sub-divided further according to their form and function. The closed word class of pronouns can also be further sub-divided and classified. It is with these three word classes, nouns, verbs and pronouns, that this unit is primarily concerned.

The grammatical explanations given in this unit aim to give you an overall description of different sub-sets of word classes. These are accompanied by activities that illustrate further the points made. You should then be able to use a more comprehensive modern grammar book to find out further information on the finer details of the points covered.

3.1 Nouns

Nouns can be divided into two major categories, **common** and **proper**, with common nouns sub-dividing further into the three categories of **concrete**, **abstract** and **collective**.

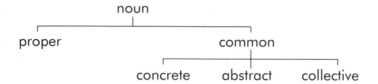

3.1.1 Proper nouns

Proper nouns refer to individual persons, places or titles. Whereas concrete nouns classify things into types, such as person, man, women, street, town, city, bands, shops and so on (see below), proper nouns refer to *actual* people, places and titles, e.g. Lucy; Harry; High Street; Leamington Spa; North Yorkshire; The Beatles; Wet, Wet, Wet; Next; etc.

Proper nouns do not usually take a determiner or article, e.g. *a Lucy* (one exception is names of pop groups, e.g. *The Beatles*), nor do they usually take a plural form (one exception is when a family is referred to by its surname, as in *keeping up with the Joneses*). Graphologically, proper nouns can be distinguished from any other kind of noun in that they usually begin with an upper-case (capital) letter, e.g. *Coronation Street; Vanity Fair;* August. However, some titles or names, particularly those of bands, album, titles and shops, use lower-case (small) letters throughout, rather than upper-case, e.g. *shades of blue; jumping the gun; is,* etc. It is very rare, though (except as a mistake), to see a proper noun that mixes upper- and lower-case letters, e.g. *the Smogs* or *Johnny winter.* The exception to this is where the main words of a title are marked with an upper-case letter and 'little' words with a lower-case letter, e.g. *Little House on the Prairie.*

3.1.2 Common nouns

Common nouns, as their name implies, form the largest category of nouns; they include every kind of noun apart from proper nouns. They typically refer to physical phenomena, that is, things you can see and feel, e.g. *cat, baby, girl, window, table,* and to things we cannot actually see, such as feelings, concepts and events, e.g. *justice, truth, love, hate, birthday.* They refer to things generally rather than uniquely (see proper nouns above).

Concrete nouns

Concrete nouns refer to physical phenomena that we can see and feel. They name things which we perceive externally in the world, and their meaning is often unproblematic, e.g. *eye, window, plate, car, aeroplane,* etc.

Collective nouns

Collective nouns refer to collections or groups of people, animals or things which have something in common, e.g. *family, government, herd, gaggle.* Although, strictly speaking, collective nouns are singular, they can take either a plural or a singular verb form, as in *Her family live/lives in Birmingham.* The difference is usually to do with whether the collective noun is seen as an individual unit in its own right or as made up of a collection of individuals. This example illustrates the idea of a grammatical convention that is determined by the meaning being conveyed.

Abstract nouns

Abstract nouns refer to more general things, such as events, states, processes, concepts and occasions, e.g. *birth, happiness, revival, birthday.* As their name implies, they are usually used to name less tangible phenomena than concrete nouns, and their meanings may be more fluid and less fixed than those belonging to any other type of noun.

The use of nouns

How nouns are used in a text can give us lots of clues as to the writer's meaning or intention and how we should interpret it. For example, it can make a difference whether a noun takes the definite or indefinite article, or whether a proper noun is used instead of a common noun. A writer may use *a girl,* or *the girl,* rather than *Joan* or any other actual name of a character, and each of these gives us slightly different information.

Similarly, adverts tend to use and often repeat proper nouns more than other kinds of texts, in order to get the reader, listener or viewer to remember the name of the product or to link the product's name to a general category associated with a common noun, e.g. *Hoover/vacuum cleaner.*

3.1.3 Count, uncount and mass nouns

Another way of categorising nouns is by whether they are singular or plural.

Count and uncount nouns

Many nouns have two forms, a **singular** form, used to refer to one thing, and a **plural**, used to refer to more than one thing, where the number can be counted, e.g. *table/tables; hour/hours; lesson/lessons.* Plural forms are usually distinguished from their singular forms by adding an 's' at the end, although a few, like *sheep,* have the same form for both. These are known as **count nouns**, since what they refer to can be counted. Most nouns can be included in this category.

Uncount nouns are those which refer to general things, rather than to individual ones, e.g. *death, money, religion, industry, care.* Uncount nouns refer to things that cannot be counted, although it is possible to quantify an amount by putting a determiner in front of the noun, such as *some* or *little,* e.g. *She needed some money.*

Mass nouns

Some uncount nouns can be quantified, in which case they are known as **mass nouns**. For example, *beer, coffee, tea* and *wine* are uncount nouns, but if we are sure that a listener or reader will understand that a specific quantity is being referred to, they become countable, as in *two beers; one tea; two coffees; two red wines.*

Types of substance or commodity, such as *soil, steel* or *cloth,* are generally categorised as uncount nouns, but in certain circumstances, usually to do with food, industry and work, a distinction may be made between different varieties of the commodity, and these varieties are made countable. For example:

Cloths such as linen, cotton and silk are produced from natural fibres.
The use of small amounts of nitrogen in making certain steels

Technical writing to do with food and materials is usually typified by using uncount nouns as mass nouns.

ACTIVITY 3.1

1 Read the three extracts below.

1 *The car ploughed uphill through the long squalid straggle of Tevershall, the blackened brick dwellings, the black slate roofs glistening their sharp edges, the mud black with coal-dust, the pavements wet and black. It was as if dismalness had soaked through and through everything. The utter negation of natural beauty, the utter negation of the gladness of life, the utter absence of the instinct for shapely beauty which every bird and beast has, the utter death of the human intuitive faculty was appalling... The Wesleyan chapel, higher up, was one of blackened brick and stood behind iron railings and blackened shrubs. The Congregational church, which thought itself superior, was built of rusticated sandstone and had a steeple, but not a very high one. Just beyond were the new school buildings, expensive pink brick, and gravelled play-ground inside iron railings, all very imposing, and mixing the suggestion of a chapel and a prison.*

D.H. Lawrence: Lady Chatterley's Lover

2 *SAME SEA, SAME PASSION, SAME LIGHT. STILL, SOMETHING'S MISSING... REMEMBER GREECE?*
Regardless of how many places you've seen or how many resorts you've been to, certain experiences are exclusive to Greece. The secluded bay you can have all to yourself; the warm hospitable smile of the people; the breathtaking sunset; the night brimming with excitement; Experience Greece.
GREECE
Makes your heart beat!
OLYMPIC AIRWAYS
THE NATIONAL CARRIER

Good Housekeeping, April 1995

3 *SUNDAY, ALL THIS COULD BE YOURS.*
The Land Rover Discovery is the best vehicle on earth. And none too shabby on tarmac. It could be yours to own for just £190 a month (plus deposit and final payment). And yours to drive away this weekend. The package is called Freedom Finance and it gives you the following:
The freedom to choose the amount of deposit; a guaranteed future value leaving you with positive equity at the end of the scheme; a Land Rover Discovery for only £190 a month; a choice of five mileage bands; insured payments with Freedom Cover; a Land Rover Discovery for only £190 a month; the reassurance that all costs involved are known from the start; a Land Rover Discovery for only £190 a month; and three end-of-agreement options (pay the final payment and keep the car; give the car back and walk away; or put the equity towards a new Discovery). And if you register the car

between 01.10.95 and 31.12.95 we'll give you 2 years free service and warranty back-up. If you're interested in Freedom Finance, there are only two things you need do. Contact your nearest dealership. And cancel Sunday lunch at Aunt Jemimah's.

Sunday Times, 17 December 1995

2 For each extract, pick out all the nouns that are used and categorise them into the seven categories: common, proper, collective and abstract, count, uncount and mass. Use a table format like the one below. Remember that some nouns may appear in more than one category.

	Passage 1	Passage 2	Passage 3
proper			
concrete			
collective			
abstract			
count			
uncount			
mass			

3 Look carefully at each category of nouns. What can you say about the number of each and the effect of this for each extract? For example, is any category used more than others in any one extract? Are any nouns repeated? What is the effect of this?

4 **a** For each extract, write out the noun phrases. Does a pattern emerge?

   b How does the use of adjectives within each noun phrase contribute to the overall effect of each extract?

   c All three extracts repeat certain words and phrases. Why do you think this is? Is the reason the same for each extract?

3.2 Pronouns

Writing, like speech, constantly refers back to people and things already mentioned or forward to things about to be mentioned (see also Section 4.1). One way of doing this is to repeat the noun we are talking or writing about each time, but more often than not we use a **pronoun** to stand in place of the noun. The use of pronouns is, therefore, grammatically and semantically linked to that of nouns. For example:

> Take three apples and peel *them*.
> Deborah recognised the knife as *hers*.
> Shilton was pleased with *himself*.
> *This* is a very busy place.

If more than one thing has been mentioned, however, you usually have to repeat at least one of the nouns, so that it is clear which one is meant. For example:

> Leaflets and scraps of paper were scattered all over the floor. I started to pick up *the leaflets*.

If the second sentence had said *I started to pick them up*, it would be ambiguous; that is, we would not know whether 'them' referred to the leaflets, the scraps of paper or both.

Although pronouns are a relatively small class of words and a closed word class, they are used a great deal in sentences. Their form changes according to their grammatical function in the sentence, among other things. The list of different forms and functions is fairly large, given how few pronouns there are. Pronouns can be categorised into at least seven different types:

> *personal*
> *possessive*
> *demonstrative*
> *indefinite*
> *relative*
> *reflexive*
> *interrogative*

3.2.1 Personal pronouns

Personal pronouns refer to yourself, the people you are talking to, or the people or things you are talking about. There are two different kinds of personal pronouns, **subject** and **object**; which one is used depends on whether the noun it replaces functions as a subject or object in the sentence (see 2.4 above). As their names imply, subject pronouns refer to a noun used as the subject of a clause, while object pronouns refer to a noun used as the object of a clause.

The following examples show subject pronouns:

> *I* think *I* made the wrong decision.
> Mary came in. *She* was a good-looking woman.
> How many people saw the BBC when *it* started broadcasting in 1937?

The following examples show object pronouns:

> The nurse washed *me* in cold water.
> A man gave *her* the car.
> We were all sitting in the cafe with *him*.

As you can see, different pronouns are used for the same person depending on whether they are subject or object pronouns. The pronouns are shown in this table.

	singular		plural	
	subject	**object**	**subject**	**object**
first person	I	me	we	us
second person	you	you	you	you
third person	he she it	him her it	they	them

Notice how the second person pronoun stays the same in both singular and plural forms and how there is no third person singular pronoun which is neutral in its gender apart from *it*. In English, the male singular pronoun *he* or *his* can refer to either male or female where the precise gender referred to is not known, whereas *she* or *her* is taken to refer to the female only; for example, *The student must feel that the essay belongs to him.*

Recently, feminism has influenced the use of personal pronouns in English, by making us more aware of their use. Because of this, *he* and *him* are no longer always used to refer to both male and female. One way of avoiding this is to use a plural pronoun, which is gender neutral, instead of a singular one, as in *The student must feel that the essay belongs to them.* (See also 3.2.8 below.)

3.2.2 Possessive pronouns

Possessive pronouns, as the name implies, are used to show that something belongs to someone or is associated with them. For example:

The baby is *hers*.
Her father fought in the war, and so did *mine*.

Possessive pronouns sometimes have the word *of* in front of them, to show that they are one of a group of things:

She is a friend *of mine*.
Barbara Cartland? I've read a book *of hers*.

The following table sums up the different forms of possessive pronouns:

	singular	plural
first person	mine	ours
second person	yours	yours
third person	his hers its	theirs

Note that the words *my, your, her, our* and *their*, while looking like the possessive pronouns, are actually **possessive adjectives**, since they usually describe a noun, e.g. *my pen, his book*, rather than standing in place of a noun.

3.2.3 Demonstrative pronouns

Demonstrative pronouns are used when there is a sense of pointing things or people out. *This* and *that* refer to one thing, being singular forms, and *these* and *those* refer to more than one thing, being plural forms. For example:

He paused at a photograph which stood on the dressing table. 'Is *this* your wife?'
Vitamin tablets usually contain vitamins A, C, and D. *These* are available from any child health clinic.
That looks interesting.
Those are easy questions to answer.

Note that the words *this* and *that* and their plural forms *these* and *those* can also function as determiners in front of nouns, e.g. *this coat; these people; that table; those children*. In some grammar books, you might find them being called **demonstrative adjectives**.

3.2.4 Indefinite pronouns

If we want to refer to or talk about people or things but do not know exactly who or what they are, or it is not important, we use an indefinite pronoun. For example:

What was needed was *someone* practical.
'*Everybody* stand still and put your hands up! *No-one* move!'
Before doing *anything* please read the instructions.

Indefinite pronouns include words such as:

anybody	*everybody*	*nobody*	*somebody*
anyone	*everyone*	*no-one*	*someone*
anything	*everything*	*nothing*	*something*

3.2.5 Relative pronouns

Relative pronouns can do two things at the same time. Like other pronouns, they refer to somebody (*who, whom* and *whose*) or something (*which* and *that*). They can also, at the same time, be used as **conjunctions**, because they join clauses together, so that a relative clause begins with a relative pronoun:

...a region *which* was threatened by growing poverty.

The difference between *who* and *whom* is that, in the past, *who* was used to add information about the subject of the sentence, e.g. *Pilgrims who had come to pray at the shrine of a local saint disembarked*, while *whom* was used as a direct or indirect object, e.g. *The person to whom I referred earlier*.

However, this distinction is not as strictly adhered to in either speech or writing as it once was. *Who* is more likely to be used these days with both the subject and the object, and *whom* is used less.

Nowadays, the distinction between *who* and *whom* is observed mainly in formal writing styles, as in academic, legal or religious texts, rather than in more informal contexts, such as tabloid newspaper articles and contemporary fiction. In speech, *who* is becoming much more common than *whom*, except in the speech of speakers who believe it to be more correct to use *whom*.

The main difference between *which* and *that* is that *which* is used to refer to things, while *that* is used to refer to both things and people.

Who and *which* can also function as interrogative pronouns, depending on how they are used within a sentence (see 3.2.7 below).

3.2.6 Reflexive pronouns

Reflexive pronouns are used when the object of a verb is the same as its subject, e.g. *They gave themselves a holiday; I treated myself.* You can usually recognise them because they end in *-self* for singular forms and *-selves* in the plural.

The reflexive pronouns are:

	singular	plural
first person	myself	ourselves
second person	yourself	yourselves
third person	himself herself itself	themselves

3.2.7 Interrogative pronouns

Interrogative pronouns are used when asking a question. *Who* and *whose* are usually used when the question relates to a person, and *which* and *what* if it refers to anything else. For example:

Who was that at the door?
What is the answer to the question?

3.2.8 Nouns, pronouns and gender

Unlike the nouns of most other European languages (for example, French, Spanish or Polish), English nouns are not generally associated with or assigned to a gender, and are usually thought of as neutral with regard to gender. Even nouns that apply to people can be gender-common, applying to both male and female (e.g. *doctor, teacher, lawyer,* etc.).

In recent years, however, the influence of feminism has caused some people to look at how gender is associated with words in English, and in particular at the relationship between nouns and the pronouns which stand in place of them. For example, gender-common words, particularly those to do with occupation, such as *doctor, lawyer, nurse, housekeeper* or *builder,* have tended to be associated with a particular gender, when either sex can do the job. Contemporary writing, therefore, generally tries to avoid using a gender-specific pronoun to relate to a noun that can apply to either sex, to avoid any charges of sexism in language.

Some nouns can be gender-specific, applying either to male or to female, e.g. *actor, actress; warder, wardress; cow, bull*, etc. Others may take a feminine pronoun: *ship, country* and *car* may be referred to as *she*. Again, the influence of feminism has led to the gender-specificity of these words being abandoned, so that women are just as likely to call themselves actors as men, and objects previously assigned a gender, such as cars, are more often referred to as *it* than *she*.

3.2.9 The use of pronouns

Being able to identify different types of pronouns in texts should help you to recognise any ambiguity, and to identify how pronouns are used to make links within and across sentences (see 4.1.1 below). Different types of text may also favour one type of pronoun over others, whilst others may not use them at all, and you should be able to recognise this and comment on its effects.

3.3 Verbs

Verbs, like nouns, are a major word class in English and are the central or pivotal element of a clause: in other words, they are very important. There is a lot that can be said about verbs and their various forms and functions, but this section will limit itself to a consideration of three of the more common aspects of verbs: **auxiliaries**, including **modality**; **tense**; and the **active** and **passive voice**.

3.3.1 Auxiliaries

The majority of verbs, sometimes called full verbs, belong to an open word class. A verb is the main element of a verb phrase, with other words in the phrase usually functioning as **auxiliaries**, sometimes called **operators**, before the main verb, or as adverbs following the main verb. Auxiliary verbs fall into two main categories: **primary** and **modal** verbs. These are generally considered to be closed word classes.

Primary verbs

There are three primary verbs in English, whose use is very important: **be, have** and **do**. It is important to remember that these three verbs can function either as full or main verbs when used on their own, or as auxiliaries when used with other verbs. They are very irregular, as the following table illustrates:

infinitive	present	past	present participle	past participle
be	am, are, is	was, were	being	been
have	have, has	had	having	had
do	do, does	did	doing	done

A primary verb can be used as an auxiliary and be followed by a main verb which is another primary verb: for example, *What have you done? What are you doing? What do you have?*

Modal verbs

Modal verbs are those which signal attitudes, concerns, requests, suggestions, wishes or intentions, or are used to be tactful or polite. Unlike primary verbs, they are always used in conjunction with a main verb.

The list of modal verbs is generally thought to be invariable; in other words it is a closed word class. There are ten of them:

> *can*
> *could*
> *may*
> *might*
> *must*
> *ought to*
> *shall*
> *should*
> *will*
> *would*

Could, would, might and *should*, confusingly, are also the past tense forms of *can, will, may* and *shall*.

The degree to which any text uses modals can be significant, since their use with a verb alters the meaning of a sentence from a definite statement of fact or question, allowing for degrees of uncertainty or choice. Similarly, we tend to use modals to soften commands and requests. We would not normally say to a stranger, for example, *Shut the door*, but something like *Will you please shut the door?* or *Shut the door, would you?*

Some texts, such as horoscopes, hypotheses, fiction and political speeches, are more likely to use modals than others, such as instructions and legal documents, particularly if they contain speculation and are considering alternatives.

3.3.2 Tense

In any piece of writing, or whenever anyone makes a statement of any kind, it is usually necessary to indicate whether the situation being referred to exists now, existed in the past, or is likely to exist in the future. The point in time to which a statement relates is usually indicated in part by the verb phrase, which is written in a particular **tense**. Two main tenses are recognised in English: the present and the past.

Present tense

The present tense is used to discuss or describe an existing state of affairs. For example:

> I'm awfully busy.

'I' is the subject and the abbreviated 'm' for *am* is a present tense form of the verb *be*, used here as a main verb.

> He lives in the French Alps.

'He' is the subject and 'lives' is a present tense form of the verb *live*. The present tense used in this way is sometimes called the **simple present**.

When a process is happening now and will go on happening, a present tense form of *be* is added before the present participle of the verb to form the **present continuous** tense. For example:

> The village is changing but it is still undisturbed.

'The village' is the subject and 'is changing' the present continuous form, which tells us that the change carries on. It is formed by using *be* with the present participle, in this case *is* plus *changing*. In the second clause, the pronoun 'it' refers to the village as a subject, while 'is' is the simple present tense of *be*, with the adjective 'undisturbed' as the complement.

Past tense

The past tense is used to discuss or describe events that have happened in the past. To describe something that happened at a particular time in the past, the **simple past** is used.

A time expression usually appears somewhere in the clause or sentence to specify the particular time you are referring to. A common way of doing this is to use a **time adjunct**. For example:

> The Israeli Prime Minister *flew* into New York *yesterday* to start his visit to the US.

'The Israeli Prime Minister' is the subject and 'flew' is a simple past tense form of the verb *fly*. 'Yesterday' tells us the time when the event happened.

Not all time adjuncts are so specific: *later*, *earlier*, *shortly* and *punctually* are all adjuncts that can be used.

If you want to describe something that happened in the recent past and over a period of time, the **present perfect** tense is used. The auxiliary *have* is placed in front of the past participle of the main verb. For example:

> They have raised £180 for a swimming pool.

'They' is the subject and 'have raised' is a present perfect form of the verb *raise*. We do not know exactly when this happened, only that it was in the recent past and still has some connection to the present (for instance that the money has not yet been spent).

Talking about the future

The future is not as certain as the past or present. It concerns what might happen or what is intended to happen. Talking or writing about the future is not as straightforward as talking about the present or the past. When we describe the future, the modal *will* or *shall* is often used in front of the base or infinitive form of the verb to indicate a future state. For example:

> Nancy *will arrange* it.

'Nancy' is the subject and 'will arrange' a future tense form of the verb *arrange*.

> I *shall do* everything I can to help you.

'I' is the subject and 'shall do' a future tense form of the verb *do*.

The following activity asks you to consider tense in more detail.

ACTIVITY 3.2

1 Photocopy page 50 and read the six extracts.

2 For each extract:

   a Underline the verb phrases, using a different-coloured pen for each different tense: past, present or future. Identify the subject of the verb phrase and any adjuncts used.

   b Identify which tense, past or present, is used in each sentence where there is also a future aspect.

3 What is the effect of any change of tense in an extract?

4 **a** Do any extracts use modals?

   b What is their effect?

You could do this activity in pairs, with each pair working on one or more extracts, and discuss your work all together at the end.

1 *Many insurance companies will only pay you the original cost of the items for which you make a claim. With Royal Insurance, however, you enjoy extra peace of mind with 'new for old cover.' This means that we'll replace items claimed for at today's prices, if they cannot be economically repaired.*

Leaflet for Royal Insurance

2 *The rectory stood half way up the hill, with its face to the church and its back to the High Street. It was a house of the wrong age, inconveniently large, and faced with chronically peeling yellow plaster. Some earlier Rector had added, at one side, a large greenhouse which Dorothy used as a workroom, but which was constantly out of repair. The front garden was choked with ragged fir-trees and a great spreading ash which shadowed the front rooms and made it impossible to grow any flowers.*

George Orwell: A Clergyman's Daughter

3 *When it comes to customer service, no organisation can claim to have all the answers. So with the help of regular research, we have made it our business to ask you, the customer, exactly what you want from your Post Office.*
As you may have already noticed, there is now a poster which gives you the latest information on waiting times at this Post Office. We also plan to keep you up to date on our performance in other important areas of activity.
The idea behind this brochure is that we let you know what our service aims are and that you, in turn, let us know where you feel we're succeeding or falling short.
At the back, you'll find a reply card which we hope you'll use to let us have your comments and ideas.

Post Office brochure: The Customer Charter

4 *McDonald's cheese slices are made exclusively for McDonald's to our own exclusive recipe. English cheddar-cheese is the starting point: A blend of cheeses of different ages which gives a mouth-watering smoothness and bite.*

McDonald's advert

5 *Just before noon he had garaged the Cooper Bristol in Lexington Street and was walking towards Bloomsbury and the Cadaver Club.*
The Cadaver Club is a typically English establishment in that its function, though difficult to define with any precision, is perfectly understood by all concerned. It was founded by a barrister in 1892 as a meeting place for men with an interest in murder and, on his death, he bequeathed to the Club his pleasant house in Tavistock Square. The Club is exclusively masculine; women are neither admitted as members or entertained.

P.D. James

6 *They crossed by night on the ferryboat to Dover, and since Lord De La Warr, then Lord Privy Seal, had arranged that they be accorded diplomatic privileges, none of their luggage was examined there or in London. He also arranged with the railway authorities that the train to Victoria should arrive at an unusual platform so as to circumvent the battery of cameras and the huge crowd of welcoming or curious visitors.*

Ernest Jones in The Pelican Book of English Prose, Volume 2

3.3.3 The active and passive voice

Verbs can be used either actively or passively, and the effect in each case is very different, as the following explanation shows.

The active voice

The active voice of a verb will have a recognisable subject, who performs the action of the verb in any clause or sentence. The subject can also be called the **agent** of the verb. For example:

> The dog ate its dinner.

'The dog' is the subject and the agent of the verb 'ate', and 'its dinner' is the object of the verb.

The active voice of a verb will make it quite clear who or what is performing the action of the verb, and who or what the action is done to, if this is appropriate. A sentence in the active voice is also more likely to follow the SVO/CA pattern outlined in Section 2.4.

The passive voice

A writer may want to change the focus of the sentence from the subject to the object; that is, to the thing or person being affected by the action. This is achieved by doing two things. Firstly, the order and function of the subject and object is reversed, so that the object becomes the subject of the verb. Secondly, a passive verb form is used. This is made up of the appropriate tense of the verb *be* (*am, is, are, has been, were*, etc.), followed by the present or past participle of the main verb. (Remember, though, that *be* is also a verb in its own right, so that recognising a passive involves more than simply identifying use of the verb *be*.) For example:

> Their dinner *was eaten* by the dog.

Here, 'their dinner' is the subject of the verb 'was eaten', but 'the dog' is still the agent, since it performed the action.

Changing the voice from active to passive means that the agent can be made to disappear completely:

> Their dinner was eaten (by the dog).
> Their dinner was eaten.

Using the passive form of the verb is a very useful way of hiding the agent of the verb. For example, instead of saying, *'Sorry, I've just broken a plate'*, which makes it quite clear who has done the breaking, you could say, *'Oh dear, the plate's been broken'*, thus putting the emphasis on what has happened rather than on the person who caused the plate to break.

When you use the active form of a verb, you cannot avoid mentioning both the subject and the object of the clause or sentence. Using the passive voice gives you the option of whether or not to mention the person or thing, the agent, responsible for the action, as in the example given above. One effect of the passive voice is that it puts the focus on *what* happens or has happened, the consequences of the action, rather than on who or what *makes* something happen. Reports of scientific experiments and processes generally use the passive voice because of their need to emphasise what happens. For example:

> *The principle of bottling is very simple. Food <u>is put</u> into jars, the jars and their contents <u>are heated</u> to a temperature which <u>is maintained</u> long enough to ensure that all bacteria, moulds and viruses <u>are destroyed</u>.*

Using the passive voice is also a useful way of hiding the agent's identity. This is a device which certain kinds of text, such as newspaper headlines and political speeches, typically use to achieve a particular effect, such as deliberately creating ambiguity.

The practice of paring structure down to the minimum in newspaper headlines gives us phrases such as:

Black Youths Shot

This is a contraction of the passive sentence *Black youths were shot*; it leaves out the agent of the verb, the person who did the shooting, and throws the emphasis on the victims. In this instance, there may be political or social reasons for hiding the identity of the perpetrators of the crime.

Leaving out the appropriate tense of the verb *be* needed to make a passive construction makes the phrase *black youths* take on the subject position. This is then followed by an active form of the verb *shoot*. Thus in syntactic terms the victims of the crime are placed in the position of being its perpetrators, which may lead us to think that they in some way caused the shooting.

The following activity asks you to consider the active and the passive voice in more detail.

ACTIVITY 3.3

1 In pairs, read the following sentences.

2 **a** For each one, write out the verb phrases and decide whether each one uses the active or the passive voice.

   b Discuss what the effect is in each case of using either the active or the passive voice.

3 **a** Decide on the type of text from which each sentence is taken.

   b How, if at all, did the voice in which each sentence was written inform your decision?

---

a *He knocked at the door, sick with fear and embarrassment.*

b *The government was forced to say that the report would be implemented.*

c *She escaped uninjured, but her boyfriend was shot in the chest and died.*

d *My grandfather was a most extraordinary man.*

e *The average Briton moves house once every seven and a half years.*

f *More people have been treated in hospital this year than at any time since the start of the Health Service.*

g *Such items should be carefully packed in tea chests.*

h *If you are studying part-time (21 hours or less a week) you can claim supplementary benefit.*

Collins Cobuild Grammar. HarperCollins, 1990

ACTIVITY 3.4

1 Read the following extracts.

2 Write a brief summary of what each one is about and any comments you might have about it.

3 For each extract, identify:

   a the verbs used, their tense, whether they are in an active or passive voice and any modals used

   b the nouns and pronouns used, within the categories described in Sections 3.1 and 3.2 above.

4 How does your analysis contribute to your understanding of each text?

---

1 *Lancaster has a population of about 50,000; in the whole built-up area and surrounding villages there is a population of some 130,000. Lancaster is an administrative centre and market town, with some manufacturing industry.*
The city centre has been extensively restored and now has a large and picturesque pedestrian area, and a maze of small streets and alleyways full of interesting shops. It is dominated on one side by the Castle, where visitors can see the Georgian courtrooms, the medieval dungeons and the beautiful Shire Hall, and nearby the fifteenth century Priory Church; and on the other side by the Ashton Memorial, an Edwardian baroque folly set in Williamson Park, a landscaped quarry. In the late 18th century St. George's Quay was at the heart of a thriving port but today its restored stone warehouse and the Gillow Custom House, now converted to house the Maritime Museum, serve as a vivid reminder of the past.

Lancaster University Postgraduate Prospectus, 1994/95

---

2 *I have never been made homeless. To have nowhere to go, perhaps for the rest of my life, to face every day the uncertainty of the night and fear of the elements, is almost unimaginable. I say 'almost', because in writing about the homeless I have gleaned something of their powerlessness once they are snared in what used to be known as the 'welfare state'. This was true before Thatcher.*
The difference these days is that there are no 'typical' homeless any more. They are also from the middle classes and the new software classes. They are both old and young – an estimated 35,000 children are homeless in London alone. My friend is typical in that he bears the familiar scars of homelessness: such as a furtiveness that gives the impression of a person being followed; a sporadic, shallow joviality that fails to mask his anxiety; and a deferential way that does not necessarily reflect his true self. The latter, because it is out of character, is occasionally overtaken by melodramatic declarations of independence. When he told me he had to go to hospital one day for a stomach operation and I offered to take him, he said, 'No! I can walk! Of course I can!' And he did.

John Pilger: Distant Voices

---

3 *'Oh, you wicked wicked little thing!' cried Alice, catching up the kitten, and giving it a little kiss to make it understand that it was in disgrace. 'Really, Dinah ought to have taught you better manners! You ought, Dinah, you know you ought!' she added, looking reproachfully at the old cat, and speaking in as cross a voice as she could manage – and then she scrambled back to the armchair, taking the kitten and worsted*

with her, and began winding up the ball again. But she didn't get on very fast, as she was talking all the time, sometimes to the kitten, and sometimes to herself. Kitty sat very demurely on her knee, pretending to watch the progress of her winding, and now and then putting out one paw and gently touching the ball, as if it would be glad to help if it might.

Lewis Carroll: Through the Looking Glass

3.4 Compounds

One way of making new words in English is to combine two lexical items to make a new one, which is then seen as a single unit, often with a different meaning from its separate 'parts': e.g. *greenhouse* from *green* and *house; handbag* from *hand* and *bag.* Confusingly, compounds can be written as a single word – *handbag* – hyphenated – *green-eyed* – or written as a phrase – *green belt.* Generally, compounds are formed by combining:

a noun + a noun: *pear tree*
an adjective + a noun: *redbrick*
an adjective + an adjective: *readymade*
a noun + a verb: *horseride*

In clauses or sentences, compounds are classified according to whether they function as nouns, verbs or adjectives.

In poetry, compounds can be used deliberately to describe a different object, a practice common in Old English poetry and riddles, where such words are called **kennings**, as in *swan-path* to mean *sea,* or *battle-adder* to mean *a sword.*

ACTIVITY 3.5

1 Read the three extracts in Activity 3.4. For each one:

   a Identify any compounds used.

   b Say whether they function as nouns, adjectives or verbs.

2 How are they different from other adjectives, nouns and verbs used in the extracts? What is their effect, if any?

4 Beyond the sentence: cohesion and coherence

4.0 Introduction
4.1 Cohesion
4.2 Coherence
4.3 Imagery

4.0 Introduction

Section 1.2 above describes how written language can be studied at the three distinct, though related, levels of text, sentence and word. Units 2 and 3 explain the main ways in which words can be classified within sentences, the ways in which words combine into clauses and phrases, and how these combinations interact with the meanings produced by the words themselves. This unit will concentrate on analysis of the text as a whole.

Any piece of writing, if it is to make sense at all, uses vocabulary and syntactic structures to bond or connect its sentences together. Just as a random selection of words does not in itself make a sentence, so too a random selection of sentences does not of itself create a coherent text. There are two main ways in which sentences combine together within texts, known as **cohesion** and **coherence**.

Cohesion refers to the ways in which syntactic, lexical and phonological features connect within and between sentences in a text, while **coherence** is more to do with semantic features, referring to the way or ways a text makes consistent sense to the reader with or without the help of cohesion.

The two concepts work together rather than independently in helping us to understand ways in which texts make sense. They are relatively new ideas, which have been developed from the 1960s onwards. Before then, patterns of language within texts beyond the level of the sentence were dealt with largely within the study of literature. These well-established patterns are usually grouped under the heading of **imagery** or **figurative or literary language**. The different aspects of imagery are explained within Section 4.1.3, which is to do with sound, and Section 4.3, which is to do with semantics.

Underlying all these different textual elements is the notion of **textuality**. Section 1.1.4 above introduced this idea, namely that a text is not just a random collection of sentences. Textuality refers to the ways in which connections within and between sentences form a coherent piece of writing, rather than a series of unconnected ideas. Here stylistic analysis really comes into its own, analysing how words and sentences combine to make the text into something meaningful and coherent.

4.1 Cohesion

As well as thinking about subject matter, its associated vocabulary and the syntactic structure of individual sentences, a writer will usually help you to read his or her writing by using direction signals to make connections in and between sentences. These include the ways in which sentences are sequenced, how one thing leads to another, implication and so on.

These signals act as markers of **cohesion** or **cohesive ties** in a text; that is, the writing is held together not only because of relationships between the ideas or events (represented through lexis, semantics or syntactic structure), but through connecting forms in the lexis and syntactic structure themselves.

Cohesion can be divided into three different kinds:

grammatical cohesion
lexical cohesion
phonological cohesion

The following sub-sections take each of these in turn.

4.1.1 Grammatical cohesion

Grammatical connections between individual clauses and between sentences can be classified into three broad types. These are:

deictics/reference
ellipsis and substitution
conjunctions (or connectives)

Deictics

Deictics is a term used in stylistics to describe words or phrases which refer to a specific time, place, person or thing in a text, without actually naming them by using a noun. Typically, speech often uses deictics, since we tend to rely on context a great deal in natural conversation; for example:

Come *here* and look at *this* mess.
Go over *there* and look at *that* mess.

These two statements point to two different scenarios: one where the mess is physically close to the speakers and one where it is further away, although both are within sight.

Deictics is also used to describe the ways in which a text links the world of the narrative with that of the reader. For example, in poetry, deictics can be used to imply that the reader takes part in or watches a scene or events alongside the poet, as in this extract:

> *Say what you will, there is not in the world*
> *A nobler sight than from* <u>*this*</u> *upper down,*
> *No rugged landscape* <u>*here*</u>...

Wilfred Blunt: Chanclebury Ring

In plays or prose, as well as within poetry, deictics or **deictic expressions** help to create and sustain the world of the play or narrative by referring to places, people, times and events that have occurred within it. Equally a further important function of deictics is to extend the world of the play or narrative to places, times, people and things we have not seen, rather than confining us to the world created by the text in front of us, as in the extract above.

Words which indicate the use of deictics include personal pronouns (*I, you, we, they,* etc.), the demonstrative pronouns (*this, that,* etc.) and adverbs of time and place. (Section 6.3 below considers the use and effects of deictics in scripted dialogue in more detail.)

Deictics can be divided into three different kinds:

> *anaphora* or *anaphoric referencing*
> *cataphora* or *cataphoric referencing*
> *repetition*

Anaphoric references   Anaphora or anaphoric reference is the term given to the use of words to refer back to somebody or something that has already been mentioned, usually by using personal pronouns such as *he, she, they* or *it* or possessive pronouns such as *mine* or *hers*. Once a **referent** has been established (that is, the person or thing referred to) it is usually replaced with a pronoun the next time it appears, unless, of course, using a pronoun would make the sense unclear or ambiguous.

The most common occurrence of anaphora is where a pronoun refers to a noun already mentioned in the same sentence or in the preceding sentence. If the noun is a male or female, or a group of people, then the pronoun used 'matches' the gender and number of the noun it replaces: *she* for Mary, *he* for John and so on.

ACTIVITY 4.1

1   Read through the following short extracts.

2   In each one, identify each pronoun and match it to the noun phrase to which it refers.

3   Where one of the pronouns *it, this, that, those* or *these* is used, does it refer to a noun phrase in the text, or to a situation?

---

1   *Connie always had a foreboding of the hopelessness of her affair with Mick, as people called him. Yet other men seemed to mean nothing to her. She was attached to Clifford. He wanted a good deal of her life and she gave it to him.*

---

2   *Davis opened a door. 'Here's your room. I'm afraid it's a bit untidy.' He picked up a dirty handkerchief off the floor and stuffed it in the drawer.*
   The keeper came loping softly up the lane with the dog padding at his heels, and we watched them through the hedge as they went by. I held her very close. My cheek was against hers.

---

3   *More and more money is being pumped into the educational system, and it is reasonable to assume this will keep on happening.*

---

4   *Only small pines are left. Many of these have twisted and stunted shapes.*

---

5   *'It was here one young prisoner was sold for a bag of corn,' said the old woman. 'That was me.'*

Anaphoric referencing can also have the effect of implying a previous existence for the text's characters. Its use plunges us immediately into the world of the text, assuming that we are familiar with the person for whom a pronoun stands when this could not possibly be the case unless we were re-reading the text. For example, the following extract, taken from the beginning of the first chapter of William Golding's novel *The Inheritors*, uses anaphora in this way:

> *He was struggling in every direction, he was the centre of the writhing and kicking knot of his own body...*

As this is the beginning of the novel, we have nothing to which we may refer back to know who 'he' is other than a male: starting the novel in the middle of a supposedly existing state of affairs immediately plunges us into the world of the narrative, rather than leading us gently into it. We are left to draw upon our own knowledge and experience to make sense of what we are reading.

Such a technique can be used to keep the reader in suspense and so reading on to discover who the *he* or *she* is. Alternatively, it may be used as a kind of delaying tactic, as in the following example:

> *'Where's that boy gone, I wonder? You, Tom!'*

In this line, the 'boy' of whom the old lady is thinking or speaking becomes the 'Tom' she can see in front of her.

Cataphoric references Just as anaphoric references refer back to a person, thing or situation in a text, **cataphoric reference** or **cataphora** refers forward. Saying that something appears 'below' in a text, for example, directs the reader to something that is about to be encountered: the reference is made before the referent itself appears. Similarly the adjective 'next' can be used to refer forward to subsequent sections of the text itself. For example:

> In the next chapter, we will examine this theory in detail.

Cataphoric references delay more precise information, thus creating an element of suspense. In the following example, cataphoric referencing gradually reveals information about a particular woman, before naming her. A pronoun is used first, followed by a noun phrase, followed by the proper noun of the person being referred to, followed by a reflexive pronoun for even more emphasis.

> And slowly down the steps in *her* magnificent ballgown comes *the young woman* of the moment we have all been waiting for, *Princess Diana herself...*

Repetition Anaphoric and cataphoric referencing use pronouns to refer outwards, backwards and forwards to something, someone or some situation, in place of the noun or noun phrase (the referent) . Sometimes, though, a noun or noun phrase is repeated rather than being replaced with a pronoun. In narrative, using repetition reinforces description and emotional effects; in public speeches and adverts, it can be used to hammer home a point or a product.

ACTIVITY 4.2

1 Read the following extracts and identify the kind of text from which each one is taken.
2 For each one, discuss what effect the repetition has, bearing in mind the type of writing it is.

1   *The rain fell heavily on the roof, and pattered to the ground... The rain fell, heavily, drearily. It was a night of tears.*

Charles Dickens: Little Dorrit

2   *We are fighting for the rights of the little man... We are fighting, as we have always fought, for the weak as well as the strong. We are fighting for great and good causes...*

Mrs Thatcher. Guardian, 13 October 1984

3
      Mine – by the Right of the White Election!
      Mine – by the Royal Seal!
      Mine – by the Sign in the Scarlet prison
      Bars – cannot conceal!

Emily Dickinson

4   *A new venture initiated by the RSPCA, it aims to give farm animals five basic freedoms:*
   1. Freedom from fear and distress.
   2. Freedom from pain, injury and disease.
   3. Freedom from hunger and thirst.
   4. Freedom from discomfort.
   5. The freedom to behave naturally.

RSPCA leaflet

Ellipsis and substitution

Ellipsis   This is the name given to the omission of part of an utterance or a grammatical structure which the listener or reader is assumed to understand easily from its context.

Because it leaves out information already given, ellipsis can help the listener or reader to focus on new or important information. It is often used where economy of words is needed, such as in note-taking and personal newspaper adverts (*Wanted: Mother's Help. Three children, 2, 4 and 7. Must drive*). The omission of words such as determiners and auxiliaries is also common in representing interior monologue in narratives; it suggests a rapid succession of thoughts or images, as the following extract from James Joyce's novel *Ulysses*, which cryptically describes the thoughts of one person, illustrates:

> *raised his eyes and met the stare of a bilious clock. Two. Pub clock five minutes fast. Time going on. Hands moving. Two. Not yet.*

This extract uses no referencing beyond *his*. Instead, a degree of cohesion is achieved through repetition and lexical cohesion (see 4.1.2 below). However, we, as the reader, have to infer far more than we are accustomed to in order to make sense of the text (see also 4.2.1 below).

Where ellipsis is used to avoid unnecessary and tedious repetition, it is typically anaphoric (see above). This is extremely common in everyday conversation, which is far more dependent on context than writing. One of the most striking differences between natural, spontaneous conversation and written dialogue that aims to represent it is the use of ellipsis. Dramatic dialogue in particular tends to be far less elliptical than natural conversation, since it lacks the context of ordinary speech (see 6.1 below). In writing which has to be explicit, such as legal contracts and advertising, there is far more repetition and referencing and consequently far less ellipsis than in other types of writing.

Ellipsis can also be used in narratives and plays, not only in the form of grammatical omission or substitution, but also as a means to speed up the action or pace of a narrative by leaving out events assumed to have happened but not described or enacted. This can be done either by omitting events altogether or by explicitly marking that they have happened: for example, *two years later...* Used in this way, ellipsis links closely with inference, as described in 4.2.1 below.

Substitution   This works in a similar way to ellipsis, except that, rather than working by omission, one word is substituted for another word, phrase or clause. The items commonly used for substitution are:

> *One(s)* I offered her a seat. She didn't want one.
> *Do* Did Frank take that letter? He might have done.
> *So/not* Do you need a lift? If so, wait for me; if not, I'll see you there.
> *Same* He chose the roast duck; I'll have the same.

Like ellipsis, substitution assumes a knowledge of the context in which it is used, and, also like ellipsis, it is a much more common feature of speech than of writing. In writing, its use is mainly in dialogue that aims to represent spontaneous speech, although again, like ellipsis, this depends upon the context having been made explicit so that it can be understood by a listener or viewer.

Conjunctions (or connectives)

Conjunctions work in a way that is different from reference, ellipsis and substitution, in that they do not search backwards or forwards for their referent; rather, they signal a relation between segments of discourse. Section 2.1.8 above described the word class of conjunctions. Conjunctions join clauses within a sentence, which can lead to ellipsis being possible in coordinating clauses. For example: *Mary walked to the car and got in (to the car)*. They also indicate that what follows in a sentence bears some relation to what has already been said, as well as grammatically joining the clauses together. As such, they commonly act as elements of coherence (see 4.2 below) as well as cohesion.

Within a text, conjunctions signal different types of relation between sentences. They can be of four different types.

Additive   These add more information, e.g. *She's intelligent. And she's very reliable.* Other conjunctions signalling such cohesion are *in addition, besides* and so on.

Adversative   These qualify the information already given, e.g. *I've lived here ten years but haven't ever heard of that pub.* Other conjunctions signalling such cohesion are *however, nevertheless* and so on.

Causal   These conjunctions introduce the reason why something happened, e.g. *He caught a cold because he fell in the river.* Other conjunctions signalling such cohesion are *consequently, therefore*, etc.

Temporal   These signal a temporal sequence; that is, that one thing happened before or after another, e.g. *I got up and made my breakfast.* Other conjunctions signalling such cohesion are: *then, subsequently*, etc.

ACTIVITY 4.3

1 Read the following extract and find conjunctions linking one sentence with another.

2 Using the four categories given above, can you say what type of conjunctive relation is signalled in each case? How do they help to develop the argument put forward?

Nicotine Addition
Nicotine is a colourless, oily compound and is the drug contained in tobacco which addicts the smoker. It is the fastest addictive drug known to mankind and it can take just one cigarette to become hooked.
Every puff on a cigarette delivers, via the lungs to the brain, a small dose of nicotine more rapidly than the dose of heroin the addict injects into his veins.
If there are twenty puffs for you in one cigarette you receive 20 doses of the drug with just one cigarette.
Nicotine is a quick acting drug and levels in the bloodstream fall quickly to about half within 30 minutes of smoking a cigarette. This explains why most smokers average about 20 per day.
As soon as the smoker extinguishes the cigarette, the nicotine rapidly starts to leave the body and the smoker begins to suffer withdrawal pangs.
I must at this point dispel a common illusion that smokers have about withdrawal pangs. Smokers think that withdrawal pangs are the terrible trauma they suffer when they try to stop smoking or are forced to stop smoking. This is in fact mainly mental and is due to the smoker feeling deprived of his pleasure or prop.
Allen Carr: The Easy Way to Stop Smoking. Penguin, 1985

The following activity asks you to consider all the aspects of grammatical cohesion – reference, ellipsis, substitution and conjunctions – covered in this section.

ACTIVITY 4.4

1 Read the following three extracts.

2 For each one, write a fifty-word summary.

3 a Note the cohesive elements within each extract.

   b Group them according to the various different types outlined in the section above.

4 For each extract, explain how cohesion helps to bind it together into a text.

1 *November 29th, a chic cafe near Edinburgh's Waverley Station: Authors aren't supposed to be recognised in public. Pop stars yes, but definitely not people who write books, unless you're Salmon Rushdie holidaying in Mecca. It's happening to Irvine Welsh a lot recently, a bit too often for the semi-reclusive writer's peace of mind. Welsh is known to disappear abroad for months at a time. But it's happening now. A scruffy student type strides towards him, as he's nursing a coffee in the corner, disguised as an Endsleigh Football League coach – thick red sports parka and pale blue eyes peering from beneath a woolly hat.*
'Excuse me, er, Irvine... er, thanks very much for the books, they're great.'

Bemused, clutching his coffee in defence, Welsh doesn't quite know what to make of the attention. The extent of his recognition unsettles him and Welsh was shocked at the attention he attracted on visiting London and Manchester earlier this year. The 37 year old former TV repairman only picked up a pen seriously five years ago, to write the stories that'd later become his debut novel, Trainspotting. Now he's 'the most important writer in Britain.' (© the national press). Only Irvine's never been a big fan of literature.

Select Magazine, February 1996

2 *The main course was dried lamb chops, dried mashed potatoes, and tinned spaghetti in tomato sauce. Cassandra, leaning across to address someone, entangled her dangling crucifix in the spaghetti. It had to be wiped clean. Julia was rigid with embarrassment; obsessed by an image of bloody loops of paste over the rigid, jewelled arms of the cross, she saw her sister ludicrous, even grotesque, and could not meet her eye. She thought she remembered, disproportionately, absurd facts of this kind; they made her books. They distracted one's attention, she thought, from the essence — although it was surely from such titbits of facts that one's attitude to people was built up? She watched, hungrily, a pair of trembling blue-veined hands, clumsy, fragile, crumble the corner of a crust. Well what was, she wondered, this essence she was missing? She looked from face to face along the table. Sexless, timid, judging, anxious, drawn-up faces, what did they want? Had they ever been like the screaming, scrawling girls beneath them? Were they, like Cassandra, in retreat from another world where things happened more perfectly and more intensely? Across the table two women had prolonged a conversation about brands and durability of sewing machines throughout the meal. Did they want knowledge or power, were they hungry for the academic praise that had singled them out in youth?*

A.S. Byatt: The Game

3 *LEN: This ain' the bedroom.*
PAM: Bed ain' made.
LEN: Oo's bothered?
PAM: It's awful. 'Ere's nice.
LEN: Suit yourself. Yer don't mind if I take me shoes off?
(He kicks them off.) No one 'ome?
PAM: No.
LEN: Live on yer tod?
PAM: No.
LEN: O.
(Pause. He sits back on the couch.)
Yer all right? Come over 'ere.
PAM: In a minit.
LEN: Wass yer name?
PAM: Yer ain't arf nosey.
LEN: Somethin' up?
PAM: Can't I blow my nose?
(She puts her hanky back in her bag and puts it on the table.)
Better.
(She sits on the couch.)

Edward Bond: Saved. Methuen, 1966

This activity shows that, taken together, these various cohesive elements create what is often called the **texture** of a text: that is, they hold it together as a connected entity, rather than it appearing as a random or accidental sequence of sentences.

Different types of text may use different kinds of cohesion to a greater or lesser extent, creating different types of texture. For example, conversations typically draw on material that is shared or taken as given, because it can be retrieved from the immediately surrounding situation; thus they generally use a lot of pronouns and ellipsis.

Fiction, such as novels and plays, depends less upon situational references and tends to use expressions referring to things which have already been mentioned in the text itself, rather than to anything outside it. For example, novels will tend to use more anaphoric reference, determiners and conjunctions and less ellipsis and fewer condensed or omitted verb forms than conversation.

4.1.2 Lexical cohesion

Lexical cohesion, as its name implies, describes ways in which items of vocabulary relate to one another across clause and sentence boundaries to make a text work as a whole. It refers to the part played by certain semantic relations between words to create textuality (that which distinguishes a text as opposed to a random sequence of unconnected sentences). The relations between vocabulary items in texts are of two main kinds: **reiteration** and **collocation**.

Reiteration

Reiteration means either repeating the same word in a later section of the text or else reminding the reader of it by exploiting **lexical relations**. These are the stable semantic relationships that exist between words and which form the basis for definitions in a dictionary or groups of words in a thesaurus. These relations are of two main kinds: **synonymy** and **hyponymy**. For example, *zucchini* and *courgette*, or *bachelor* and *unmarried man* are related by synonymy: they both refer to exactly the same thing or state. *Courgette* and *vegetable*, or *jumbo jet* and *aeroplane* are related by hyponymy: in each case the second is a **superordinate** in the family tree of the first.

Consider this example of synonymy:

> The meeting *commenced* at six thirty. But from the moment it *began,* it was clear all was not well.

In this example, 'commenced' and 'began' apply to the same event, the meeting. They do not always do so, however. For example:

> The meeting *commenced* at six thirty; the storm *began* at eight.

In this second example, 'commence' and 'began' refer to separate events; the semantic relation of synonymy between them is being exploited stylistically to create humour or irony.

Now consider this example of hyponymy:

> There was a fine old *rocking chair* that his father used to sit in, a *desk* where he wrote his letters, a nest of small *tables* and a dark, imposing *bookcase.* Now all this *furniture* was to be sold, and with it his own past.

Direct repetition of words is something we do not commonly use other than for a particular effect, such as those described in 4.1.1 above. Instead, we tend to vary items, in this case with hyponyms of the superordinate *furniture*, which taken together build a mental picture of the kinds of furniture being described.

Such variation can add new dimensions and nuances to meaning, building up an increasingly complex context. Every paraphrase of an earlier word brings with it its own semantic connotations. Where reiteration is done by superordinate, as in the example above, various elements are brought together under one, more general term. This is more likely to be a conscious choice than a chance event: both speakers and writers deliberately choose whether to repeat directly, to find a synonym or to use a superordinate.

The following newspaper report uses several types of lexical cohesion.

> *Police toughened up their anti-protest tactics at Brightlingsea yesterday and arrested 12 demonstrators who had defied their warnings against trying to block the continuing export of live animals from the port in Essex.*
>
> *Around 400 demonstrators, a lower turnout than the 1,000 anticipated by the organisers, failed in their attempt to turn back three lorries containing around 1,500 sheep. Following a clear police warning that arrests would be made if the paths of vehicles were blocked, the lorries containing the sheep began the final 400 yards of their journey to the quayside at Brightlingsea. A line of police riot vans protected the convoy, as they have through the months of protest.*

Independent, 19 April 1995

'Toughened' is being used as a superordinate of 'arrested' to indicate a hardening of the police's attitudes towards the protestors. 'Live animals' is reiterated as the hyponym 'sheep', which is itself repeated, making it clear that it is this particular live animal that is being discussed in the article. 'Lorries', 'vehicles' and 'convoy' are also used synonymously, whilst the word 'vans' (as used by the police) is a reiteration to distinguish them from the 'vehicles' used to transport the sheep. 'Demonstrators' is repeated; a more sensationalist style of reporting might have used more lurid synonyms.

Collocation

Collocation describes the way in which certain words commonly (or uncommonly) associate with others in a semantic way. Some adjectives, for example, are used with some nouns and not with others. The adjective *beautiful* collocates with the noun *woman* rather than with *man*, as do other adjectives such as *frumpy, bitchy, slender* and *pretty*. The phrase *a pretty man* is syntactically accurate but semantically rather suspect, unless used in an ironic way, since *pretty* and *man* do not normally collocate.

Similarly, we would expect to see the adjective *shabby* applied to the nouns *clothes* and *treatment* rather than to *water* or to *a baby*. Some verbs regularly collocate with particular nouns, particularly those associated with animal and insects: bees buzz, dogs bark and ducks quack. Similarly, we *drive* a car but *ride* a bike.

The reason why some words have particular associations is not all that clear. We only know that some words are more likely to combine with specific items to form natural-sounding combinations, while others do not, even though they are possible or understandable. For example, we call milk that has gone off *sour*, whereas butter that has gone off is *rancid* and eggs *rotten*. All these adjectives describe foodstuffs, yet they are not interchangeable; we would think it odd for someone to describe milk as *rotten* or butter as *sour*, yet these words essentially describe the same process.

Section 4.3 below looks at further aspects of collocation under the heading of **imagery.**

ACTIVITY 4.5

1 Read the following extract taken from a travel article in the *Mail on Sunday*.

2 Make lists of words which create lexical cohesion in this extract, through reiteration and collocation.

3 One of your lists will include wild animals and another words to do with politics or aspects of government. How do these two seemingly disparate groups contribute to the overall meaning of the text?

Before I left my Nairobi hotel, the nice lady from Abercrombie & Kent warned me: 'You must ask permission of the locals before you use your camera.'

Then she added: 'And if you bump into the president, whatever you do, don't even try to take his photograph.'

Since the chances of bumping into the president somewhere in the 224,900 square miles of Kenya was about as likely as me bumping into Hillary Clinton in Tesco in Borehamwood High Street, it was not going to be a problem.

Certainly, the locals were no problem – Kenyans are some of the nicest people on the African continent. And everywhere I went on my hunting and fishing safari they couldn't have made me more welcome.

I had been invited to spend a frenetic week hopping from one remote airstrip to another, trying to see as much of Kenya as possible and hunting big game with my camera and giant Nile perch with my fishing rod, hoping it would be strong enough to handle the reputed monsters.

I spent three nights in the Masai Mara game reserve, staying in one of the tents in Siana Springs camp.

The tents are permanent structures, 12ft high, with double bed, separate dining room, veranda and shower, and probably about the same size as the average semi-detached in Guildford.

We drank wine every evening and watched the spectacular African sunsets, and were woken in the night by the roar of hunting lions and leopards in the jungle.

We were up every morning just before sunrise, and saw every aspect of nature, red in tooth and claw – lions eating a freshly killed buffalo, hyena, jackal, zebra, cheetah, leopard, elephant, and a large number of rhinos. All in the Kenyan game parks is clearly well now that the poaching has been stopped.

But the government will have to do something about the increasing number of tourists in their Land Rovers, putting fresh pressure on the animals – no longer with guns but now with their video cameras.

On day three, we moved on to start fishing, and if I'd had any doubts about whether we'd catch any fish, particularly big fish, they were dispelled within minutes.

My powerful rod was wrenched almost off the back of our boat and my first Nile perch was landed some 20 minutes later, weighing more than 40lbs.

Michael, my gangling Kenyan boatman, who fishes every day, shook me solemnly by the hand and said: 'This could be a very good day. We might even catch some big ones.'

Frankly, with a 40-pounder already to my credit, I was more than happy, but there are some absolute monsters out there.

I was based at Mfangano Island on Lake Victoria – the fishing was tremendous and the food and wine in this luxurious camp in the middle of nowhere was superb.

The fish couldn't have been more obliging – unlike most species, Nile perch don't even require you to get out of bed early.

A typical day was a leisurely breakfast, a long, luxurious swim in water that averages about 21C (70F), and then off in the boat to hunt for the Nile perch which usually started feeding around 11 am.

They were introduced to Kenya in the Fifties, and since then they have bred and bred.

The biggest fish taken out of Michael's boat last year was caught by a woman, Jocelyn Stephens, from London. There was barely room for it in the boat and it weighed 163lb.

The biggest so far caught on rod and line was also caught by a woman, from the USA, and it weighed 203lb.

And even huge fish like that have only really scratched the surface of the Nile perch potential.

Most of the bigger fish caught by the locals break free, but one monster snared a couple of years ago weighed 540lb and fed the island for a fortnight.

Mfangano Island itself is one of the most beautiful places I've ever stayed in, although if you don't like eating fish it's probably not the place for you.

Rupert Finch-Hatton, my host at the camp – an amiably eccentric young man from Horsham, Surrey, who has lived on the island for three years – boasts that he has 365 different recipes for Nile perch.

Chris Tarrant. Mail on Sunday, 2 April 1995

4.1.3 Phonological cohesion

The aspects of text cohesion considered so far in this unit have concentrated on the grammatical and lexical elements of words. There is, however, a further important consideration which influences a writer's choice of words: how they sound, including the sound patterns they make. Sound patterns are particularly important when it comes to writing verse of any kind. For example, **alliteration**, where the first letter of two or more words is the same, is often favoured as a poetic device in languages where stress falls on the first syllable of every word. This was particularly so in Old English poetry, as in the example below:

> *Over breaking billows, with belly sail,*
> *And foamy beak, like a flying bird*
> *The ship sped on.*

Alliteration was regularly used as a means of cohesion in a form of poetry known as alliterative verse, which was common in England both before the Norman Conquest in the eleventh century and again in the fourteenth century, when poems such as *Piers Plowman* and *Sir Gawain and the Green Knight* were written. The alliterated syllables are usually strongly stressed ones, so that they relate to the rhythmic pattern of the rhyme, as in this extract:

The snaw snitered ful snart, that snayped the wilde
(The snow came shivering down very bitterly, so that it nipped the wild animals)

Sir Gawain and the Green Knight

Assonance is where a vowel sound is repeated in a word with different consonants, as in *Break! Break! Break! On the cold grey stones, O Sea!* The 'o' in 'cold' and 'stones' is repeated again as the single word 'O', stressing the poet's anguish. The linked words 'break' and 'grey', 'cold' and 'stone' also, by the use of lengthened vowels, suggest the steady movement of the sea. (See 4.3 below for other ways of patterning words.) *Cough drop* and *fish and chips* are further examples of assonance.

Phonology can therefore be a source of cohesion in a text; alliteration, assonance and rhyme, in particular, involve textual patterning created by the repetition of the same or similar sounds. An extreme form of phonological cohesion is the basis for tongue-twisters such as *She sells sea shells on the sea shore.*

Alliteration, assonance and rhyme are among the most obvious and easy ways in which a poem can be made phonologically cohesive. This means that such cohesion is often very superficial. Where these phonological aspects form the strongest element of the structure of a poem, as in the rhymes that appear in commercial cards for birthdays, Christmas and other seasonal events, then the meaning is often banal. A more complex kind of cohesion is that which is created through the interaction of phonological patterns with patterns of meaning. Even though sounds in themselves have no meaning, and the association between sound and meaning in language is arbitrary and conventional, there are ways of using sound so that it complements meaning. For example, **onomatopoeia** is the name for another kind of phonological patterning, where the sound of a word imitates the sound of the thing it refers to, e.g. *whisper, rustle.*

This kind of cohesion is discussed and exemplified in the following passage, taken from Alexander Pope's *Essay on Criticism*, written in the eighteenth century. The use of underlining in the poem reflects an eighteenth-century convention for showing emphasis, while nouns tended to be capitalised then (see 7.2 below).

> *True Ease in Writing comes from Art, not Chance,*
> *As those move easiest who have learn'd to dance.*
> *'Tis not enough no harshness gives Offence,*
> *The Sound must seem an Eccho to the Sense.*
> *Soft is the Strain when Zephyr gently blows,*
> *And the smooth Stream in smoother Numbers flows;*
> *But when loud Surges lash the sounding Shore,*
> *The hoarse, rough Verse shou'd like the Torrent roar.*
> *When Ajax strives, some Rock's vast Weight to throw,*
> *The Line too labours, and the Words move slow;*
> *Not so, when swift Camilla scours the Plain,*
> *Flies o'er th'unbending Corn, and skims along the Main.*

Pope's key advice here is that 'sound must seem an echo to the sense'. The sound, according to this advice, supports the meaning by triggering associations, with the syntax contributing further to the total effect. For example, the word 'smooth' in line 3 associates through alliteration with the 's' of 'stream', creating a sound like the ever-flowing stream itself. In line 7, the word 'loud' cues us in to the significance of low vowels, especially the diphthong 'ou', intended to echo the roaring of the waves. However, as Pope's use of the verb 'seem' in line 4 acknowledges, sound symbolism of this kind is based not on any systematic feature of language, but rather on vague and subjective impressions.

Meter

One further form of phonological patterning is **meter**. Meter in this sense refers to patterns of stress in lines of verse. Stress is a feature of language which we internalise as we learn to speak it; meter is something which is imposed on language, making the stresses fit a particular pattern. Using meter imposes a constraint upon language that we do not normally use in everyday speech. This is particularly true in a language such as English, which has a variety of patterns and degrees of stress. The most common metrical types in English are the **Iamb**, the **Trochee**, the **Anapest** and the **Dactyl**.

Pope's poem on page 67 is written using the **iambic pentameter**, which is the most common metrical form in English poetry. This meter arranges words in lines containing ten syllables, beginning with an unstressed syllable and then alternating stressed and unstressed:

> The sound | must seem | an ec | cho to | the Sense

The Trochee reverses the unstressed–stressed pattern to form a stressed–unstressed one:

> And be | fore the | Summer | ended
>
> Stood the | maize in | all its | beauty

The Anapest has two unstressed syllables followed by a stressed one:

> Not a sound | hath escaped | to thy ser | vants,
>
> of prayer | nor of praise

The Dactyl reverses the Anapest, with one stressed syllable followed by two unstressed ones:

> Lulled by the | coil of his | crystalline | streams. |

Rhythm and meter   Using meter produces rhythm in a text, but a text does not have to be metric to be rhythmic. Free verse and prose are types of text which by definition do not use a fixed metrical scheme, but in both rhythm is often a source of cohesion and sound–sense connections. Virginia Woolf, for example, is a writer whose prose is often very rhythmic, as the following extract from her novel *Mrs Dalloway* shows:

> *What a lark! What a plunge! For so it had always seemed to her, when, with a little squeak of the hinges, which she could hear now, she had burst open the French windows and plunged at Bourton into the open air. How fresh, how calm, stiller than this of course, the air was in the early morning; like the flap of a wave; the kiss of a wave; chill and sharp and yet (for a girl of eighteen as she then was) solemn, feeling as she did, standing there at the open window, that something awful was about to happen...*

Much of the rhythm in this passage comes from the repetition of similar stress patterns, either within a phrase or between two consecutive phrases. The first two sentences, 'What a lark! What a plunge!' introduce repetition, the phrases being identical in their syntax, syllable structure and stress. The fourth sentence contains two pairs of parallel phrases, 'How fresh, how calm...' and 'like the flap of a wave; the kiss of a wave', in which the similarity of stress pattern accompanies virtually identical syntactic and syllabic structure. Although this is not verse, some phrases within the prose use the iambic pentameter; for example, 'and plunged at Bourton into the open air' and 'that something awful was about to happen' at the end.

   These repetitive rhythmic patterns and mirror image phrases strongly associate with one of the novel's main themes: life as an alternation between a joyous 'lark' and a 'plunge' into despair, and the search for an equilibrium between the two.

ACTIVITY 4.6

1 Read the following poem by Anne Stevenson.

2 **a** Comment on the use of rhyme, alliteration and assonance in this poem.

   b How do they contribute to the content of the poem?

3 **a** Look more closely at the meter in the first stanza. How does it contribute to what the poet is expressing in the poem?

   b How and where does it work against our expectations?

4 How does the title of the poem relate to the rest of the poem?

Resurrection

Surprised by spring,
by the green light fallen like snow
in a single evening,
by hawthorn, blackthorn, willow,
meadow – everything
woken again after how many thousand years?
As if there had been no years.

That generous throat
is a blackbird's. Now, a thrush.
And that ribbon flung out,
that silk voice, is a chaffinch's rush
to his grace-note.
Birds woo, or apportion the innocent air they're made for.
Whom do they sing for?

Old man by the river
spread out like a cross in the sun
feet bare
and stared at by three grubby children,
you've made it again, and yes we'll inherit a summer.
Always the same green clamouring fells you that awakes you.
And you have to start living again when it wakes you.

   Anne Stevenson: Enough of Green. Oxford University Press, 1977

4.2 Coherence

A text 'makes sense' because there is continuity within the information it contains, whereas a text is 'senseless' or 'nonsensical' when there is a serious mismatch between what it describes and our prior knowledge of the world, including the textual 'world'. For example, we would find it odd if a report suddenly changed to become a narrative about something completely unrelated to the original subject of the report. Similarly, we would find it odd in a novel if characters were described who took no part in the events which followed.

As the previous section has shown, cohesion goes a long way towards establishing the coherence of a text. But a text does not have to include cohesion in order to be coherent. For example, the two sentences *Term ends next week. I've got a pile of essays to write* are coherent, even though there are no conjunctions or other commentary items such as *nevertheless* or *but* which might indicate a causal or adversative relation between the two statements. They make sense because the concepts to which they refer (*term, week, essay*) imply a relationship of cause and effect: the idea of students having essays to write because of term ending is consistent with our knowledge of the world. If we subsequently discovered that the 'I' was a teacher, lecturer or airline pilot and not a student, then we would have to rethink our interpretation of the two statements.

One important element of coherence is that known as **inference.**

4.2.1 Inference

Coherence, unlike cohesion, is not simply a matter of the grammatical, lexical and phonological features of texts. It also involves a degree of interaction between the text and the reader: when we read a text of any kind, we draw on our experiences of the world to make sense of what we read. We use our own existing knowledge to fill in the gaps or discontinuities which exist in a textual world. This is called inference. For example, take the following sentences:

> *Everything was ready. Scientists and generals withdraw to some distance and crouched down behind earth moulds. Two red flares rose as a signal to fire the rocket.*

The second sentence gives us a clue as to what the 'everything' is in the first, namely preparations for some kind of scientific experiment connected with warfare. We also infer that the 'scientists and generals' were watching the preparations being made before they withdrew to the earth moulds, and that this withdrawal had something to do with what was about to happen. Most texts we read require us to fill in gaps for ourselves in this way: they assume that a certain amount of inference will take place on the part of the reader. To record every detail would make texts repetitive and could distract the reader from the thread of what is being recounted, because it would get lost amongst all the detail.

In narratives, inference is nearly always necessary, since without taking for granted facts, details and cultural knowledge, a story would be very tedious to read. Much information is presupposed on the basis of our understanding of what happens in the real world. For example, we assume that characters go to bed at night, wash, use the lavatory and get dressed in the morning, as well as eating regularly every day, even though these events may not be described. The events that *are* described then have far more significance for the plot and characterisation in the story. This selection is known as **foregrounding**. In turn, the events which are described or foregrounded require inference in terms of their potential significance for the theme or events of the story.

Texts which do make everything explicit, such as legal contracts and Acts of Parliament, can be very repetitive and difficult to understand, for the very reason that they do have to include every detail. This makes it difficult for us to sort out what is relevant to us as opposed to irrelevant. On the other hand, instructions may be difficult to follow if the amount of inference demanded of the reader is too great: previous knowledge of car mechanics may be assumed in a car repair manual or computer literacy in a booklet on word processing. Letters between friends often assume a considerable amount of shared knowledge, which makes them perfectly understandable to the intended reader but meaningless to anyone else. Similarly, texts which do not make it clear for which particular kind of reader they are intended may lead to confusion. For example, a leaflet about drug abuse may mix information intended for the drug addict with that intended for those living with drug addicts, thus leaving the implied reader confused as to which bits of information relate to his or her particular situation.

A text, therefore, does not make sense by itself, but rather by the interaction of text-presented knowledge with readers' stored knowledge of the world, which can be very different from reader to reader. Thus the same text can be interpreted in a variety of ways, depending upon the relationship between the world presented in the text and the reader's own experience of the world within which he or she lives. Some texts are more liable to different interpretations than others; a poem, for example, may be interpreted in various ways, whereas an advert usually has far fewer possibilities.

Whatever interpretation a reader puts upon a text may be valid, rather than there being a single 'right' interpretation. In the past, literary criticism often aimed to interpret texts in the 'right' way. Since ways of approaching literary criticism have themselves become diverse, and growing attention has been given to the interaction between the reader and the text, this is no longer the case. Instead, analysis can provide an alternative means of evaluating a text, which takes much greater account of its fitness for its purpose than of its 'worth' or 'literariness'.

ACTIVITY 4.7

1 Re-read the three extracts in Activity 4.4 above.

2 Find examples of places where inference is required to make each text coherent.

3 Analyse each extract, taking into account all the elements covered so far in this book.

4 How does your analysis contribute to your own interpretation of the texts?

4.3 Imagery

Imagery is a term with which you may be familiar. It has been used in literary analysis to describe language that aims to achieve a particular, often poetic, effect. Often imagery works through exploiting unusual collocations. It may also create coherence within a text. For example:

> *I am aware of the damp souls of housemaids*
> *Sprouting despondently at area gates*
> T.S. Eliot: Morning at the Window

We do not normally associate the words 'damp' and 'sprouting' with the noun 'soul', or think of such an action as a 'despondent' one. *Damp* and *sprouting* are terms usually associated with gardening, rather than spirituality, which might lead us to think of a soul's growth in gardening terms. However, the word 'despondently' gives the growth a particular human feeling, thereby **personifying** it. These two lines deliberately exploit the connotations of various words by making them collocate with one another in ways which they normally would not do.

But poetry is not the only kind of text to exploit words in this way: it is also a common feature of advertising. Here, products are often linked with particular words or images which invite a particular inference on the part of the reader or listener (tigers with petrol, women with aftershave, etc.). One of the ways in which advertising is very like poetry is in its use of so-called poetic devices. Unlike poetry, though, which uses them to form layers of possible interpretations, advertising uses such devices to put a simple message across. Examples of such poetic devices, which often use collocation to produce more vivid visual images, are simile and metaphor.

A **simile** is the term given to an expression which compares one thing to another in order to describe it more vividly, using the word *like* or *as:* for example, *as white as snow; as warm as toast; hair like a black raven's wing.*

A **metaphor** goes one stage further than a simile and describes one thing as another. For example, Hamlet says that the world:

> *is an unweeded garden,*
> *That grows to seed...*

Act I scene 2

This metaphor applies the features of a garden to the world, as Eliot does to souls in the example given above. An **extended metaphor** is one which, as its name implies, extends an image over several lines of text.

Metaphor and simile are both ways of using language in a defamiliarising way, expressing the familiar by comparing it to or describing it as the unfamiliar; this makes them a powerful source of multiple meanings. Some similes and metaphors, though, have become so habitual or common that they are known as **clichés.**

A **mixed metaphor** is one in which the combination of qualities suggested is illogical or ridiculous, usually because two different metaphors are applied to the same thing: for example, *those vipers stabbed us in the back.*

Other unusual word associations are ones which work through metonymy and synecdoche. **Metonymy** is where a writer (or speaker) replaces the name of one thing with the name of something else that is closely associated with it: for example, *the press* for journalism, *the bottle* for alcoholic drink, *the Oval Office* for the US presidency. Visual images as well as words can be metonymic, as in a tree representing a forest on stage, or a row of houses standing for a town. A common form of metonymy is known as **synecdoche;** here, the name of a part is substituted for a whole, as in *hand* for worker and *names* for famous people. In both metonymy and synecdoche, the associated meanings belong to the same semantic area, unlike metaphor, which transfers the field of reference.

All these forms of imagery may be found in all types of text, and are not restricted either to literary language or to other self-conscious forms of language such as advertising. We use or come across hundreds of similes, metaphors and metonyms every day in different kinds of text, both spoken and written, ranging from everyday speech such as slang to public speeches, poetry and novels. The difference is that in poetry such imagery is generally used self-consciously, whereas in everyday speech and writing we do not think of it as being anything unusual (*the pound recovers; the war against inflation; green issues*, etc.).

ACTIVITY 4.8

1 Read the poem below, which is by Robert Browning.

2 Write a brief summary of about thirty words saying what you think the poem is about and what happens in it.

3 Why do you think the poem is called *Meeting at Night*, without either a definite or an indefinite article?

4 **a** Identify and list examples of cohesion and coherence.

   b How do these different features contribute to the meaning of the poem? Do they all contribute in the same way?

5 **a** Identify any imagery the poet uses.

   b How does this contribute to the meaning of the poem?

Meeting at Night

The grey sea and the long black land
And the yellow half-moon large and low:
And the startled little waves that leap
In fiery ringlets from their sleep,
As I gain the cove with pushing prow,
And quench its speed i' the slushy sand.

Then a mile of warm sea-scented beach;
Three fields to cross till a farm appears;
A tap at the pane, the quick sharp scratch
And a blue spurt of a lighted match,
And a voice less loud, thro' its joys and fears,
Than the two hearts beating each to each!

5 Who's telling the story?

5.0 Introduction
5.1 Perspective: narration, authorial voice and point of view
5.2 Representing speech and thought in fictional texts
5.3 Representing speech and thought in factual reporting

5.0 Introduction

So far, the units in this book have given a general introduction to grammatical structures and the terminology associated with analysing words, sentences and texts. This unit begins to look at some of the different ways in which texts and the sentences within them are structured, starting with aspects of narrative structure.

Even the simplest narrative follows a pattern of development, with the listener or reader being steered through the course of a tale by the teller or author, as Activity 1.1 demonstrated. Generally, we are unaware that we are being guided, and it is only when we begin to look more closely at the way in which the language is structured that we begin to realise it. Two important aspects of the way in which a narrative develops are the way in which the writer chooses to tell the story and the way in which speech and thought are represented within it. Sections 5.1 and 5.2 of this unit consider these two aspects in terms of fictional narrative, whilst 5.3 considers them in connection with factual reporting.

5.1 Perspective: narration, authorial voice and point of view

Texts which tell a fictional story usually describe the events, characters and setting from a particular perspective, which may be the author's, a character's or, more usually, a combination of both. This sense of perspective is conveyed mainly through the **authorial voice** and the **point of view**. As the following explanations describe, there is a certain amount of overlap between these terms, according to how the writer has chosen to use them.

5.1.1 Narration and authorial voice

Any written text has an author, whether known or unknown. In factual texts, the author is usually at pains to keep him or herself at a distance from what is written, whereas in fiction the author can take a more active and positive role in telling the story. The degree to which a writer makes him or herself known to readers as the **narrator** of the story can vary, according to how much he or she chooses to intervene directly in the telling, creating either a **personal** or an **impersonal narrator.** In either case, the author must then choose to have a narrator who knows everything about the characters and events (**authorial omniscience**), or to restrict the narrator's perspective (**authorial reportage**). Both these perspectives can be referred to as an **authorial voice**. Taken altogether, the way in which the narrative is told, with either an impersonal or a personal narrator, and an omniscient or reporting authorial voice, contributes to the particular perspective or **point of view** from which a story is told.

Personal narrator

A personal narrator may be the author or a character within the narrative, who intrudes into the story to address us, the readers, directly, making comments, passing judgements or moralising about the characters and events. This type of personal narrator often appears as an *I* outside the story. Such an intrusion was fairly common in early novels, such as Henry Fielding's *Tom Jones* (1749). In this novel, Fielding interrupts the telling of the story for whole chapters whilst he passes comment on the events that have just occurred. A very general characteristic of the development of the novel is that this kind of personal intrusion has been used less and less often, and has now virtually disappeared, so that where it does reappear, as in John Fowles's novel *The French Lieutenant's Woman*, its appearance is startling and seems something new.

Another category of personal narrator appears in narratives which are or purport to be autobiographical. Using the personal pronouns *I* and *we*, the author or the main character tells an autobiographical story about himself or herself: examples are J.D. Salinger's *The Catcher in the Rye* and Roddy Doyle's *Paddy Clarke Ha Ha Ha*. This is known as a first-person narrative.

Impersonal narrator

An impersonal narrator is one who is less intrusive, simply reporting the events of a story without passing comment on them. This narrator is much more likely to use the third person in telling the story; that is, to use characters' names and the personal pronouns *he, she* and *they*. Written narratives are unlikely to use the second person, *you*.

It is perfectly possible for both types of narrative reporting to be used within the same text. For example, the nineteenth-century novelist George Eliot generally uses an impersonal narrator in her novels, but occasionally she addresses her readers directly, changing to a personal narrative style.

Authorial omniscience and authorial reportage

Telling a tale also involves a writer in deciding the extent to which details of characters are to be portrayed. He or she may choose to be authorially omniscient, deliberately entering the characters' minds and thus telling us, the reader, the characters' thoughts as well as their actions. The nineteenth-century writer Thomas Hardy, for example, uses a generally impersonal narrative style but is authorially omniscient, able to reveal his characters' innermost thoughts and feelings. Alternatively, an author may choose to report only events which are external to the characters, leaving their thoughts alone, as does the twentieth-century writer Graham Greene. What characters think or feel is represented only through their speech, rather than through descriptions of their thoughts.

5.1.2 Point of view

A writer may choose to tell the tale from the perspective of a particular character (or characters), with whom we as the reader are invited to identify. This character may or may not be the chief narrator of the tale, but is usually the first one to whom we are introduced in the book. Usually, narratives are told from the point of view of the main character, and the events of the story are told as they relate to him or her. Other characters appear in relation to the main one, and our opinion of them tends to be formed by that of the main character. Examples would be novels such as *Jane Eyre* by Charlotte Brontë, *Emma* by Jane Austen and *The Passion of New Eve* by Angela Carter. Such novels are often written in the first person, where the point of view is that of the *I* telling the story, but may also be written in the third person, with an omniscient author presenting the point of view of the main character.

Alternatively, and especially where there appears to be no one main character in a story, a writer may choose to tell a tale from more than one perspective, moving from one character's point of view to another's. A novel such as *Women in Love* by D.H. Lawrence does just this, moving between descriptions of the actions, thoughts and feelings of two sisters and those of two men with whom they form relationships, using an omniscient authorial voice. Telling the tale from more than one character's perspective provides authors with the opportunity to develop different narrative strands or sub-plots within the main one, which may be used to keep the reader guessing, as in detective fiction, or to create suspense, as in thrillers. It also enables the author to create a wider text world than one seen by a single main character, as in *Little Dorrit* by Charles Dickens or *The Man Who Made Husbands Jealous* by Jilly Cooper.

Often, particularly within twentieth-century fiction, writers may use different varieties of authorial voice and different points of view within the same novel, or even within paragraphs of the same novel. Throughout this century, novelists have experimented with language and narrative technique in a much more self-conscious way than in previous periods. Language is no longer seen as a transparent medium through which a tale or some universal moral truth shines; instead, language itself and how it is used are important parts of the author's concerns. Analysing the way in which language is used to tell a story can tell us as much about the assumptions, social values and prejudices of the period in which it was written as its content and intended point of view, in ways which the writer probably never realised.

ACTIVITY 5.1

Photocopy pages 79 and 80 and read the four extracts. Then answer the following questions on each one.

1 Decide whether it is written in the first or third person.

2 Decide whether its narrator, authorial voice and point of view are consistent or not. If they are, decide what they are.

3 For those extracts which are inconsistent, mark any changes in authorial voice or point of view that occur within each extract by underlining each separate point of view with a different-coloured pen. You should end up by underlining *all* the text. Mark any passage about which you are unsure two or three times with different-coloured pens.

4 For each extract, consider what the effect of the particular point or points of view within it is. What is the effect of changing the point of view or not changing the point of view?

5 What does what you have done so far tell you about the kinds of considerations writers need to take into account when presenting action through a particular point of view?

6 Choose either extract 2 or extract 3 and continue writing the story from a different point of view, using any other character already mentioned or introducing a new one of your own. What effect does this have on the story?

1 *I took off my jumper so there wouldn't be a smell of smoke off it. It was cold now but that didn't matter as much. I looked for somewhere clean to put the jumper. We were at the building site. The building site kept changing, the fenced-in part of it where they kept the diggers and the bricks and the shed the builders sat in and drank tea.*

Roddy Doyle: Paddy Clark Ha Ha Ha

2 *The High School term ended on the Wednesday before Easter. On Good Friday Miss Sigglesthwaite attended the Three Hours' Service, listened, during the afternoon, to Bach's St Matthew Passion broadcast from York Minster, then went to tea with Miss Burton in her office at the school. After tea she wandered out along the cliffs south of Kiplington, wondering what she really ought to do.*
I ought to resign. She's quite right. She's a good girl.
Agnes Sigglesthwaite had been trained in justice and charity. She recognised the quality of her new head mistress. The school was a different place since she had been there.
She's intelligent – modern, enterprising; the children like her; she stands up to the governors, yet they don't quarrel with her. She's clever enough to give way about the things that don't matter; but she stands firm as a rock for those that do.
She's quite right that the staff should be sacrificed to the girls. 'I'm thinking of the girls, Miss Sigglesthwaite.' She meant that. There was no malice in her. She said that she respected my mind. She told Miss Jameson that the school was lucky to have such a distinguished scientist on its staff. But that sigh when she said, 'I'm thinking of the examination results.' That told everything.

Winifred Holtby: South Riding

3 *When his interview with the barrister was over, it was too late to go back to the office. His sight of Katherine had put him queerly out of tune for a domestic evening. Where should he go? Go walk through the streets of London until he came to Katherine's house, to look up at the windows and fancy her within, seemed to him possible for a moment; and then he rejected the plan almost with a blush as, with a curious division of consciousness, one plucks a flower sentimentally and throws it away, with a blush, when it is actually picked. No, he would go and see Mary Datchet. By this time she should be back from her work.*
To see Ralph appear unexpectedly in her room threw Mary for a second off her balance. She had been cleaning knives in her little scullery and when she had let him in she went back again, and turned on the cold-water to its fullest volume, and then turned it off again. 'Now,' she thought to herself, as she screwed it tight, 'I'm not going to let these silly ideas come into my head... Don't you think Mr Asquith should be hanged?' she called back into the sitting room, and when she joined him, drying her hands, she began to tell him about the latest evasion on the part of the Government with respect to the Women's Suffrage Bill. Ralph did not want to talk about politics, but he could not help respecting Mary for taking such an interest in public questions. He looked at her as she leaned forward, poking the fire, and expressing herself very clearly in phrases which bore distantly the taint of the platform, and thought, 'How absurd Mary would think me if she knew that I almost made up my mind to walk all the way to Chelsea in order to look up at Katherine's windows. She wouldn't understand it, but I like her very much as she is.'

Virginia Woolf: Night and Day

4   *It was a fine and quiet afternoon, about three o'clock; but the winter solstice having steadily come on, the lowness of the sun caused the hour to seem later than it actually was, there being little here to remind an inhabitant that he must unlearn his summer experience of the sky as a dial. In the course of many days and weeks sunrise had advanced its quarters from north-east to south-east, sunset had receded from north-west to south-west; but Egdon had hardly heeded the change.*

Eustacia was indoors in the dining-room, which was really more like a kitchen, having a stone floor and a gaping chimney-corner. The air was still, and while she lingered for a moment here alone sounds of voices in conversation came to her ears directly down the chimney. She entered the recess and, listening, looked up the irregular shaft, with its cavernous hollows, where the smoke blundered about on its way to the square bit of sky at the top, from which daylight struck down with a pallid glare upon the tatters of soot draping the flue as sea-weed drapes a rocky fissure. She remembered: the furze-stack was not far from the chimney, and the voices were those of the workers.

Her grandfather joined in the conversation. 'That lad ought never to have left home. His father's occupation would have suited him best, and the boy should have followed on. I don't believe in these new moves in families. My father was a sailor, so was I, and so should my son have been if I had had one.'

Thomas Hardy: The Return of the Native

5.2 Representing speech and thought in fictional texts

You may have noticed in doing Activity 5.1 that one way in which point of view is represented is by the reporting of speech and thought. Speech that we speak to one another face to face is very different to speech that is written down. One immediate and important reason is that they use different mediums of expression: speech uses sound and our hearing, whereas writing uses graphology and our sight as the vehicle for words. Once spoken speech has been spoken, it is gone forever, unless it is recorded, whereas written language is much more permanent: it can be returned to again and again, and altered and changed as spoken speech can never be.

Spoken speech is also interactive, usually involving at least two people taking turns to speak, which makes it a **dialogue**. Depending on the situation, there is no limit to what will be talked about. Where speech requires little or no interaction, as in a lecture, an after-dinner speech or a parliamentary speech, then it has usually been scripted and rehearsed, and is more in the form of a **monologue** than a dialogue. Written dialogue and thought is interactive in a completely different way. The interaction happens on two levels: between the reader and what is read, and between the characters represented. A writer is also far more in control of what characters say than participants in 'live' speech.

The most extreme case of the representation of speech in written form is the dramatic text, where the entire story unfolds through talk. In a film script, dialogue may be interrupted with camera shots, presenting aspects of the story in a way unavailable to written fiction and drama (see 6.4 below). The report of what someone has said is also a major feature of many factual texts, such as police statements, court proceedings and news items in the press and on television. Section 5.3 below considers the reporting of speech in these texts in more detail. In the case of fictional texts, there is a narrator who reports any conversation: what is said is either attributed directly to the characters or presented indirectly by the narrator. The narrator is, therefore, in charge of selecting what to report and of organising how it is reported in ways that simply are not possible for participants of the everyday conversation which the reported speech seeks to imitate.

The other characteristic of written speech is that we are given more than the actual words that are spoken. Information that we can see and hear in 'live' speech – such as who is speaking and their tone of voice – has to be written alongside the words themselves, to give us more details about what was said and how it was said.

There are four main ways in which speech or thought can be represented in narrative. They are:

direct
free direct
indirect
free indirect

5.2.1 Direct speech or thought

Direct speech or thought reports someone's actual words. Consider this example:

> 'Do you see her much?' she said, half-concerned.

In this sentence, there are two independent voices at work. One is the quote, which gives us the actual words spoken, bound by speech marks: 'Do you see her much'. The other is the narrator's voice in a clause which reports information about the quote, in this case who said it, with further information on how it was said: 'she said, half-concerned'. This clause could also tell us to whom the question was addressed.

Reporting speech in this way is called direct speech: the actual words spoken by a character are given, within a sentence which provides further information about the speech. Punctuation marks are used to identify the actual words spoken. The **reporting verb** (the verb which describes the process of speaking) may well tell us a lot about the purpose, emotions and intentions of the utterance. It may also tell us about the expression on a person's face and his or her emotional state. For example:

> 'Go away,' she screamed.
> 'Go away,' she said.

Adding an adverb or a prepositional phrase after the reporting verb, as in the following examples, is another way of conveying more information about what is said.

> 'Most of them were too young,' she replied.
> 'Most of them were too young,' she replied sorrowfully.
> 'Most of them were too young,' she replied with disgust.

5.2.2 Free direct speech and thought

Throughout this century, writers have increasingly experimented with speech representation, for example presenting speech directly but without the usual accompanying punctuation or the reporting clause characteristic of direct speech. Such variations from the representation of direct speech are known as free direct speech or thought. For example:

> She said, 'I want to see the elephants.'
> 'I want to see the elephants.'

Sometimes, writers may use dashes instead of conventional speech marks, or omit punctuation altogether, depending on the particular effect they want to achieve. This tends to make actual speech appear more like free indirect speech (see 5.2.3 below). For example:

> *— I found it, I told him.*
> *My finger was in the book, where George Best's autograph was.*
> *— Did you? he said. — Good man. What?*
> *— What?*
> *— What did you find?*
> *— The autograph, I told him.*

He was messing.
— Let's see it, he said.
I put the book and opened it on his knees.
— There.

Roddy Doyle: Paddy Clarke, Ha Ha Ha. Minerva, 1993

Representing speech in this way tends to minimise the narrator's role and foreground the character and his or her speech.

In free direct thought, speech marks are omitted from a character's thoughts. *'What was to become of him?' she wondered* becomes *What was to become of him, she wondered.*

5.2.3 Indirect speech or thought

Indirect speech or thought is the narrator's report of what was said, rather than the actual words spoken. Consider this example:

She asked him whether he saw her much.

Here, there is only one voice and one point of view. The narrator is using his or her own version of the speech rather than the words that were actually used by the character. There is a **reporting clause** ('she asked him') and a **reported clause** ('whether he saw her much'). No speech marks are needed. Reporting speech in this way usually has the effect of foregrounding the narrator rather than the character who has spoken.

5.2.4 Free indirect speech or thought

Sometimes, speech or, more often, thought is reported in the narrator's words, but from the character's point of view. This is called free indirect thought. Consider this example, from *Women in Love* by D.H. Lawrence.

He thought of Ursula, how sensitive and delicate she really was, her skin so over-fine, as if one skin were wanting. She was really so marvellously gentle and sensitive. Why did he ever forget it? He must go to her at once. He must ask her to marry him. They must marry at once, and so make a definite pledge, enter into a definite communion. He must set out at once and ask her, this moment. There was no moment to spare.

Here, although the character's thoughts are being narrated, the narration shifts to the character's point of view. We can hear the voices of the narrator and of the character speaking at the same time, but at different strengths, a bit like the instruments of an orchestra. The use of free indirect thought or speech within narrative has become more common in modern fiction, particularly in stories which aim to present events through the characters' eyes and minimise the presence of a narrator.

5.2.5 Summary

The different ways in which writers represent speech and thought in writing are summarised in the table below.

	speech	thought
direct	He said, 'I'll come back tomorrow.'	'What will they say of me?' she wondered.
free direct	'Am I too late?'	Am I too late, she wondered.
indirect	He said that he would return the next day.	She wondered what they would say of her.
free indirect	He would come back tomorrow.	What would they say of of her?

Generally, the narrator's role or function is to inform the reader of what is going on and/or to interpret a particular or whole situation for the benefit of the reader.

The characters' role or function is usually to make claims, express doubts and desires, display all sorts of emotions, and evaluate themselves and/or others and/or a particular situation from their individual point of view.

A writer may represent speech or thought in any of these four ways to varying degrees, and may use two or three of them in one paragraph.

The following activity asks you to consider the use of speech and thought in more detail.

ACTIVITY 5.2

1 Read the extract below.
2 What is being reported?
3 What kind of speech or thought representation is being used? What is its effect?
4 What does 'here' relate to in line 2?
5 How can you explain the use of parenthesis (dashes) and brackets in terms of who is speaking?
6 Why does the narrator use 'ought to be happy' instead of 'would be happy'?
7 What does the last sentence mean?

Nor had Adela much to say to him. If his mind was with the breakfast, hers was mainly with her marriage... There were real difficulties here – Ronny's limitations and her own – but she enjoyed facing difficulties, and decided that if she could control her peevishness (always her weak point), and neither rail against Anglo-India nor succumb to it, their married life ought to be happy and profitable. She mustn't be too theoretical...

E.M. Forster: A Passage to India

8 a Write a short speech (two or three sentences) in which you are the speaker, informing someone about something. Include your opinion, concerns or emotional reactions to this piece of information.

b As a narrator, report your speech in the third person. Rather than using the reporting verb *say* or *tell* in each reporting clause, vary the verb so that it produces a particular effect.

c Keeping to the third person, rewrite your speech again, this time making the character's point of view stand out.

d Explain how the different points of view (or different voices) can be picked out from the passage you have created.

For example:

'I am here to inform you that your mother is waiting for you at Reception; she looks very upset and doesn't want to tell me what has happened. So you can leave the class now to meet her.'

'Your mother is waiting for you at reception,' he told the student. 'She looks very upset and doesn't want to tell me what has happened,' he continued very quickly. 'So leave the class now and go and see her,' he ordered.

There she was, waiting for her son to meet her. She felt very upset and didn't want anyone to know what was happening, only her son. Ten minutes! Wasn't he worried about her feelings? Here he was now, coming from his class.

5.2.6 Why report speech at all?

Why is speech represented in narrative at all? In other words, what does it do? It is perfectly possible to recount a tale without using speech at all, but its use has become a common feature of fiction; it is part of what we expect writing which tells a story to include. Generally, including representation of speech and thought in writing does three things.

Firstly, it interrupts the general flow of the narrative, slowing it down and concentrating attention on a particular character, event or relationship.

Secondly, it develops and brings out relationships between characters: their personalities may be revealed by what they say, by their reaction to what is said and/or by what others say about them.

Thirdly, it adds to the sense of a social background, with each character's concerns and speech mannerisms enabling the reader to place him or her in a social context. For example, if a character speaks with a regional accent, this may lead us to make assumptions about the character's social position.

Conversation in fictional texts is, by definition, imaginary, and although it may follow the rules of natural conversation there is nothing natural about it. It is artificial, contrived and interwoven into a wider creative structure, where it always does more than just represent talk, no matter how natural it may appear.

ACTIVITY 5.3

Read the following two extracts and answer these questions on each one.

1 Identify the type or types of speech and thought representation used.

2 What is the function of the dialogue within the narrative? (It may be any or all of the three points listed above.)

3 Do the characters interact with one another in fairly short utterances, in longer ones or a mixture of both? What is the effect of this?

4 a Is the dialogue presented as 'bare', or is it interspersed with references to characters' behaviour and appearance or comments about other things?

   b Do the narrator's words just describe actions, or do they have a wider significance, such as indicating the characters' states of mind, their personality or their relationship to other characters?

5 Is typography used in any way to suggest tone, intonation or styles of speech?

6 How does the speech contribute to the overall development of the narrative?

---

1 *The children were now happily settled on the long red velvet sofa.*

'And so Robin is a big man now and he chooses smoked salmon,' said Ingeborg. 'Do you think you will like that? It is only red fish, you know, with lemon.' But when Robin solemnly registered his choice, she said to the waiter with mock seriousness, 'The gentleman wants a good portion of smoked salmon.'

'What about you Kay?' asked Gerald.

Kay, in her disfiguring chamber-pot velour school hat, wriggled nervously.

'I don't know daddy,' she said.

'Little Kay will have hors d'oeuvre,' said Inge; 'it is the same as our favourite smaabrod *you know. But not so good, perhaps,' she laughed. 'You will have your dear* smaabrod, *won't you Johnnie?'*

John looked primly down the menu. 'I don't see the sense in having it if it's not so good,' he said. 'I will have plover's eggs.'

'Oh, you won't eat the little birds eggs!' cried Inge.

'He'd better eat them while he can,' said Gerald; 'They're being prohibited after this year.'

'And I should like sole mornay to follow,' added John.

'I shan't have fish,' Robin said, with the importance of the eldest child, 'I will have a steak.'

'And what will you have Kay? It's your birthday. You choose what you like.' Gerald looked at his leggy daughter with affection. But Kay looked at her mother.

'What shall I have, Mummy?' she asked.

'Oh, you must not ask me. Ask Papa, who is giving this lovely birthday to a lucky little girl.'

Kay looked at her father obediently. It annoyed Gerald that she apparently had no views of her own, after all she was thirteen, but he guessed the agony this spotlight was causing her and thought it better to order for her. 'Lobster Thermidor,' he said to the waiter. 'There you are Madam,' he said, hating himself for his facetiousness which he could not avoid with his children, 'the lobster is being boiled at your command.'

Kay became very red in the face.

'Oh, Gerald my dear, what have you said? cried Inge. 'She will never eat it now! Poor little Kay! You don't want the lobster to be cooked for you, do you, dear?' Then she whispered fussily to the waiter. 'I've ordered her some fried sole,' she told Gerald.

'Kay's turned red instead of the lobster,' Robin declared with glee.

'Shut up,' said Gerald.

Angus Wilson: Anglo-Saxon Attitudes

2 *'I think, sister, we need not keep Miss Lee any longer, when Fanny goes to live with you?'*

Mrs Norris almost started. 'Live with me, dear Lady Bertram, what do you mean?'

'Is she not to live with you? – I thought you had settled it with Sir Thomas?'

'Me! Never. I never spoke a syllable about it to Sir Thomas, nor he to me. Fanny live with me! the last thing in the world for me to think of, or for anybody to wish that really knows us both. Good heaven! what could I do with Fanny? – Me! a poor helpless forlorn widow, unfit for anything, my spirits quite broke down, what could I do with a girl at her time of life, a girl of fifteen! the very age of all others to need most attention and care, and put the cheerfullest spirits to the test. Sure Sir Thomas could not seriously expect such a thing! Sir Thomas is too much my friend. Nobody who wishes me well, I am sure, would propose it. How came Sir Thomas to speak to you about it?'

'Indeed, I do not know. I suppose he thought it best.'

'But what did he say? – He could not say he wished me to take Fanny. I am sure in his heart he could not wish me to do it.'

'No, he only said he thought it very likely – and I thought so too. We both thought it would be a comfort to you. But if you do not like it, there is no more to be said. She is no encumbrance here.'

'Dear sister! If you consider my unhappy state, how can she be any comfort to me? Here am I a poor desolate widow, deprived of the best of husbands, my health gone in attending and nursing him, my spirits still worse, all my peace in this world destroyed, with barely enough to support me in the rank of gentlewoman, and enable me to live so as not to disgrace the memory of the dear departed – what possible comfort could I have in taking such a charge upon me as Fanny! If I could wish it for my own sake, I would not do so unjust a thing by the poor girl. She is in good hands, and sure of doing well. I must struggle through my sorrows and difficulties as I can.'

'Then you will not mind living by yourself quite alone?'

'Dear Lady Bertram! What am I fit for but solitude? Now and then I shall hope to have a friend in my cottage (I shall always have a bed for a friend); but the most part of my future days will be spent in utter seclusion. If I can make both ends meet, that's all I ask for.'

Jane Austen: Mansfield Park

5.3 Representing speech and thought in factual reporting

As the first activity you did in Unit 1 showed, fiction is not the only kind of writing that tells stories. Newspapers report what they call 'stories' every day, telling of events that have happened in the world. Magazines also tell stories that have happened in real life to real people. Such writing is generally thought to be 'telling the truth' or 'telling it as it was' in ways which distinguish it from fiction. But reporting any event involves a process of selection, involving not only the facts themselves but the words used to describe them, which can result in the same event being presented from completely different perspectives.

One way in which a process of selection can be seen to be at work is in the reporting of speech. Direct and indirect reporting of words in the news has the function of legitimising what is reported. The representation of speech is a strategy commonly used by the media to show that what is being reported is reliable. The same words, however, can be interpreted and therefore retold in various ways, according to different points of view and social conventions.

First of all, the selection of a reporting verb can have a significant effect on how a story is interpreted. For example, take these two sentences, which report two views of the same event:

> The Prime Minister explained that the Budget measures were necessary.
> The Leader of the Opposition claimed that the Budget measures were unnecessary.

The choice of the verb 'explained' in the first statement implies the truth of the Prime Minister's statement, whereas the verb 'claimed' in the second implies an opinion. In fact, both politicians' statements are expressing an opinion.

Similarly, which facts and which quotes are selected for reporting can affect the story. Although it seems to be reporting all the facts of a case in a neutral way, a story may in fact be presenting facts from one participant's point of view, or giving several participants' points of view as a single one. The following activity looks at this in more detail.

ACTIVITY 5.4

1 Read the following newspaper report, which appeared in the *Sunday Times* on 1 May 1994.

2 In which voice, active or passive, is the headline? Why do you think this is?

3 Who is this report about, President Clinton or Paula Jones?

4 **a** Pick out the main verb of each sentence. Decide which ones are reporting factual statements and which speculative ones, paying particular attention to the use of modals. What is the difference between the two sets of sentences?

   b In which category did you place the verb 'claim'? Why?

5 Look at sentences 2, 6, 8, 9, 10, 12 and 13 again. Divide them into those with direct and those with indirect speech representation. What kind of considerations do you think the news reporter took into account in deciding to represent speech as direct or indirect?

6 Divide the direct speech representation according to who is supposed to have said what. Why do you think the writer chose to represent these particular utterances as direct rather than indirect speech?

7 How many different 'speech voices' are represented in the extract? What is the effect of this?

8 Two facts are given about Paula Jones in sentence 11. Why do you think these particular facts have been selected for reporting?

President Clinton to be sued for sexual harassment
(1) President Clinton is to be sued for sexual harassment by a woman who was employed by the state of Arkansas when he was governor. (2) She claims he demanded sex in what she says was a crude and gross abuse of power when he was her boss.
(3) It is the first time an American president has faced such damaging charges in court and already the White House is making preparations to limit the political damage. (4) But legal costs and punitive damages could amount to several million dollars, potentially bankrupting Clinton. (5) The president is unable to use government resources because the incident happened before he was elected to the White House. (6) Paula Jones, 27, claims Clinton summoned her to a room in the Excelsior Hotel in Little Rock during the Arkansas Quality Management Governor's Conference on May 8, 1991, where she was working on the registration desk. (7) Allegedly on Clinton's orders, she was approached by a state trooper and told that the governor wanted to see her. (8) The trooper escorted her to the room where, according to her sworn affidavit, Clinton sexually harassed her, demanding oral sex as well as exposing himself.
(9) 'He took my hand. He was loosening his tie. He told me, "you have nice curves, I love the way your hair goes down your body,"' Jones has said. (10) But she insisted that she fended off his advances after he exposed himself and that she immediately left the room. (11) Jones, whose father is a Nazarene lay minister, was at the time engaged to be married. (12) She says that she went up to Clinton's room because she had hoped he might give her a better job. (13) 'She thought it was an honour. She thought about asking about job opportunities,' said Daniel Traylor, her Little Rock attorney. (14) He will file the suit this week in Little Rock, giving the president 20 days to respond.

Unlike speech representation in fiction, one of the main criteria for representing speech in factual reporting is that of 'significance': in other words, the reporter selects those parts of the exchange which are significant to him or her according to the particular view represented in the text as a whole. Rather than incorporating stretches of dialogue, factual texts such as news reports are more likely to select one or two significant 'utterances'. Sometimes, utterances are curtailed even further, and are reported only in part, as in the following example:

> *Mr. Gilbert Gray, QC, defending, claimed that prosecution witnesses had lied to 'send a man of God like a lamb to the slaughter'.*

> Daily Telegraph, 13 February 1987

One thing which factual and fictional representations of speech have in common is that what is or has been said is reported by a writer, who has chosen to make particular sayings significant. Like fictional texts, factual ones are filtered by an author, who has selected some propositions over others and has a particular point of view towards them.

A fundamental difference between fictional and factual reports of speech, however, is that fictional speech is created by one person, whereas factual reporting of speech is created by two. In a factual report, the reporting of the represented speech depends on its actually having been said by someone. It has, in a sense, two authors: the speaker him or herself and the writer who selects what to report. By contrast, speech in fiction has one author, who may base his or her dialogue on fact, but who is also at liberty to create speech that has never, in fact, existed, because the readers do not expect it to have existed.

Because news stories report facts, we tend to assume that the speech being quoted was actually spoken, as well as that the events reported actually happened. However, this is not always the case, as the following explanation by a crime reporter illustrates:

> *When I needed quotes, I used to make them up, as did some of the others... for we knew what the 'bereaved mother' and the 'mourning father' should have said and possibly even heard them speak what was in our minds rather than what was in theirs.*

> Bird and Dardenne in W.J. Carey (ed): Media, Myths and Narratives, 1988

Factual reporters, therefore, can distort what has been said. They can also be extremely powerful when it comes to reproducing, under the guise of 'fact', what it is most convenient for them to convey, in terms of their aims, particular perspective or point of view. At one extreme, they can make the speech itself up, but more usually they will select parts of a conversation or even single utterances which they think are important. By cutting and pasting speech, they can also change the order of the utterances, which can completely alter the meaning of what was said, although we as readers assume that the speech occurred in the altered sequence. In cases such as this, the distinction between a fictional and a factual saying can be blurred. The quoted words can be presented through many different voices and the 'real' speech becomes as fictionalised as any dialogue created by a novelist.

6 | Analysing scripted dialogue

6.0 Introduction

Some written texts are primarily intended to be read by their audience; others are primarily intended to be spoken. Spoken speech itself can be divided into two types, the **monologic** – that is, spoken by one person – and the **dialogic** – interactive speech between at least two participants. Examples of scripted monologic speech texts include public speeches and lectures, whilst dialogic speech texts include stage, radio and TV plays and films. These two different types of text are not exclusive categories, as a variety of different types of speech text are possible in between. For example, a television advert, or a TV or radio investigative programme, may mix or interweave monologic speech with dialogic.

As 6.1 below points out, there are at least as many differences between spontaneous and scripted speech as there are similarities. Scripted speech is planned and usually has a single author, which enables a far greater degree of control to be exercised over it than can ever be the case in spontaneous speech.

This unit looks at the ways in which speech is scripted in texts other than prose, exploring how it is structured and the implications of various structures for the interpretation of the text.

6.1 Spontaneous and scripted speech

Most scripted speech, especially dialogue, aims to reproduce spontaneous, natural, everyday speech. However, there are several important differences between real spoken speech and written speech intended to imitate it.

Firstly, in scripted speech, one person has usually written the words that a different person speaks, whereas in normal conversation the speakers are the authors of their own words.

Secondly, we are active participants in any conversation with which we are involved, whereas with scripted speech we take the part of onlookers. We see and hear, but do not engage directly with the speakers, although we may be appealed to in a way that invites a response. Scripted speech has an audience in much the same way as any other form of written language, which has implications for the pace at which something is spoken, its phrasing and the degree of implied context.

Scripting speech means that it is written in advance of being spoken and can be edited, unlike everyday, ordinary conversation.

Finally, scripted speech may look like spoken language written down, but if you compare a transcript of a normal conversation with scripted speech you will immediately see many differences. For example, spontaneous speech:

- is repetitive (*'tell me who you saw in the television shop tell me who you saw'*)
- has phrases or clauses which are re-structured or self-corrected halfway through (*'I wanted to go to I wanted to ride my horse'*)
- contains words which would be 'wrong' in written speech, such as lack of subject–verb agreement (*'the film were really good – it were brilliant'*)
- has two or three people talking at once
- has lots of pauses and words to fill pauses (fillers) that we do not use in writing (*ur, um, erm*).

In spontaneous speech, we cannot predict whether or to what extent these features are present. Written speech, on the other hand, tends to use few of these features, if any at all. It is a much more self-conscious form of speech presentation than anything that happens naturally, not least because a writer is in control of what is being said in a way that is impossible in everyday speech. Changes of subject may occur unexpectedly at any time in spontaneous speech, whereas in scripted speech such changes are part of the plan.

In conversation, we usually take it in turns to speak: this is known as *turn-taking*. Often, though, we interrupt before someone has finished their turn, while scripted speech allows each character to take his or her turn.

Spontaneous speech can also be heavily dependent on the context in which it is spoken, relying on the shared knowledge and background of the speakers, which makes specific reference to names and places unnecessary:

Do you think she meant to... I don't know, but she did it anyway... Oh yes, well, she would...

Scripted speech cannot assume such a shared understanding on the part of its listeners. For example, in scripts, even those of long-running soap operas or series, characters nearly always refer to one another by name and explain details of events which in spontaneous conversation would be taken for granted, so that viewers new to the serial or series or those who haven't watched it for a while can pick up the thread of the story. Scripted speech also tends to be about one particular idea, event or person at a time, whereas spontaneous speech can hop about from one topic to another and back again in a seemingly haphazard way. In scripted speech, characters nearly always finish what they start to say without being interrupted, and talk to only one person at a time, using hardly any of the normal features of spontaneous conversation such as repetition, re-structuring and fillers.

Writers of scripted speech have total control over the content of what they write and a great deal over how it is to be spoken. It is then up to the people speaking the words to interpret the script by adding tone of voice, expression, gesture and so on. Scripted speech, then, can have two different audiences: the actors or people who are to do the talking and the audience for whom they interpret the script.

ACTIVITY 6.1

1 Read the following transcript of spoken speech.

2 In pairs, re-write the transcript as scripted dialogue.

3 What changes did you have to make? Why?

A: *you got a cold*

B: *no just a bit sniffy cos I'm I am cold and I'll be alright once I've warmed up do I look as though I've got a cold*

A: *no I thought you sounded as if you were*

B: *mmm*

A: *pull your chair up close if you want is it*

B: *yes I'll be alright in a minute it's just that I'm*

A: *what have you got*

B: *stupid I had about five thousand books to take back to the library yesterday and I got all the way through the college to where the car was at the parking meter at the other end and realised I'd left my coat in my locker and I couldn't just*

A: *mmm*

B: *and I thought well I'll get it on tuesday it's a bit silly cos I need it*

A: *mmm it's gone very cold hasn't it*

B: *mmm it's freezing*

A: *I'm*

B: *you're knitting (laughter) what are you knitting that's not a tiny garment*

A: *no*

B: *no it's for me but it's very plain*

A: *it is nice*

B: *yeah I never did I could never take to knitting except on these double 0 needles with string you know that's my sort of knitting*

A: *yeah*

B: *it grows quickly*

A: *yeah I get very fed up*

B: *the process though do you sew I used to sew a lot when*

A: *no I don't*

B: *in the days when I was a human being*

Crystal and Davy: Investigating English Style

When a script is written down on a page, *all* the words on the page, including any stage directions and camera angles, form part of the script, as well as the actual words the characters speak. What we see or hear is the actors' interpretation of the writer's words and accompanying directions. Scripts, like any other kind of writing, can also be edited and changed. After a script has been written, a director may choose to make his or her own alterations. For example, he or she may decide to cut certain lines, to encourage actors to improvise on the words in the text or to change aspects of the location of a scene (for example, changing it from indoors to outdoors or vice versa).

ACTIVITY 6.2

1 In pairs, read through the following script, intended to be shown as a stage play. The spoken words have been included, but any stage directions have been left out.

2 Write the script out, adding stage directions to do with:

   a setting and location

   b movement

   c how characters should speak.

3 Compare your version with those of others in the class. Do any differences of representation emerge?

Dysart: *So, did you have a good journey? I hope they gave you lunch at least. Not that there's much to choose between a British Rail meal and one here.*
Won't you sit down?
Is this your full name? Alan Strang?
And you're seventeen. Is that right? Seventeen... Well?
Alan: *Double your pleasure*
Double your fun
With Doublemint, Doublemint
Doublemint gum.
Dysart: *Now, let's see. You work in an electrical shop during the week. You live with your parents and your father's a printer. What sort of things does he print?*
Alan: *Double your pleasure*
Double your fun
With Doublemint, Doublemint
Doublemint gum.
Dysart: *I mean does he do leaflets and calendars? Things like that?*
Alan: *Try the taste of Martini*
The most beautiful drink in the world.
It's the right one –
The bright one –
That's Martini!
Dysart: *I wish you'd sit down, if you're going to sing. Don't you think you'd be more comfortable?*

Peter Shaffer: Equus, Act I scene 3

6.2 Scripting factual speech texts

Scripting speech which deals with factual events, like representing speech in factual reporting, as discussed in 5.3, involves selecting the content of what is to be said from a wide range of possibilities. The speech in spoken news items, for example, will be selected and edited in ways which fit the content of the programme. When you see or hear an interview on radio or television, what you hear are usually edited extracts taken from the whole interview, just as when you read an interview that, too, will have been edited. The way in which material such as interviews or commentary is edited can highlight particular elements of what people have said or what a camera has filmed. This selection of facts for a particular purpose becomes, in its most blatant form, propaganda.

It is probably because of the ways in which speech can be edited that prominent public figures such as politicians, actors and members of the royal family not only ask to see the questions they will be asked before an interview, in order to prepare their answers, but also ask to see, hear or read the final edited interview before it is published or transmitted. Nearly everything that we see and hear on television and radio has been scripted, edited and previewed before it is transmitted or broadcast, and very little television these days is broadcast 'live'.

Scripted speech can, however, involve monologic speech interspersed with extracts of spontaneous, natural conversation. For example, in television and radio news reporting, the scripted monologue may be interrupted by an extract from an interview, either in the studio or 'vox pop' (that is, interviews with randomly chosen people recorded in a natural setting).

6.3 Scripting dialogue in plays and films

Scripted dialogue has to convey to its viewer or listener all the things normally described through narration in prose writing. For example, what the characters say and do has to convey emotions and actions and move on the plot, as in the extract from the play *Equus* used in Activity 6.2 above. We do not have access to the thoughts in the characters' heads as we do in novels, short stories or poems. All our information about their personalities and motivation comes from the words which they say. An analysis of a script, then will need to look very closely at ways in which the language spoken by characters and the stage directions give us clues to the characters' personalities and reasons for their actions, as well as indicating the actions themselves.

A further consideration in analysing scripts is their reference to deictic time, space and place. Section 4.1.1 above introduced deictics in considering ways in which cohesion is achieved in a text. Since a playscript is written to be spoken, deictics serve as a way not only of binding the text together but also of extending the text world beyond the stage or set to incorporate elements of a wider world. For example, in the conversation given in Activity 6.1 above, speaker A comments on the weather. As this is an example of natural speech, we can assume that the remark was about the actual weather at the time the conversation took place. When a dialogue is being performed on the radio, stage or screen, any world outside the scene cannot actually exist, but we are invited to believe in it as part of the process of engaging with the scenes that are being acted out.

As 6.1 above pointed out, much of our everyday conversation relies on a shared understanding of the context within which it is taking place, and the more we have in common with the people we are talking to the more assumptions we make. References to places, times, people and events will also usually imply a common understanding of those elements within our daily lives.

Dialogue in scripts, too, will refer to places, times, people and events, which may occur 'outside' the script (see 4.1.1 above). As the audience, we are drawn into the script world both through events and settings we actually experience *and* through references to places, times, people and events which we do not actually see but which may have a direct bearing on the action played out on stage or set.

The following activity takes an extract from a television play to consider the interrelationship between dialogue, action and representation.

ACTIVITY 6.3

1 Read the following extract taken from Willy Russell's television play *Terraces*.

2 What information does the dialogue by itself give us on:
   a each of the three characters (e.g. how they speak and their verbal mannerisms, as well as their personalities)
   b their relationships with one another
   c what is happening
   d anything else (e.g. the significance of the crossword clues)?

3 Overall, what do the staging directions add to the dialogue?

4 Where is the 'going down there' Susan refers to?

Scene 5: Danny's House – Lounge Interior. Day: Day 1

(SUSAN IS PAINTING HER NAILS. DANNY IS READING A NOVEL. THEIR SON, MICHAEL, IS DOING A CROSSWORD IN THE PAPER).

SUSAN:
Are we goin', Danny?
DANNY: (ABSENT)
Mm?
SUSAN:
Are we goin' down there or not?
MICHAEL:
Dad ... what's a (READING) a 'Historical gang' beginnin' with M...
DANNY:
A what?
MICHAEL:
Three letters?
DANNY:
'ere are ... let's have a look.
MICHAEL: (GETTING UP TO SHOW DANNY THE PAPER)
A historical gang.
DANNY:
Historical! Hysterical ... you nutter!
MICHAEL:
Oh yeh.
(SUSAN WALKS OVER TO THE MIRROR TO APPLY LIPSTICK)
SUSAN:
Are we goin'?
DANNY:
D'y' fancy it?
SUSAN:
I thought y'd want to celebrate gettin' through to the final.

DANNY:
That's not celebratin'. It's just drinkin' for the sake of it an' going over every last detail a thousand times.
SUSAN:
Oh, you're a real killjoy, you are.
MICHAEL:
Dad ... what's a ten letter word that means 'one who always agrees'?
DANNY:
Who's supposed to be doin' this crossword?
SUSAN:
Other fellers would be overjoyed if their team got through to the final.
DANNY:
I am overjoyed. I just can't see much point in goin' over it again an' again. Eddie an' that lot, they're like bloody TV commentators.
SUSAN:
So we're not going out?
DANNY:
I didn't say that. Do you want to go out, love?
SUSAN:
Well, it is Saturday night.
DANNY:
Yes, but do you want to go out?
SUSAN:
Yes. Yes!
DANNY:
Well get your coat on then. If you want to go out, we'll go out.
SUSAN:
Well why didn't you say that in the first place? Come on. Hey – I bet it's a riot down there tonight!

6.4 Presenting point of view in scripted speech

As Section 5.1 above pointed out, an important feature of narrative texts is that events are portrayed from a particular point of view. Stage plays, films and television and radio drama are not able to present point of view in the same way as written narratives. Reading a novel gives us the time to absorb descriptions as well as the intricacies of the plot, whereas a film or play condenses its story into a much shorter time span. However, sometimes in film and television, a narrator is used, in what is known as a 'voice-over'; here, the voice of one of the characters (usually the main one) is heard off-screen, telling us their thoughts, whilst an image is presented on-screen. *The Color Purple, Dances with Wolves* and *The Age of Innocence* are all films where this technique has been used. In radio, too, voice-over can be used, with a narrator as well as other characters, as in Dylan Thomas's *Under Milk Wood.*

   Actions, thoughts, background, character and plot are all conveyed to us through images and voice in scripted drama, or through voice alone in the case of radio. In the visual medium of film, a coherent and intelligible story emerges through the way the scenes are shot and edited together, according to conventions which have evolved. For example, as a dialogue between two people progresses, there is usually a gradual focusing down on the individual protagonists, so that each is shown in close-up. Camera instructions, therefore, form part of a script for film or television, alongside the speech itself and the movements the characters make. Film is thus able to employ narrative structures more often associated with fiction, such as point of view, in ways stage plays cannot.

ACTIVITY 6.4

1 Photocopy pages 99 and 100 and read the extract, taken from E.M. Forster's novel *A Passage to India*.

2 In pairs, turn the extract into a script for a stage play, including details of your set. You might find it helpful to get you started to go through the text first highlighting those parts of it you think you will use in your script. Remember that you will not be able to use everything and may have to change or add speech to capture in sound what is presented in the narrative.

3 How is your script different to the original text? What did you have to leave out or add? What other decisions did you have to make in turning the text from one type into another?

4 Read or act out your script aloud to the rest of the class. Then discuss your answers to question 3 above.

5 *A Passage to India* was made into a film in 1978. You might like to compare the prose extract with the film script given in Appendix 2.

6 How does your version compare with the film version? Do they involve different interpretations and realisations of the novel? If so, in what way?

Adela Quested, an Englishwoman, has gone to India to get married. This extract from the novel tells of a visit she makes to a site of local interest – the Marabar Caves – with Aziz, an Indian doctor. Adela is preoccupied with thoughts about her forthcoming marriage to Ronny Heaslop, an English colonial officer. Dr Aziz is preoccupied with the organisation of the trip, for which he is responsible.

Miss Quested and Aziz and a guide continued the slightly tedious expedition. They did not talk much, for the sun was getting high. The air felt like a warm bath into which hotter water is trickling constantly, the temperature rose and rose... Aziz had never liked Miss Quested as much as Mrs Moore, and had little to say to her, less than ever now that she would marry a British official.

Nor had Adela much to say to him. If his mind was with the breakfast, hers was mainly with her marriage... There were real difficulties here – Ronny's limitations and her own – but she enjoyed facing difficulties, and decided that if she could control her peevishness (always her weak point), and neither rail against Anglo-India nor succumb to it, their married life ought to be happy and profitable. She mustn't be too theoretical; she would deal with each problem as it came up, and trust to Ronny's common sense and her own. Luckily, each had an abundance of common sense and goodwill.

But as she toiled over a rock that resembled an inverted saucer, she thought, 'What about love?' The rock was nicked by a double row of footholds, and somehow the question was suggested by them. Where had she seen footholds before? Oh yes, they were the pattern traced in the dust by the wheels of the Nawab Bahadur's car. She and Ronny – no, they did not love each other.

'Do I take you too fast?' enquired Aziz, for she had paused, a doubtful expression on her face. The discovery had come so suddenly that she felt like a mountaineer whose rope had broken. Not to love the man one's going to marry! Not to find out till this moment! Not even to have asked oneself the question until now! Something else to think out. Vexed rather than appalled, she stood still, her eyes on the sparkling rock. There was esteem and animal contact at dusk, but the emotion that links them was absent. Ought she to break her engagement off? She was inclined to think not – it would cause so much trouble to others; besides, she wasn't convinced that love is necessary to a successful union. If love is everything, few marriages would survive the honeymoon. 'No, I'm all right, thanks,' she said, and, her emotions well under control, resumed the climb, though she felt a bit dashed. Aziz held her hand, her guide adhered to the surface like a lizard and scampered about as if governed by a personal centre of gravity.

'Are you married, Dr Aziz?' she asked, stopping again, and frowning.

'Yes, indeed, do come and see my wife' – for he felt it more artistic to have his wife alive for a moment.

'Thank you,' she said absently.

'She is not in Chandrapore just now.'

'And have you children?'

'Yes, indeed, three,' he replied in firmer tones.

'Are they a great pleasure to you?'

'Why, naturally, I adore them,' he laughed.

'I suppose so.' What a handsome little Oriental he was, and no doubt his wife and children were beautiful too, for people usually get what they already possess. She did not admire him with any personal warmth, for there was nothing of the vagrant in her blood, but she guessed he might attract women of his race and rank, and she regretted that neither she nor Ronny had physical charm. It does make a difference in a relationship – beauty, thick

hair, a fine skin. Probably this man had several wives – Mohammedans always insist on their full four, according to Mrs Turton. And having no one else to speak to on that eternal rock, she gave rein to the subject of marriage and said in her honest, decent, inquisitive way: 'Have you one wife or more than one?'

The question shocked the young man very much. It challenged a new conviction of his community, and new convictions are more sensitive than old. If she had said, 'Do you worship one god or several?' he would not have objected. But to ask an educated Indian Moslem how many wives he has – appalling, hideous! He was in trouble how to conceal his confusion. 'One, one in my particular case,' he spluttered, and let go of her hand. Quite a number of caves were at the top of the track, and thinking, 'Damn the English even at their best,' he plunged into one of them to recover his balance. She followed at her leisure, quite unconscious that she had said the wrong thing, and not seeing him, she also went into a cave, thinking with half her mind 'sight-seeing bores me,' and wondering with the other half about marriage.

7 Written language change

7.0 Introduction

So far, this book has looked at the various ways in which language is used to create a text and at texts of particular kinds. This unit now turns to look more closely at the ways in which writing itself has changed over the centuries, particularly since the fifteenth century, when printing began.

The history of writing as a medium of communication is a much shorter one than that of speech. In terms of language history, written English, being some 500 years old, is a very young, developing phenomenon.

The development of written texts as a medium of communication in English has been closely connected with technological advances, starting with the introduction of the printing press in the fifteenth century and progressing to developments in printing and publishing technology in the nineteenth and twentieth centuries.

The more widespread use of printing during the nineteenth century, together with a growth in the number of people who could read, made printed material such as song sheets, adverts, newspapers, magazines, novels and textbooks accessible to a far wider audience than had ever been possible before.

Throughout the twentieth century, printing and the technology associated with it have continued to develop, bringing with them new ways of publishing using computers. Visual means of communication such as film, radio and television broadcasting have also added to the variety of written, scripted forms.

Different forms of written text have a history in themselves. For example, the novel as a form began to develop in the eighteenth century, whilst plays have been around for much longer, and religious texts longer still. The language used has changed, too. As a written code, the English language we know today was standardised during the eighteenth century. Since then, changes in language have continued to happen and will go on doing so. The idea that language stopped changing 200 years ago is clearly a false one: it is likely that the English language, in all its spoken dialect varieties, as well as in its written forms, is changing just as much in the present has it has in the past, although the *rate* of change may be different, as 7.1 below explains further.

The spoken language of previous centuries is lost to us, but written forms have survived. It is these surviving texts which provide evidence for the fact that language does change in all kinds of ways, to such an extent that the 'English' of the Middle Ages appears to us to resemble a foreign language. The example below is a cure for wolfsbane poisoning, written in the tenth century:

> *Gif mon þung ete, āþege buteran ond drince; se þung gewīt on þā buteran. Eft wiþ þon stande on hēafde; āslea him mon fela scearpena on þām scancan; þonne gewit ūt þæt ātter þurh þā scearpan.*

Could you make sense of it? Spelling, word formation (morphology) and grammar are so different as to seem like another language. A modern translation of this passage is as follows:

> *If you eat wolf's bane, take butter and drink; the poisonous plant will transfer to the butter. Then stand on your head. You should be scratched many times on the shanks; then the poison will pass out through the scratches.*

Coming closer in time, fourteenth-century English becomes easier to understand, but is still very different to modern English, as the following example, written by John of Trevisa (died 1402) shows:

> *Also Englyschmen, þeyʒ hy hadde fram þe begynnyng þre maner speche, Southeron, Northeron, and Mydell speche in þe myddel of þe lond, as hy come of þre maner people of Germania, noþeles by commyxstion and mellyng, furst wiþ Danes and afterward wiþ Normans, in menye þe contray longage ys apeyred, and som vseþ strange wlaffyng, chyteryng, harryng, and garryng grisbittyng.*

This is still a long way from the English of today, as the following translation illustrates:

> *Also though Englishmen had from the beginning three kinds of speech, southern, northern and middle speech from the middle of the country, as they are descended from three kinds of Germanic people, and also by mixing, first with the Danes and then with the Normans, the country language has deteriorated in many, and some use strange stammering, chittering, snarling and grating gnashing of teeth.*

7.1 A framework for analysing language change

One way of considering the various ways in which language has changed is to consider the words on the page before us. This can be done in relation to the following areas:

> *graphology* typeface, print size, punctuation, spelling
> *vocabulary* both lexis and semantics
> *syntax* word order
> *phonology* sound

Every one of these different aspects of language is subject to change, but the rate at which this happens varies considerably: it can take place over decades or even centuries. The element that changes most quickly is probably vocabulary, followed by graphology. Syntax and phonology tend to change at a much slower rate generally, and in writing change much more slowly than in speech. The reasons why any of these aspects of language changes are many and varied, but they are nearly always to do with developments in the wider social environment, such as war, invasion, new technologies and new ideas.

The next three sections in this unit describe ways of analysing aspects of change within these four areas in more detail. Taken together, they will provide you with a useful starting point in your analysis of texts written in previous centuries.

ACTIVITY 7.1

1 Take both of the texts reproduced in 7.0 above and comment briefly on each one in terms of the four categories:

a graphology
b vocabulary
c syntax
d phonology

7.2 Graphology and vocabulary

7.2.1 Graphology

The graphology of texts has changed considerably since people first started to write. The invention of publishing in the fifteenth century revolutionised the reproduction of written texts, which before then had always been handwritten. Graphological conventions, **orthographic** features, including spelling, and typographic elements such as size and type of print have themselves changed significantly since the fifteenth century, and can provide valuable clues as to when a text was written.

Generally, modern texts tend to use different styles of typeface and to be less densely printed on a page than those of even fifty years ago, with far greater use of pictures, photographs and, increasingly, colour. The actual production of written texts has changed dramatically, with handwritten manuscripts giving way to printing, which in turn has been superseded by computer-generated publishing, such as desktop publishing and electronic texts. These inventions have had a significant impact on the writing, design and editing processes, including typographical and graphological conventions.

The following sections look at two particular features of graphological change: punctuation and spelling.

Punctuation

How we perceive a sentence is closely connected to the way it is punctuated. But conventions of punctuation, both within words and between them, have changed over the centuries. Today, the use of punctuation is closely connected to the grammatical construction of sentences, but this has not always been so. In the fifteenth and sixteenth centuries, punctuation was more closely connected to rhythm and elocution. This began to change during the seventeenth century, when its function became more grammatical and logical.

For example, the conventions we associate with the apostrophe, such as its use to show possession, did not become established until the second half of the seventeenth century, while direct speech was not punctuated until the eighteenth. The question mark appeared much later than either the comma or the full stop, two of the first punctuation marks ever used.

One of the consequences of editing ancient texts has been that each new edition standardises not only the spelling and syntax but also the punctuation, to accord with current conventions. Thus the most recent editions of texts such as the Bible, the Oxford English Dictionary and the plays of William Shakespeare look physically very different to the original text. When we come across an ancient text, therefore, we cannot assume that it will use all the conventions we take for granted. If the typography, spelling and punctuation of a text from an earlier century conform to modern conventions, you can be fairly certain that an editing hand has been at work.

ACTIVITY 7.2

1 Compare the two extracts below, taken from the play *King Lear* by William Shakespeare. The first is taken from the 1972 Penguin edition and the second from an edition printed in 1623.

2 List the particular aspects of language which have been changed in the modern edition.

3 What significance do you think the differences have for reading and performing the text?

---

1   *LEAR: ...Tell me, my daughters,*
   since now we will divest us both of rule,
   Interest of territory, cares of state,
   Which of you shall we say doth love us most,
   That we our largest bounty may extend
   Where nature doth with merit challenge. Gonerill,
   Our eldest born, speak first.

   GONERILL: Sir, I love you more than word can wield the matter,
   Dearer than eyesight, space, and liberty,
   Beyond what can be valued rich or rare,
   No less than life, with grace, health, beauty, honour,
   As much as child e'er loved or father found;
   A love that makes breath poor and speech unable;
   Beyond all manner of 'so much' I love you.

   King Lear, I.1.48–61

---

2   *LEAR: ...Tell me my daughters*
   (Since now we will diuest vs both of Rule,
   Interest of Territory, Cares of State)
   Which of you shall we say doth loue vs most,
   That we, our largest bountie may extend
   Where Nature doth with merit challenge. Gonerill,
   Our eldest borne, speak first.

> *GONERILL: Sir, I loue you more than words can wield the matter,*
> *Deerer than eye-sight, space and libertie,*
> *Beyond what can be valewed, rich or rare,*
> *No lesse then life, with grace, health, beauty, honor:*
> *As much as Childe ere lou'd, or Father found.*
> *A loue that makes breath poore, and speech vnable,*
> *Beyond all manner of so much I Loue you.*

Spelling

How words are spelt, too, changes over time. Before the seventeenth century, written texts varied enormously in terms of spelling as well as punctuation. English replaced Latin and French as the language of official documents during the early part of the fifteenth century, which gave the impetus to the adoption of a standard spelling system, in contrast to the huge variety that had prevailed in Middle English. The introduction of the printing press by William Caxton in 1476 consolidated the need for a standardised system.

From the seventeenth century onwards, when printing became more widespread, printed texts began to look more like modern English texts. Samuel Johnson wrote the first English dictionary in the eighteenth century, and also in that century grammarians published the first English grammar books. These adopted a very prescriptive approach to language, based on notions of 'correctness' and 'good' uses of language. Before the eighteenth century, variation in spelling was accepted and tolerated: the ability to spell was not linked to the notion of literacy in the same way as it is today. William Shakespeare, for example, writing in the seventeenth century, spelt his own name in several different ways. Sometimes words could be spelt in two or more ways within the same paragraph: *idolatry/idolatrie; doth/dooth; heere/here; with/wyth; heart/hart; forbidden/forbiden*.

With the introduction of printing, capital letters were usually used for names and for the initial letter of the first word of a sentence, as they are today. During the seventeenth century, capital letters were also used for other words, particularly those which were thought to be important in a text, but this particular orthographic feature had declined by the mid-eighteenth century.

However, whilst spellings have stabilised, pronunciation continues to change, so that spellings which once corresponded to pronunciation no longer do so. (See Section 7.4 below.)

Generally speaking, the more unfamiliar a text appears in terms of its spelling and its use of words, the older it will probably be.

7.2.2 Vocabulary

New words are entering the English language all the time, just as others fall out of use. Dictionaries, most commonly thought of as a record of word usage, are constantly being updated and revised to account for changes of usage and meaning. There is no one single reason why vocabulary changes, but several. For example, changes in work practices in an area such as printing also include changes in the vocabulary associated with the work. The widespread use of computer technology in printing has brought along with it a whole new vocabulary – *word processing, mouse, hardware, software* – as well as causing the vocabulary associated with the old methods to fall out of use. Changes in work practices are generally associated with changes in the wider social sphere, to do with economic and political change. New vocabulary thus often indicates more far-reaching changes in society as a whole.

Similarly, as lifestyles change, so too does the vocabulary associated with them. For example, there were once wide areas of vocabulary associated with horses and coaches as a form of transport and with domestic service. This vocabulary has narrowed and fallen out of use as a result of changes in methods of transportation and ways of cleaning and cooking. Similarly, vocabulary associated with the fashion of men's and women's clothes changes as the fashions themselves change.

Take, for example, the following article, which appeared in a New Zealand newspaper during 1988:

> A senior citizen is one who was here before the Pill, before television, frozen food, credit cards or ball point pens. For us, time-sharing meant togetherness, not computers, and a chip meant a piece of wood. Hardwear [sic] meant hard wear, and software wasn't even a word. Teenagers never wore slacks. We were before pantyhose, drip-dry clothes, dishwashers, clothes driers and electric blankets. Girls wore Peter Pan collars and thought that cleavage was something that butchers did. We were before Batman, vitamin pills, disposable nappies, jeeps, pizzas and instant coffee, and Kentucky Fried had not even been hatched. In our day, cigarette smoking was fashionable, grass was for mowing and pot was something you cooked in. A gay person was the life and soul of the party, and nothing more, while AIDS meant beauty lotions or help for someone in trouble. We are today's senior citizens. A hardy bunch, when you think how the world has changed and of the adjustments we have had to make.

The words that are in common use at any one period of time, therefore, closely reflect the world or society of that time. As society alters, so, too, do the words people use within it, either through new words coming into use and others falling out of use, or through changes in meaning. For example, the word *punk* was often used in the sixteenth and seventeenth centuries to mean a down-and-out, more like our current word *tramp*. The word fell out of use during the eighteenth and nineteenth centuries, to be revived in the twentieth, with a change of meaning. During the 1970s the word was applied to a particular music and fashion movement, and this is how most people would now understand it. Reading texts written in previous centuries, such as those written in the sixteenth and seventeenth centuries by William Shakespeare, may be difficult for us because not only are some words no longer used, but ones we are familiar with may have had different meanings then.

The influence on society of foreign cultures and of war or invasion can also have a major impact on the vocabulary of a language. The vocabulary associated with food, for example, has been significantly widened as restaurants and foreign travel have introduced us to food of different cultures. The Cold War between East and West and attempts at international cooperation in the 1990s have given us new vocabulary in news reporting, such as *peace-keeping force* in place of *army*.

Such changes reflect wider changing attitudes, in this case the role of soldiers not directly involved in defending their own countries.

Changes in different areas of vocabulary happen at different rates. Slang, for example, is most usually associated with spoken language; in its written form it appears in texts which imitate natural conversation, such as popular fiction, plays and television programmes, or in those which appeal to a particular age group, such as comics. Slang is commonly associated with youth culture, and each generation invents its own words, making the previous vocabulary outdated and old-fashioned. People who were teenagers in the late 1950s and 1960s, for example, used words such as *smashing* and *fab*, which have since been superseded by others. Some slang words may become part of the dictionary, such as the 1980s word *yuppie*, but generally they do not survive long enough to become established. Slang, like fashion, dates very quickly, and in its turn dates any text which uses it.

ACTIVITY 7.3

1 Read the two extracts below. Make a brief summary of the content of each one.

2 Discuss and compare their use of punctuation, spelling and vocabulary.

3 From your discussion and your own reading, can you make an informed guess as to the century in which each one was written?

4 On which particular aspects of the graphology and vocabulary did you base your opinion?

5 What other information provided you with clues?

---

1 *The kynge bithoughte hym and marked how many a yonglyng departed from thens al wpying/which were nyghe of his kynne/and sayde to hym self/heir behouth other counseyl herto/Though reynart be a shrewe/ther be many good of his lignage/tybert the catte sayde/sir bruyn and sir Isegrym/how be ye thus slowe. it is almost euen/hier ben many busshes and hedges. yf he escaped from vs. and were delyuerd out of this paryl he is so subtyl and so wyly and can so many deceytes that he should neuer be taken agayn.*

The History of Reynard the Fox, translated from the French by William Caxton

---

2 *May it please your Majesty,*
A work, having for its objects, to lay the solid foundation of literary knowledge amongst the Labouring Classes of the community, to give practical effect to the natural genius in the Soldier, the Sailor, the Apprentice, and the Plough-boy, and to make that genius a perennial source of wealth, strength and safety to the kingdom; such a work naturally seeks the approbation of your Majesty, who, amongst all the Royal Personages of the present age, is the only one that appears to have justly estimated the value of The People.
The Nobles and the Hierachy have long had the arrogance to style themselves, the Pillars that support the Throne. But, as your majesty has now ascertained, Royalty has, in the hour of need, no efficient supporters but The People.

William Cobbett: A Grammar of the English Language

7.3 Syntax

7.3.1 Word order and clause structures

The pace of change of syntax is much slower than the pace of change in vocabulary, but a glance at any Old or Middle English text, such as those given in 7.0 above, is enough to indicate that changes have certainly happened. For example, in the early form of English known as Anglo-Saxon or Old English (covering the period AD400 to the early Middle Ages) the order in which words were written in a sentence was fairly flexible, unlike in modern English, where there is far less flexibility. Some aspects of this flexibility survived into the English of the seventeenth century; for instance, allowing parts of sentences – such as a verb or object – to be moved to the beginning. This use of word order, however, survived mainly in literary texts, and not in other forms of writing of the time, such as letters and diaries.

Until the fourteenth century, within the period of Late Middle English, sentence structure was relatively simple, and sentences tended mainly to consist of single or coordinate clauses. During the Renaissance period in the sixteenth century, when the study of ancient Latin and Greek flourished, a syntax derived from Latin was increasingly applied to English. One of the consequences of this was an increase in subordination within sentences. Long, controlled sentences of the kind to be found in Latin texts by writers such as Cicero were much admired, and the sentence structure found within them was applied to the construction of written English.

In the fourteenth century, subordination with conjunctions other than *when*, *while* and *as* was uncommon. From the Renaissance onwards, the use of subordination became increasingly associated with sophistication, and the earlier typical pattern was relegated to 'unsophisticated' texts such as popular fiction and diaries. In recent years, there has been a move (especially within the Civil Service) to design material aimed at a public audience – forms and leaflets in particular – to be simple and more accessible in style. This is done by using active rather than passive constructions, less subordination and more single or coordinate clauses.

ACTIVITY 7.4

1 Photocopy page 109 and read the three extracts.

2 With a pen or pencil, mark the clause divisions within each sentence and decide what kind each clause is.

3 How does the clause structure relate to the content of each extract?

1 *Ethiope is departed in two princypall parties; and that is in the Est partie, and in the Meridionall partie, the whiche partie meridionall is clept Moretane. And the folk of that contree ben blake ynow, and more blake than in the tother partie; and thei ben clept Mowres. In that partie is a well, that in the day is so cold that no man may drynke thereoffe; and in the nyght it is so hoot that no man may suffre hys hond therein.*

John Mandeville: Travels. c. 1400

2 *There dwelt in London a rich Merchant that kept a great Ape, which when he had broke loose, would doe mischief, and he could not see any thing done before him, but he would be a doing the like. There dwelt a Cobler ouer-against this Gentlemans, which the Ape would view how he cut out his Leather, and when the Cobler was gone abroad, Iacke would come ouer & play such reakes [pranks], spoyling all the shoes & leather he could come neere; which was much hinderance to the poore man, and he knew not hoow to be reuenged, because he had all his worke from thence; yet at last a crotchet came into his head, and spying the Ape looking vpon him: to work hee went cutting his leather, and then whetting his knife of his whetstone, and then would he with the backe of the knife seeme to cut his throat.*

The Tale of the Cobler and the Ape. 1632

3
Of man's first disobedience, and the fruit
Of that forbidden tree whose mortal taste
Brought death into the World, and all our woe,
With loss of Eden, till one greater Man
Restore us, and regain the blissful seat,
Sing, Heavenly Muse, that, on the secret top
Of Oreb, or of Sinai, didst inspire
That shepherd who first taught the chosen seed
In the beginning how the heavens and earth
Rose out of Chaos: or, if Sion hill
Delight thee more, and Siloa's brook that flowed
Fast by the Oracle of God, I thence
Invoke thy aid to my adventurous song,
That with no middle flight intends to soar
Above th' Aonian mount, while it pursues
Things unattempted yet in prose or rhyme.

John Milton: Paradise Lost, Book 1. 1667

Throughout the Renaissance period, the number of conjunctions and prepositions used in writing increased. New prepositions were created by using participles of verbs, such as *considering, during* and *notwithstanding*. One important addition to the word class of conjunctions was the word *because*, formed by the condensing of the phrase *by the cause that. Because* was very rare in Middle English; the Oxford English Dictionary records its first known use as in 1386, with an example taken from Chaucer. Even so, the conjunction *for* or *that* was much more commonly used until the seventeenth century. During that century, long Ciceronian sentences came to be seen as old-fashioned, though Milton wrote most of his epic poem *Paradise Lost* in such a style.

It was in the seventeenth century that something approaching a fixed standard for forming sentences was reached, with a much sharper distinction between coordination and subordination. From the eighteenth century onwards, the written dialect we know as standard English (which first became dominant in the fifteenth century) became the established and favoured form, and was the one to which grammars of English applied. During the eighteenth century, prescriptive attitudes towards the use of grammar, based on the grammar of Latin, resulted in some strict rules as to how sentences should and should not be constructed. These rules included not ending a sentence with a preposition *(the chair she sat on)* and not splitting infinitives *(to clearly explain)*. In Latin, these grammatical forms are contained in a single word, rather than being separate words. Of course, in reality, writers as well as speakers do construct their sentences in this way. The novels of Jane Austen and George Eliot, for example, contain sentences which end in prepositions, and perhaps the most famous popular use of a split infinitive is Captain Kirk's statement in the television programmes and films of Star Trek: 'to boldly go...'.

More recent twentieth-century systems of grammar, such as functional grammar, aim to base their approach very much on describing how language is actually used rather than prescribing how it ought to be used. Thus, along with changes in the language itself over the centuries, there have also been changes in attitudes towards language use and changes in the way grammar itself is described.

7.3.2 Archaism

Using outdated forms of language is known as **archaism.** This technique is generally associated with poetry, and survived well into the nineteenth century, when it was used by poets such as William Wordsworth (see Activity 7.5). One common archaic form is the inversion of the verb phrase and a noun phrase that would usually follow it. The effect of this is to give the impression that a poem was written in a much earlier time than it actually was.

ACTIVITY 7.5

1 Read the following stanza from a poem by William Wordsworth called *The Last of the Flock* (1798).

2 A more usual sequence for the first line in modern English would be to have the subject ('I') first, followed by the verb ('have been') and then the rest of the clause. Rewrite the rest of the stanza, placing the underlined phrases after the appropriate verb phrase, rather than before.

3 What is the effect of this rewrite?

> *In distant countries I have been,*
> *And yet I have not often seen*
> *A healthy man, a man full grown,*
> *Weep in the public roads alone.*
> *But such a one, on English ground,*
> *And in the broad high-way, I met;*
> *Along the broad high-way he came,*
> *His cheeks with tears were wet.*

English legal texts continue to use archaic forms of language. Their writers have resisted changing their use of language and the register in which they write to a more modern idiom. Why this is so is not really clear. Some would say it is to intimidate the general public and force them to employ solicitors and barristers to represent them, whilst others maintain that such intricate and specific language use is necessary to make what is being explained absolutely clear and unambiguous.

Consider, for example, the following extract taken from a legal notice printed in the *Glasgow Herald*:

> *Notice is Hereby Given, That ... the sheriff at Campbelltown, by Interlocuter dated 30th December 1986, ordered all parties desirous to lodge Answers in the hands of the Sheriff Clerk at Castlehill, Campbelltown within 8 days after intimation, advertisement or service, and in the meantime, until the prayer of the Petition had been granted or refused, nominated Alistair White to be Provisional Liquidator of the said Company on his finding caution before extract.*

When one is faced with a text of this kind, it is possible to analyse it by looking at the three different categories considered so far: graphology, vocabulary and syntax.

Graphology   A distinctive feature of the extract is its archaic orthography, since it makes extensive use of capitalisation for words which are no longer capitalised in modern English. Despite this archaism, the spelling itself conforms to modern patterns, as does the punctuation.

Vocabulary   This text uses a lot of unusual vocabulary, which suggests it belongs to a particular register of language. For example, phrases such as 'Provisional Liquidator', 'said Company' and 'finding caution before extract' are all terms specific to the legal field. There are also archaisms – 'desirous', 'notice is hereby given' – and a highly Latinate vocabulary: that is, words which have derived from Latin, such as 'Interlocutor', 'petition' and 'intimation'.

Syntax   The extract is one single, complex sentence, containing several subordinate clauses. Their relation to one another is very difficult to follow, with the clauses containing relevant information interspersed with those containing additional or minor information.

The following activity asks you to analyse texts using the same framework.

ACTIVITY 7.6

1 Read the two extracts below, one of which was written in 1816 and the other in 1944.

2 Analyse each one according to the three categories of graphology, vocabulary and syntax.

3 What are the main differences between the two extracts?

4 What effect do the differences have on your understanding of each text?

---

1 *Report of the Parliamentary Committee on the Education of the Lower Orders in the Metropolis and Beyond. 1816.*

The Select Committee appointed to inquire into the Education of the Lower Orders in the Metropolis, and to report their Observations thereupon...

...have found reason to conclude, that a very large number of poor Children are wholly without the means of Instruction, although their parents appear to be generally desirous of obtaining that advantage for them.

Your committee have also observed with much satisfaction, the highly beneficial effects produced upon all those parts of the Population which, assisted in whole or in part by various Charitable Institutions, have enjoyed the benefits of education.

Your committee have not had time this Session fully to report their Opinion upon the different branches of their Inquiry, but feel persuaded that the greatest advantages would result to this Country from Parliament taking proper measures, in concurrence with the prevailing disposition in the Community, for supplying the deficiency of the means of Instruction which exists at present, and for extending this blessing to the Poor of all descriptions.

---

2 *The Education Act 1944*

Part 1

1. It shall be lawful for His Majesty to appoint a Minister (hereinafter referred to as 'the Minister') whose duty it shall be to promote the education of the people of England and Wales and the progressive development of institutions devoted to that purpose, and to secure the effective execution by local authorities, under his control and direction, of the national policy for providing a varied and comprehensive educational service in every area.

Part 11.6

Subject to the provisions of Part 1 of the First Schedule to this Act, the local education authority for each county shall be the council of the county, and the local education authority for each county borough shall be the council of the county borough.

7.3.3 Second person personal pronouns

Another syntactic change over the past 200 years has been the disappearance of the distinction between the second person personal pronouns *thou* and *you*. The distinction in use between these two forms corresponded to a similar distinction still current in French, *tu* and *vous*. Late Middle English typically distributed them as shown in the table:

	singular	plural
subject	thou/ye	ye
object	thee/you	you

From the late thirteenth century, when French was the official language of England, the influence of the French *vous* meant that the plural *ye/you* began to be used as a polite singular. *Ye/you* thus contrasted with the singular *thou/thee*.

During the fifteenth century, *you* began to be used as a singular subject pronoun. This singular *you* tended to be used by inferiors to superiors, for example by children to parents, or by servants to masters, while *thou/thee* was used to signal intimacy and when addressing God. Amongst themselves, the upper classes preferred to address one another as *you*, whereas the lower classes used *thou*. Even so, switches between *you* and *thou* happened often, both within and between social classes, particularly for emotional reasons. An angry person might say *thou* even to a superior, and the upper classes might use *thou* to one another to signal anger, intimacy or affection. In Shakespeare's plays, and in Renaissance literature generally, changes of pronoun between *thou/thee* and *you* are indicative of the continually fluctuating relationships between characters.

During the sixteenth century, increasing social mobility and competition between the rising merchant class and the aristocracy meant that by Shakespeare's time there was considerable confusion about the use of the two different forms. The radical Quaker movement in the seventeenth century used *thou* for everyone as an act of levelling social relationships between people. The distinction eventually collapsed, with only the pronoun *you* surviving. *Thou* now appears only in registers where archaism is intended, including poetry.

In religious texts, *thou* tends to function as a mark of respect rather than of inferiority, as in the King James Authorised Version of the Bible, written in 1611, where biblical characters address God as 'thou'. Even at that time, the form had already become archaic in speech, surviving in print because the King James Bible used as its source an earlier (sixteenth-century) version. The Authorised Version was the most widely used translation of the Bible until the middle of this century. The New English Bible, published in 1961, adopted a translation more in keeping with modern forms of English. In recent years, some Christian groups and churches have adopted this version or other recent translations, whilst others have kept to the King James version.

ACTIVITY 7.7

1 In pairs, choose an extract from a text first printed in the sixteenth or seventeenth century, such as a Shakespeare play, which uses both *you* and *thee/thou*.

2 How can you account for the variation between the two forms?

3 Underline or write out any words which are unfamiliar to you.

   a Can you make a guess at what they mean from their context?

   b Why do you think these words are no longer in common use?

4 What other comments can you make about the syntax, vocabulary and
graphology of the extract?

5 In what ways does your analysis add to your understanding of the text?

7.4 Phonology

7.4.1 Rhyme

Another element that has changed is the way in which we pronounce our words.
Between the time of Chaucer and that of Shakespeare, a definite change in the
way English was pronounced occurred: this is called the Great Vowel Shift. The
precise reasons for this change are somewhat uncertain, although several
attempts have been made to explain it. Whereas we would find it difficult to
understand Chaucer were we to meet him in the street today, we would not have
too much of a problem with Shakespeare, particularly if we drew on the resources
of modern English dialects other than standard English. For example, the West
Country dialect and its corresponding accent have preserved the sounds of
sixteenth-century English in ways which current southern dialects have not. Even
so, just as there was no standardised way of spelling words during the period
from 1400 to 1700, so too was there a tremendous variation in pronunciation,
particularly of vowel sounds.

One area where these changes can be perceived in writing is in poetry which
uses rhyme, where words have so altered their pronunciation that where once
they would have rhymed, they no longer do so.

For example, the 'a' in a word like *have* is usually pronounced as a short vowel
today, but in the Middle Ages its pronunciation varied between short and long, so
that it could rhyme with words like *gave* and *crave*, as it does in Spenser's poem
The Faerie Queen (1590–96). 'A' as in *shall* also had a variant pronunciation that
made it possible to rhyme it with *call* and *all*. The combinations 'ea' and 'ee',
which are indistinguishable today, would have had different pronunciations in
the sixteenth and seventeenth centuries. For example, the 'ea' in the word *sea*
would have been pronounced [e:], that is as a Scot would pronounce *say* or a
French person *né*, whereas *see* would have the vowel it has today, [i:]. It was not
until the eighteenth century that 'ea' words began to rhyme with 'ee' words,
although the identification of 'ea' with a long 'a' has lingered in words like *break*,
great and *steak*.

The 'k' at the beginning of words like *knee* and *knight* was also pronounced in
the sixteenth and seventeenth centuries, as was the '-ed' at the end of words if the
metre in which the verse was written required it. Shakespeare wrote many of his
plays in the verse metre known as an iambic pentameter (see 4.1.3 above). In lines
6, 10 and 30 of Gloucester's opening speech in *Richard III*, the '-ed' in each line
must be sounded for the rhythm to emerge as an iambic pentameter:

> *Our bruiséd arms hung up for monuments*
> *And now – instead of mounting barbéd steeds*
> *I am determinéd to prove a villain*

7.4.2 Stress

One of the features of speech is the stress we place on syllables of words. Some languages have a regular pattern of syllabic stress, but English does not. In some English words, where the stress is placed can vary. For example, take the word *fifteen*. If this word comes at the end of a sentence, we stress the second syllable: *He's only fifteen*. But if a stressed word follows *fifteen*, we stress the first syllable, as in *Looking back fifteen years...*

Deciding which syllable to stress in English is not easy, because there is no regular syllabic patterning to guide us. In poetry, however, a sense of rhythm can be achieved by ordering words with a regular number of syllables into lines which form a particular stress pattern. One of the most well-known poetic meters in English is the iambic pentameter, the meter in which Shakespeare wrote much of his poetry and many plays (see 4.1.3). Such a regular patterning of sound in poetry gives words a rhythm they don't usually have in ordinary speech.

Where the stress falls within a word can also change over time, so that the syllable on which the stress falls in the iambic pentameter of Shakespeare's verse may not be the syllable on which the stress most commonly falls today. For example, in the following two lines, the stress on the word *antique* falls on the first syllable, rather than the second, which is more usual today:

> FIRST PLAYER: *Striking too short at Greeks. His antique sword*
>
> > Hamlet II.2.471–2
>
> SALISBURY: *In this antique and well-noted face*
>
> > King John IV.2.21

However, it is very difficult to generalise about patterns of stress in English, particularly as different dialects of English may stress words differently. When you are reading poetry and verse, it may help to establish first of all if a meter is being used and the pattern of stress within it, since this will give you some clues as to how to say the words in a way that is consistent with the intended rhythm of the verse. If the stress patterns are different to your own, the chances are that the poetry is not modern.

Stress in words which had a foreign origin also used to be much more flexible than it is now. The word *comrade*, for example, from Spanish/French, was sometimes stressed on the second syllable, as in the first two examples below, but in the third it is stressed on the first, as in modern usage.

> POLONIUS: *Of each new-hatched unfledged comrade. Beware.*
>
> > Hamlet I.3.65
>
> HOTSPUR: *And his comrades that daffed the word aside*
>
> > Henry IV Part 1. IV.1.96
>
> LEAR: *To be a comrade with the wolf and owl*
>
> > King Lear II.2.382

Given the many ways in which both spoken and written language have changed over the centuries, it is no wonder that texts written in earlier times appear so strange to us now. Nevertheless, as this section suggests, it is possible to trace connections between present forms and earlier ones which will help you to understand those earlier texts.

7.5 Engineering language change

The changes discussed so far in this unit have been those which have not happened in any conscious way, but have evolved independently. Another type of change is that which is made deliberately. One example of this in recent times have been changes to the words used to describe ethnic groups. Words which had been commonly used are now perceived as derogatory. The use of words such as *yid, nigger* and *sambo,* for example, is viewed as offensive to those they describe and their use in contemporary writing tends to be avoided except in examples.

One major area of influence on language in recent years has been the increasing recognition of the fact that there are many elements in language which are sexist and which offend women. To counter this, attempts have been made to reform language in a variety of ways, which have altered its use in both speech and writing. For example, discriminatory words have been replaced by neutral ones: *chair* or *chairperson* in place of *chairman, humankind* instead of *mankind, staff* instead of *manpower,* and so on. Another strategy has been to use derogatory words such as *crone, dyke* and *virago* in a positive way, or to coin new words to mark women's difference from men, as in using the word *herstory* in place of *history.*

Much of the influence of feminism has centred on vocabulary, but some would argue that the very grammar of the language is sexist as well. The most obvious example of this is using the pronoun *he* to refer to both men and women, making women invisible. This is now far less common than it once was.

However, although it is possible to make conscious changes to language on a small scale, getting them adopted is not so easy. Although in Britain we do not have an established 'keeper' of language, like the Académie in France, we do have 'defenders' of language: institutions such as the media, education, the government and so on. All too often change is perceived as 'corrupting' or 'debasing' the language, as letters on this subject printed in newspapers every day testify. If change itself is seen as undesirable, then engineering language change may, to some, appear even less so. Engineering language change itself has given rise in the 1990s to a new phrase, 'political correctness', meaning a conscious adoption of non-sexist, non-racist forms of language.

Generally, though, changes in English occur outside the conscious control of particular individuals or groups. Even if the 'defenders of language' attempt to resist change, there is no guarantee that they will be successful. Attempts to keep language 'pure' – i.e. unaffected by change – are inevitably doomed to fail.

Equally, although the influence of ideas such as feminism on language is an example of how language can change, deliberate attempts to change language can be unacceptable. A prescriptive attitude towards change rooted in feminism has as little change of succeeding as the attempts of the eighteenth-century grammarians. Although feminism has had some effect on changing language use, particularly in vocabulary and the use of pronouns, its attempts at prescribing change have sometimes backfired. For example, we differentiate titles for women in a way we do not for men: the alternatives *Miss* or *Mrs* for women depend on their marital status, whereas *Mr* for men does not. An attempt was made in the 1960s to introduce an alternative, neutral form of address for women which would not reveal marital status and would have the same status as *Mr*. However, this alternative, *Ms* rather than being used instead of *Mrs* or *Miss,* has in fact been used in addition, so that women are now faced with three choices when it comes to filling out a form, rather than the one that was intended or the two that existed previously. This illustrates how language change cannot be brought about artificially: attitudes have to change, too.

As we have seen, the reasons for changes in written language are many and varied, but in general it seems that it happens as a result of alterations to the way we live, be they due to wars, inventions or changes in social attitudes.

7.6 Language change and the literary canon

One of the largest and most accessible categories of text to survive through the centuries has been fiction, in the form of novels, plays and poems. Many of these are frequently chosen for study as part of examination courses and in college and university departments of English.

7.6.1 Historical periods in literature

You may find it helpful to familiarise yourself with some of the writing that has survived from different historical periods. The following is a brief guide to some of the most well-known writers, divided into broad groups by date.

The Renaissance
This period (late sixteenth to late seventeenth century) is associated mainly with plays and poetry of writers such as William Shakespeare, Thomas Middleton, Ben Jonson, John Donne and John Milton. It includes a period sometimes called the Restoration, in the late seventeenth century, notably the works of playwrights such as John Dryden and William Congreve.

Neo-classicism
This period (mid-eighteenth to early nineteenth century) is associated with poetry, particularly that of a group of poets known collectively as the Romantics, which included William Blake, John Keats, Samuel Taylor Coleridge, William Wordsworth, Percy Bysshe Shelley and Lord Byron; it is also known for the plays of William Goldsmith and the novels of Jane Austen.

Realism
This period (mid to late nineteenth century) is associated most often with the development of the novel, particularly those of Thomas Hardy, Charles Dickens, George Eliot, Oscar Wilde and William Thackeray.

Modernism
This period (first half of the twentieth century) is associated with writers who consciously experimented with all three literary genres – novels, plays and poetry – such as Virginia Woolf, James Joyce, E.M. Forster and T.S. Eliot.

Post-modernism

This period (since 1945) has seen developments in all three literary genres by writers such as Harold Pinter, Tom Stoppard, Angela Carter, Jack Kerouac, W.H. Auden and Philip Larkin.

During the latter half of this century, the number of writers writing in English about a post-colonial life has increased, as generations of post-colonial children and immigrants to England have grown up. This has also led to a widening and diversification of language use, with considerable variations from standard English. Poets such as Lynton Kwesi Johnson, for example, write their poetry and song in a written equivalent of their spoken dialect. In many modern literature courses, the range of writing offered for study is wide ranging, and it is possible to specialise in American, African or Afro-Caribbean literature as well as in English literature.

7.6.2 Analysing language in literary texts

The divisions given above are by no means fixed or definitive, nor do they encompass all writing, but they may give you some idea of the range of writing available to you. As well as these historical divisions, you may also encounter divisions by type or genre, such as gothic, romance, historical, science fiction, horror or detective fiction, including works by some of the authors listed above. These categories organise fiction into type rather than historical period.

If you are faced with a text that is set in a historical period, there are usually plenty of clues within it as to what period it is. Stories, plays and poems which describe characters and/or events usually provide us with a description of where the action is set. However, although the content of fiction, and particularly its use of vocabulary, will give us plenty of clues as to when it was written, writers may also use a historical setting for a contemporary novel or play. For example, many of Shakespeare's plays, especially his history plays, are set in the past. Robert Bolt's play *A Man For All Seasons* is set in Tudor England, but was written in the 1960s. Historical novels or plays written today but set in a different time may use archaic vocabulary as well as a period setting. On the other hand, although graphology can provide clues as to when texts were printed, aspects of graphology such as typography and spelling are also modernised as older texts get reprinted, making it difficult to tell from the print used how old a text is, unless we have an older version in front of us.

There are, however, clues to when a text was written in its sentence structure. Modern writers will probably use contemporary sentence construction, while writers of the past, writing of events that were contemporary to them, would have used the written language style of their time, which seems archaic to us. Considering graphology, vocabulary, syntax and phonology together will help you to identify the period in which a text was written, particularly if editing practices have not altered the original text.

ACTIVITY 7.8

Read the three extracts below and answer the following questions on each one.

1 Decide in which century you think the extract was written and when it is set.

2 What is each extract about? How did this help you to decide the period in which it is set?

3 Which particular features of the writing helped you to decide when each extract was written?

4 Pick out and note down any words or phrases which helped you to decide this and discuss why they did.

5 What can you tell about where each extract is set?

6 Is the 'thirty years ago' referred to in extracts 1 and 2 the same thirty years? How can you tell?

7 Pick out any sentences you found difficult to understand. Think about why this was so (for example, whereabouts in the sentence the subject and the verb group or groups appear).

8 Choose one of the three extracts and rewrite it in modern English, as if it were a historical novel or play being written now.

9 What changes have you made? What do these changes tell you about the ways in which language itself has changed?

---

1 *Thirty years ago, Marseilles lay burning in the sun, one day. A blazing sun upon a fierce August day was no greater rarity in southern France then, than at any other time, before or since. Everything in Marseilles, and about Marseilles, had stared at the fervid sky, and been stared at in return, until a staring habit had become universal there. Strangers were stared out of countenance by staring white houses, staring white walls, staring white streets, staring tracts of arid road, staring hills from which verdure was burnt away. The only things to be seen not fixedly staring and glaring were the vines drooping under their load of grapes. These did occasionally wink a little, as the hot air barely moved their faint leaves...*
Far away the dusty vines overhanging wayside cottages, and the monotonous wayside avenues of parched trees without shade, drooped beneath the stare of earth and sky. So did the horses with drowsy bells, in long files of carts, creeping slowly towards the interior; so did their recumbent drivers, when they were awake, which rarely happened; so did the exhausted labourers in the fields. Everything that lived or grew, was oppressed by the glare; except the lizard, passing swiftly over rough stone walls and the cicala, chirping his hot dry chirp, like a rattle.
Charles Dickens: Little Dorrit

---

2 *About thirty years ago, Miss Maria Ward of Huntingdon, with only seven thousand pounds, had the good luck to captivate Sir Thomas Bertram, of Mansfield Park, in the county of Northampton, and to be thereby raised to the rank of a baronet's lady, with all the comforts and consequences of an handsome house and large income. All Huntingdon exclaimed at the greatness of the match, and her uncle, the lawyer himself, allowed her to be at least three thousand pounds short of any equitable claim to it. She had two sisters to be benefited by her elevation; and such of their acquaintance as thought Miss Ward and Miss Frances quite as handsome as Miss Maria, did not scruple to predict their marrying with almost equal advantage. But there certainly are not so many men of large fortune in the world, as there are pretty women to deserve them. Miss Ward, at the end of half a dozen years, found herself obliged to be attached to the Rev. Mr Norris, a friend of her brother-in-law, with scarcely any private fortune, and Miss Frances fared yet worse.*
Jane Austen: Mansfield Park

3   *One knock without.*
        VOLPONE: Who's that? Away! Look, Mosca.
        MOSCA: Fool, begane!
                (Exuent NANO, CASTRONE, and ANDROGYNO.)
                'Tis Signior Voltore, the advocate;
                I know him by his knock.
        VOLPONE: Fetch me my gown,
                My furs, and night-caps; say my couch is changing,
                And let him entertain himself awhile
                Without i' th' gallery.
                (Exit MOSCA.)
                                Now, now, my clients
                Begin their visitation! Vulture, kite,
                Raven, and gorcrow, all my birds of prey,
                That think me turning carcass, now they come,
                I am not for'em yet.
                (Enter MOSCA with gown, furs, etc)
                                How now? What news?

        [changing = being made]

                                            Ben Jonson: Volpone. Act 1

Re-representing Texts

8 | Re-representing texts

8.0 Introduction
8.1 Strategies, considerations and approaches
8.2 Text organisation
8.3 Summary: a successful text

8.0 Introduction

Part 1 of this book has stressed the interrelation between the way words and sentences are used to create a text and their meaning. The following two units apply the same principles used in the first part of the book, but this time to your own writing and creation of texts, especially where you are required to write in a particular format with a particular audience in mind, using pre-selected source material. This unit considers ways of approaching a writing task of this kind that can be applied to virtually any task you may be asked to do, whilst Unit 9 contains a range of practice activities based on a wider selection of material.

As Part 1 of this book has shown, there is a wide variety of textual forms, many of which you will probably not be used to writing: reports, booklets, articles for newspapers and magazines and scripted talks, amongst others. Even if you have had some experience of writing in these different forms, you may not have given too much thought to the particular audience for whom you were writing. Much of the writing you will have done, in whatever form, will most probably have been for a limited audience. You will probably have been involved in the writing process all the way through, from finding out your information to writing your text and presenting it in a final format.

The writing you are asked to do in text transformation tasks requires you to use your reading and writing skills in very specific and possibly unfamiliar ways. It is with these that this unit is concerned.

A writer's success in communicating information owes much to his or her ability to write in a particular form and style. This is true of any writing that we do. There are, though, many different types of writing, each with their own textual conventions. Rather than attempting to describe each one, the remaining sections of this unit will describe general principles and approaches to text transformation tasks, which can be applied to any task, whatever its particular requirement may be.

8.1 Strategies, considerations and approaches

One important consideration that you will have to take into account before you approach your re-representation task is that all the information you will need will have been gathered for you already, usually from a variety of different textual sources. This aspect of writing is usually a time-consuming one, and re-representing this material may seem an easy and straightforward thing to do, since someone else has already done all the donkey work for you. You may well think that it simply involves sorting through and selecting the material you have, then cutting it out and arranging it in a particular sequence to match the typographical requirements of the text you have been asked to produce.

It's not that simple!

Your task is to use the information given in the material, which will be on a particular topic, to write a *new* text in a specified format, such as a prepared talk, magazine or newspaper article, information booklet or chapter of a book. There is far more to a task of this kind than simply finding the relevant information and writing it out or cutting and pasting it into the appropriate format, such as a booklet or exhibition notes. Even though you will be expected to use the information provided within the material that has been gathered for you, your task will be to re-represent that material as a completely new text, written for a particular purpose and a specific audience.

Your re-representation will almost certainly require a substantial rewrite of the information contained within the source material if it is to achieve any sense of coherence or if its message is to reach its intended audience. Writing of this kind does not involve you so much in showing that you know the information you have been given, which is the purpose of most writing you do in school or college, as in proving that you can present it in a way which communicates the message successfully to the intended audience. These two different approaches might appear to be similar, but they are in fact very different, and require very different skills.

You will need to **understand** the source material, **interpret** it and **adapt** it to make a new text. This will involve you in **re-representing** and **editing** the source material for an audience which will be different to the one for which each text within the source material was originally intended.

8.1.1 Understanding the source material

Fulfilling your task requires you to understand the content of the source material in order to make appropriate selections from it to write your particular text.

First of all, you can be certain that the material you are given to do your task will always be more than you actually need. The success of your completed task will depend on your ability to combine material from a number of different sources, which have been written for a variety of audiences and in different formats, to form a new, coherent text. Your text will also need to bear in mind its specific, intended audience, which may affect the particular language style you adopt. This style may be different from any used in the source texts. Thus, although your source material will provide you with all the information you need, you will almost certainly need to select what is relevant and appropriate for the target audience before rewriting it.

The first part of the process, understanding your source material, can be achieved by following the procedure below.

Skim the material first; this means reading it through quickly to get an overall feel for its content and to make initial judgements about its purpose. It might help to make notes on a separate sheet of paper for each extract as you go along, leaving space to add further information later on.

Read the material through again, this time making sure that you understand it all and checking the meaning of any words with which you are unfamiliar. Familiarise yourself with which parts of the material are giving facts, and which are opinion. You may find it useful to use a highlighting pen or make notes in the margin as you go along.

Summarise each text which forms part of your source material. On a sheet of paper list the titles and write a brief summary of each different text in two or three sentences.

Remember that you should use *only* the information given in this source material when you write your own text. How you use the information and how much of it is up to you, and will probably depend to a large extent on the nature of the task set. It does not help in any way to add any extra information other than that contained within the material.

8.1.2 Interpreting the source material

Once you have read through the source material and made sure you understand it, you will need to be certain that you are sufficiently familiar with it to express it in a variety of potential different ways. The context for which and within which each text of your source material was written will almost certainly have been different in every case. Each text will have been written with a different audience and purpose in mind. As you read each one, therefore, it is important that you should keep in mind the context within which it was produced. For example, a newspaper article may include people's personal details and quoted speech, whereas a scientific report would list facts and figures in a much more impersonal way. Both are presenting facts and information, but in very different ways. You need to be able to separate the facts the source material contains from the contexts in which they are used, so that you can re-use them in an entirely different context.

Before you are ready to do this, it will be helpful to **categorise** the source material according to the different areas of the topic which it covers. Although there will be a central theme or subject, this will probably have between three and five different aspects, covered to varying degrees by the various texts. Give each different aspect a sub-heading and list the texts which belong to it. You may find that some texts belong under more than one sub-heading.

8.1.3 Adapting the source material

Once you have been given and/or chosen your task, you can begin to consider how to adapt the source material to create your own text. Before you begin to write, you will need to **select** the material containing the relevant information you know you are going to use, and abandon the rest. You can do this in a variety of ways: by highlighting the parts of texts you are going to use and drawing a line through the rest, by separating your chosen material from the rest, or by a combination of both. You will probably find that you will use between half and three-quarters of the information that can be found in the texts that make up your source material. The rest you will not use at all.

One important consideration in adapting the information given in the source material is that the text you create will need to be written in a coherent way. It may be appropriate for you to use scissors to cut and paste material you have been given into the text you are writing. However, it is important to remember that you are creating a text of your own, with its own unique tone and style. Including long extracts in someone else's tone and style will make your own text appear disjointed, as they will almost certainly have been written for different purposes and with different audiences in mind. Nevertheless, if there are a few lines that you feel are appropriate, or would work well as a quote, then it may be quicker to cut and paste than copy out. This will not be the case for single sentences: it would be far quicker to write these out.

There can be no hard and fast rules as to how much of your final text is in your own words and how much is taken from what has already been written, but as a rough guide it is unlikely that more than a third of your total word count will consist of text lifted straight from its original source.

8.1.4 Re-representing the source material

Once you are familiar with both the source material and your task, and have selected the relevant information from the texts that make up the source material, you can then begin to think of re-representing it in a text of your own. Before you begin, there are some further general points you need to be clear about to help you undertake your task.

Audience

Everything we write is written not in a vacuum but within a context of some kind. Whatever we write, we write for someone. A diary, a shopping list or attempts at writing a novel may be for our own eyes only, an audience of one, but the majority of writing that we see around us is targeted at a wider audience. Comics and general interest magazines, for example, are written with a specific audience in mind, which determines not only their format but also their content: children, teenagers, young or old people, men or women, and so on. Special interest magazines are usually written to appeal to people with a reading age of sixteen or above who share a common interest, such as computing, fashion, sport, babies, music, gardening or fishing. Alternatively, such magazines can be specifically aimed at a younger audience, which in turn will affect the way in which information is written and presented.

Other texts are written for a more specialist audience, assuming a degree of shared knowledge: academic text books, in-house company newsletters, technical and legal reports, and so on. It is highly unlikely that you will be asked to write such a text for a specialist audience of any kind. All the information you will need to re-represent will be contained within the source material, and you will not have to have any prior knowledge of its subject matter.

Equally, the task you are set will not ask you to write a text where the material is beyond the capability of an average adult: the audience for your task with be either the general public or children or young people of a specified age up to eighteen. It is likely, therefore, that you will be asked to write a text which will have general appeal.

Whom we are writing for affects the **register** that we use (see 1.3 above). Texts written for a younger audience, say up to sixteen years of age, tend to have vocabulary that is usually simpler or less sophisticated, with more explanation of unfamiliar terms. Even so, the ideas contained in them may be just as complicated as those in writing intended for an older audience.

Purpose

A further important consideration that you must bear in mind is what your writing is aiming to do. Is it to entertain, persuade, inform or instruct? Whichever category your writing falls into will affect how it is written to achieve its purpose. Some or all of the texts you will be given to work with will have been written for a different purpose to the one you will have in mind. Even if the purpose is the same, the audience for which you are writing will probably be different.

Section 2.5 above distinguished between four different functions of sentences: as statements, commands, exclamations and questions. When you are re-representing information in your text, it is important to consider the kind of sentences you are going to use. Commands may be appropriate in an instruction manual, for example, but not in an information booklet. If you are going to write commands, are they going to be uncompromisingly direct (*First place the material on the table*) or will it be more appropriate to modify them with modals to make them more user friendly (*It may be a good idea to...*)? Exclamations are used frequently in poetry, and it is a good idea to ask yourself the reason for using an exclamation instead of a statement. Similarly, if questions are asked it is important that they are answered.

Your selection of material will also be linked to what your specific purpose is. Part of your task in re-representing information taken from a variety of different texts is to be consistent in your approach, so that your text clearly matches its purpose. One way in which this can be done is by making sure that the tone of your writing is appropriate to its audience. Take care, for example, that you do not make your writing complicated or over simplified for the intended audience.

You will also need to make your presentation of the topic interesting, even if you do not find it interesting yourself. This is perhaps one of the most challenging aspects of this kind of task, since usually we have some degree of interest in the subject about which we are writing. It is hard to write about computers or music, for example, if you know absolutely nothing about either and find the topic completely dull. Nevertheless, you will need to keep your intended audience interested. How you weave your text together will play an important part in keeping up the momentum of your writing.

Text type

Generally, different types of text are written and organised according to
conventions, particularly those of layout and graphology. This aspect of the
process is one that needs to be borne in mind when you are drafting your writing,
although this does not necessarily mean that you have to include all those
features, for example making your text physically look like a booklet.
Nevertheless, considerations of what your finished text might look like will
probably affect the way you write and do need to be taken into account, which is
where notes to an editor or publisher come in (see 8.1.5 below). Booklets, chapters
of textbooks and radio scripts are examples of three distinctive text types which
you may be asked to write.

Booklets   These usually present their information in a very visual format,
interspersing text with pictures and breaking it up into sections. In your draft,
you will probably want to indicate somewhere how the information you have
written is to be presented. For example, you may want some information to
spread across a double page, or to have columns of text interspersed with boxed
or highlighted blocks of text. You may design and write the text for the front and
back covers of the booklet separately to the main text.

There are all kinds of ways of approaching this task without producing an
actual booklet, although that is one way of doing it. Another alternative is to
write your script as one continuous draft, carrying one page over onto another.
When you finish writing, you could then draw a mock-up of how you would
wish the finished text to appear.

Magazine articles share common principles of typography with booklets, in that
they are self-contained pieces of writing, where the text is usually presented in a
variety of different ways, rather than simply reading left to right across the page.

Textbook chapters   Unlike booklets, textbook chapters will, by their very
nature, be part of a much longer text. Nevertheless, a chapter is a complete unit
within a much larger one. It is probably safe to assume that the layout you
envisage would apply to the whole book, and you could even make reference to
previous or forthcoming chapters in the book.

Textbooks may be designed with writing running across the page from left to
right, or the text may be broken up into columns. A page of dense print is not
very appealing to look at, and often it will be broken up with illustrations,
suggested activities or questions which relate to the main part of the text. As the
writer, you have a choice as to how you draft your writing; you could write the
main text first, then draft additional elements afterwards, or draft your chapter as
a continuous script. It will not be necessary for you to consider the front and back
covers of the book, although you will have to give your chapter a title.

Radio scripts   These are meant to be spoken and listened to, rather than read,
and this affects the way in which they are presented. Usually, a radio script will
give information on who is speaking, what is said and any sound effects to be
included. Any text which involves representing spoken speech – talk, audio
cassettes, speeches or lectures, as well as radio and play scripts – will involve a
special kind of writing. It is important to break up the potential monotony of a
long monologue by having different speakers, a narrator, dramatised parts and so
on; this is particularly true in a radio programme, which relies on sound as its

medium rather than sound and sight. Radio programmes very often make use of sound effects and music to break up the monotony of spoken sound (see also 8.2.2 below).

A sample radio drama script is reproduced below. This is taken from a booklet called *Writing for the BBC*.

	(FADE UP EXTERIOR ACOUSTIC.
	SKYLARKS HEARD DISTANTLY.
	CLOSER TO, THE RUSTLING OF BUSHES AS
	A MAN BREAKS THROUGH)
MAN:	(Close to mike, pants heavily)
JOHNSON:	(A little away) You're late.
MAN:	(Sharp intake of breath)
JOHNSON:	You are precisely two minutes and fifty seconds late.
MAN:	There was a hitch. The train was late. Where the devil...
	(BUSHES RUSTLE AGAIN)
JOHNSON:	(Approaching) Right behind you. I was waiting.
MAN:	I told you, the train was delayed. I came as quickly as I could.
JOHNSON:	And the old lady?
MAN:	It's all right. She just caught it.
JOHNSON:	Just caught it?
MAN:	(Wearily) First-class compartment, three carriages from the front, corner seat facing the engine. A non-smoker, of course. Just as you said.
JOHNSON:	Good.
	(A PAUSE)
MAN:	So what now?
JOHNSON:	So what now? That's all. You're finished.
MAN:	Finished? But I thought -
JOHNSON:	(Softly) I said, you're finished.
	(A PISTOL FIRES CLOSE TO MIKE.
	CUT TO THE SCREAM OF A SIREN AS A DIESEL
	TRAIN RUSHES PAST.
	CROSSFADE FROM CLATTERING WHEELS TO INTERIOR
	OF TRAIN, A CLOSE ACOUSTIC IN WHICH TRAIN NOISE IS
	MINIMUM. HOLD BRIEFLY TO ESTABLISH)
MISS TREE:	(Gently, close to mike) Young man.
YOUNG MAN:	I beg your pardon?... Oh, I see.
MISS TREE:	Thank you so much. But it is a non-smoker. I always make a point of insisting, you know. Trains nowadays are so dirty anyway, don't you think?

These three examples should enable you to take layout into account when approaching your draft script. You need not worry too much whether what you have written looks like or imitates the actual published text form. What matters is that your draft is written in such a way that it is clear what its final published or recorded version will be like.

Length

The instructions for your task will usually specify how long your text is to be, either in word length or the time it takes to speak. How long the text is to be is usually a fair indication of how detailed its content is to be.

Your success as a writer of jingles or adverts, for example, will be very short-lived if they are twenty lines or ten minutes long. Similarly, a brief report which turns out to be 200 pages long or an in-depth study of 200 words is not going to go down well with its intended audience. The word or time limit set will usually reflect the length of texts similar to the one you are writing.

Word count   It is a good idea to get used to what 100, 200 and 500 words of your own writing look like, and to calculate the average number of words you write on a line. Covering a side of A4 paper with average-sized handwriting will usually take approximately 250 words, although individual handwriting varies considerably. To get a rough idea of how many words you write, take a line of your writing and count up the number of words you have written. Total the number of lines you have written and multiply the two numbers together. For example, the approximate word count for a piece of writing which averages ten words a line and is 200 lines long will be 2000 words.

It is also important to remember that the total word count is just that: the total number of words you are to write, which includes any instructions such as the title, instructions for editing, etc.

Time count   As well as getting an idea of how many words you usually write on a page, it is also a good idea to estimate how long your text will take to speak. This can be done by timing yourself saying a given number of words aloud, using a watch or clock, so that you get an idea of how many words will fit into a minute (usually between 100 and 150, depending on any pauses that may be included).

Conclusion

None of the various considerations described above works independently of the others. Rather, they work together to form a coherent, organised and communicative text which will fulfil its purpose. For example, you may write the required number of words, but not make it clear who is the intended audience for your writing or take sufficient account of conventions associated with the particular text form. It is worth taking a minute or two when you are reading or listening to different kinds of text – a schools' broadcast, magazines, brochures, programme notes – to take note of their particular conventions and the effect these have on the presentation and content of the material.

8.1.5 Editing

There are several stages to the editing part of the re-representation process. First of all, you will need to select the material which contains the information that is most suitable to your assignment. You will have to take it from one context and fit it into another, or **recontextualise** it.

The text you write may however have two audiences. If it is a text that is to be printed, then as well as the text itself you may be asked to write notes for an editor to help him or her to turn your writing into its final, published form. If it is a text that is to be spoken, it will include information for the director and the speakers of the text as well as the words themselves.

In theory, what you write will not be the final version, since most public writing that we do passes through the hands of a publisher, editor or director. Even speeches or talks that are given to a public audience can be subsequently published, which will almost certainly include editing. The task that you are doing is continuing on from something someone else has already done, the research, and will be handed on to a further person, a publisher. It may be helpful to think of the task you are involved in as part of a process that has already started and will be completed by someone else. The stages of this editing process are as follows.

First stage   Selecting a topic and finding information on it. This stage will already have been done for you, and you have no need to find any other material to add to it.

Second stage   This stage will require you to select the information you need to fulfil your specific task before you begin writing. This is where your part of the editing process begins.

Third stage   Once you have selected the relevant information you need, your task is to write a draft script, in a way which is appropriate to its intended form, purpose and audience. There is usually no need to make your writing look like the text you are aiming to write, such as a glossy brochure or a typed radio script, since these form part of next stage. Section 8.2 below goes into this writing process in much more detail.

Fourth stage   Publishing or making public the final text. You are not expected to take part in this final stage, which would usually, in real life, be carried out by someone else. In order to have some control over what is done, however, you may find it helpful (or you may be specifically asked) to include notes to the editor, publisher or director which would help them to fulfil your intentions. For instance, you might indicate such things as typeface and type size, the position of illustrations, captions and so on, which are additional to the text you are actually writing. For an audio cassette, you might write notes about the type of background music, or the accent of the narrator. You will need to imagine what your text would be like in its final version, though not produce it as such yourself.

8.2 Text organisation

How you organise and sequence your information into a new text will be of crucial importance to the success of your task. Section 1.1 above described various ways of categorising written language, which it may be useful to read again. The one which will apply most in your own writing will probably be whether your text is organised chronologically or non-chronologically.

8.2.1 Chronological and non-chronological patterns of textual organisation

The content of a piece of writing can be organised in two main ways: chronologically or non-chronologically (see 1.1.3). If the text you are writing is chronologically organised, then to a certain extent its sequence will be determined by the order in which events took place in time. For example, if you are writing a magazine article following the death of a public figure or marking the anniversary of that death, then events in that person's life will probably feature prominently in your article, and the organisation of the writing will be based around them.

Non-chronological writing does not depend on time or on a sequence of events for its organisation. Instead, presenting an argument or different perspectives on one topic could form the organisational basis for your particular text. For example, an information booklet on health and diet is unlikely to be organised according to a time sequence; nor is a talk on areas of outstanding natural beauty in a particular area. Non-chronological textual organisation allows for many different patterns of organisation.

When faced with your task, deciding which of the two different kinds of writing yours will be is a helpful first step in approaching the organisation of the information you are required to present.

Alternatively, the requirements of your task may mean that different parts of the text will use different kinds of textual organisation. For example, you may be asked to write a tour guide (chronological) which also includes information about local places of interest (non-chronological). Again, it is important that you are clear about the conventions associated with either kind of textual organisation.

8.2.2 Scripted texts and written texts

Another important aspect of organising your text is whether it is intended to be read or spoken. In either case, you will need to consider different types of text organisation. To maintain their readers' or listeners' interest, writers have a variety of techniques at their disposal, usually associated with different kinds of text organisation.

Written texts

Variety in written text is usually achieved by its graphology and typography as well as by the language style itself. These include such things as:

- laying the writing out in columns broken up with sub-headings
- boxing information to highlight key points
- large, bold-type headings
- illustrations

Although your draft does not have to look like the finished, published text, it is important that you bear these features in mind as you are writing, as well as in giving editorial guidance. Breaking writing up into columns, for example, does not of itself make a magazine article; it is important that your writing in its draft form reflects the characteristics that relate to its final, published form.

Scripted texts

As has already been pointed out, a wide variety of written texts are meant to be spoken, particularly radio scripts and audio tapes such as information guides. In this case, your draft script will probably reflect the final format more closely than the draft of a written text, since it is meant to be heard, not read. Variety within this kind of writing depends upon aural rather than visual elements, which can include things like:

- using several different speakers
- varying the speakers regularly and introducing new speakers
- varying tone of voice
- interspersing talk with reading
- use of sound effects

Because a scripted text is meant to be heard, it is important that the writer maintains the hearer's interest by varying the speaker and the tone whilst at the same time making it easy to follow so that the hearer does not get confused by the different voices.

8.2.3 Structuring your text

Once you have established the overall pattern of textual organisation and the medium within which you are going to be working, you can turn your attention to the structure and organisation of the text itself.

Whether your text is organised chronologically or non-chronologically, and is intended to be speech or writing, starting your task with a blank sheet of paper in front of you may appear very daunting. It is useful to think of the information, together with the number of words and the space you will eventually cover on paper, as a frame. Within the frame, you can structure your writing into different sections to make sure that you cover the aspects of the topic you have selected evenly. How the segments relate to one another will then depend upon the overall organising principle of your writing. Structuring your material in this way should make it easier for you to weave all its different elements together into a coherent whole.

It is far more difficult to structure non-chronological writing than chronological, and the examples of text frames given in the rest of this section refer to this particular kind of textual organisation.

Presenting information

One typical type of non-chronological writing is one which presents information on a particular topic. An informative text may follow a pattern based on the following frame:

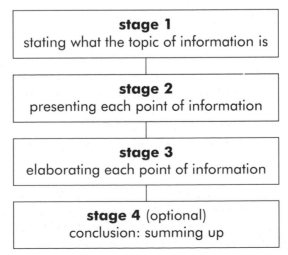

stage 1
stating what the topic of information is

stage 2
presenting each point of information

stage 3
elaborating each point of information

stage 4 (optional)
conclusion: summing up

Since non-chronological writing by its very nature does not follow a linear, time-defined structure, it is likely that the text will weave backwards and forwards between stages, particularly stages 2 and 3. A text may present some topics in stage 2, elaborate on them in stage 3, then repeat the cycle for further points. Another might present each point and elaborate on it in turn. You might leave stage 4 out altogether, depending upon the purpose of the text. For example, consider the following text:

Introducing Gîtes

A gîte is reasonably priced self-catering holiday accommodation in France – part of a house or an entire house – and almost invariably in the countryside, although some are within reach of the coast. Some gîtes are on farms, others in small villages. Some are quite detached and rather remote, others in a group of farm buildings, in a house containing more than one gîte, or are self contained flats in the owner's house. But they are all in France, and they all bear the trademark of the Fédération Nationale des Gîtes Ruraux de France, which is why we call them Gîtes de France.

GÎTE STANDARDS

In all gîtes, the accommodation is simple and adequate. So DO NOT EXPECT LUXURY. It should be stressed that the accommodation is self-catering and can never be compared with that of a three star hotel. Gîtes are equipped for everyday living by owners who have taken care in some instances choosing furniture of a style to match the gîte, fitted bedside lamps etc... Exceptionally a gîte might be quite grand, in a château for instance, but such is very far from being the general rule.

Whatever the standard of the gîte you will stay in, which should never be compared to a luxurious villa or hotel, you can rest assured that the 45,000 properties registered with the Fédération Nationale des Gîtes Ruraux (our head office) have all been approved and that each and everyone meets the standards of quality and comfort laid down in the charter of our organisation. All the properties listed in this handbook (over 2,300) have been carefully selected to provide the gîte holiday maker with a good standard of self-catering accommodation at a reasonable price. The vast majority of the gîtes featured in this guide have been included in our selection for many years and we know that they have always met these criteria.

GÎTE RATINGS

Gîtes are classified by ears of corn and the corresponding rating from 1 to 3 can be found in the 3rd digit of the reference number of every gîte. For example: Gîte Ref: 242725

24=Departmental number (Dordogne)

2= No. of ears of corn

725= Ref No. of the property

The standard which the rating is supposed to represent varies from one area to another, often a matter of taste and opinion. The rating may depend on the geographical location of the gîte, the recreational activities available within 20km and/or the degree of comfort, but this should only be regarded as a relative indication of what to expect.

HOW TO FIND YOUR GÎTE

Almost all our gîtes are rural and are located outside large towns or cities. Practically none of them have a house number nor do they have a street name linked to their address. Therefore DO NOT WORRY if the full address you are given is simply the name of the house or hamlet and the name of the nearby village. The description of the gîte in the guide will first give you the name of the village in **BOLD TYPE** and capital letters followed by the name of the hamlet in **Bold, Small Print.** If the gîte is in the village itself the description will point this out. First obtain a very detailed map (e.g. I.G.N. maps – see page 320) which will show you where the village is (you may even find the name of the hamlet!). On your arrival in that village, simply ask anyone to show you the way to the hamlet or gîte itself.

Please note that we shall be providing you with summary directions to your gîte at the last stage of the booking procedure (with your holiday voucher and travel wallet). It should be stressed that the information of how to get to the gîte is from the point of view of the owners – it may not necessarily be the shortest or the quickest way, so should you find a better route, please let us know and we shall amend our records and inform other gîte holidaymakers. You are on a gîte rural holiday – you may well spend half an hour finding the gîte but then again, where's your pioneering spirit!

ARRIVAL TIME AT THE GÎTE

Again, you are advised to obtain a large-scale, detailed map of the area in which the gîte is located, since for the most part, gîtes are situated in or outside quite small villages.

You should try to arrive at about 4 p.m. – the time that you are due to take possession of your gîte for the term of your holiday. Similarly, you should arrange to leave by or before 10a.m. on your last day. If, for any reason, you cannot get ▶

to the gîte on the arranged day, or if you seem likely to arrive late in the day, please contact the owner before leaving (or, if possible, write or send a telegram, see sample letter on page 320).

THE OWNERS

It is important to know that most gîtes are owned by people who are working – generally small farmers and other country people. Like all humanity, they have their own quirks or customs, but the bonus is that, as non-professional operators in the world of tourism, they will feel a natural obligation to welcome guests who are strangers to their country. This feeling is almost a "Golden rule" and has considerably contributed to the success of the Gîtes de France movement over the years. Do not hesitate to ask the owners about the locality, about their way of life, about their family. Talk to their children, introduce yours to theirs! Be friends – even the language difficulty, if it exists, can be overcome by human under-standing and gesticulations.

FRENCH RURAL LIFE

The gîte is a product of the everyday and the unusual. Suddenly, for a week or two, you enter the somewhat different world of rural France and its unpretentious farm or village life. You will discover, for example, what it is like to live on a French farm and buy direct from the farmers almost all you need to put in the pot or frying pan. You will (we hope!) enjoy the tranquillity and beauty of the French countryside and, perhaps, come to terms with the tractor setting out early in the morning for the fields and the cockerel crowing a few hours before you intended to rise! If you cannot, perhaps this type of holiday is not for you!

HOLIDAYING IN THE COUNTRYSIDE

Life in the country has many advantages but also little inconveniences. In the countryside, you may encounter insects, flies, dormice and fieldmice (although they have on occasions been confused with rats,

the latter two are harmless – a dormouse is in fact a protected species in France). This applies to any rural area of the world, be it in England, Wales, Scotland, Ireland or France.

If you cannot accept this, then you ought to reconsider your decision about staying in the country. If you can, you will find a Gîtes de France holiday the ideal choice for you and you will wish to book again (75% of our customers have been doing so regularly over the past 13 years!)

YOUR INCLUSIVE PACKAGE

All gîte holidays are offered on an inclusive gîte accom-modation, vehicle insurance cover and ferry crossing basis. However, we realise that a small number of you (e.g. ferry company shareholders) may wish to book a holiday without ferry travel. We shall obviously be very happy to offer this alternative, if requested, although you will find that booking the all-inclusive package with us generally works out cheaper.

WHEN DOES YOUR HOLIDAY BEGIN AND END?

The gîtes listed in this brochure are bookable either from Saturday to Saturday only or from Tuesday to Tuesday only. (But in the case of 'gîtes court-séjour' – short-break gîtes – you can arrive any day of the week and stay 2, 3 or 4 nights – see details on p. 342). Whichever choice you opt for though, please bear in mind that booking a ferry and on-board accommodation for departures on bank holidays or weekends in high season may sometimes prove difficult, so travelling during other periods is well worth considering. By travelling to France mid-week (i.e. Sunday to Thursday) you will save time and money and gain other benefits (see below) so we strongly recommend this option!

ADVANTAGES OF TRAVELLING MID-WEEK

If you choose to travel mid-week – i.e. from Sunday to Thursday – you will reap lots of benefits:

★ Far less traffic both in the UK and in France.

★ Ease of finding car space and on-board accommodation on the

long Western Channel ferry crossings.

★ Ease of booking your choice of en-route hotels.

★ Shops and banks open during the week (some are closed on Mondays).

★ Local Gîtes de France offices open just in case their assistance is required (they are usually closed over the weekend).

★ Finally, look out for our discounted ferry rates when crossing Sunday to Thursday!

EUROP ASSISTANCE PERSONAL AND VEHICLE COVER

Europ Assistance is the household name in France in the field of personal and car insurance. In other words, you can motor to France safe in the knowledge that Europ Assistance will be instantly acknowledged by all, should you require their help. What is more, the highly competitive rates we can offer you, as well as your vehicle insurance cover built into your basic holiday price at a fraction of public rates, are sure to put you in good stead when it comes to savings. The added bonus is that Europ Assistance will operate a special Travel Advice Helpline especially for Gîtes de France customers. In addition to our telephone number, this special helpline will provide you with holiday information or pre-travel advice ranging from route planning, roads and tolls to climate information, or even urgent message relay. Details on page 336.

From the 1994 Gîtes de France Official Handbook

The text frame for this extract might look something like this:

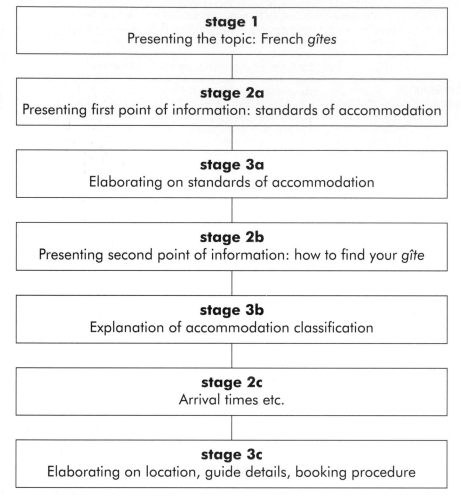

stage 1
Presenting the topic: French *gîtes*

stage 2a
Presenting first point of information: standards of accommodation

stage 3a
Elaborating on standards of accommodation

stage 2b
Presenting second point of information: how to find your *gîte*

stage 3b
Explanation of accommodation classification

stage 2c
Arrival times etc.

stage 3c
Elaborating on location, guide details, booking procedure

In this particular text, each point of information is introduced and elaborated upon in turn after the initial introductory stage. Each stage is clearly marked with a bold-type sub-heading to introduce each new topic. The purpose of the text is as an introduction to a brochure, so there is no summing up (stage 4) at the end of it. It is obvious, though, that there is a clear structural pattern to the way the information is organised and presented.

The register shows markers of informality: for example, the text addresses the reader directly in the second person as *you*, and identifies the writers of the text as the people actually responsible for providing holidays, by using *we*. However, there are no contractions of words, shortened or incomplete sentences or other aspects associated with informality (see 1.3 above), which makes the register semi-formal, recognising the distance between the reader and the text whilst at the same time trying to make it 'user friendly'. The vocabulary is straightforward, with any unfamiliar terms explained, so that anyone new to holidaying in a *gîte* will be just as comfortable with the material as those who have done it before.

Within the text frame, therefore, the organisational structure, the vocabulary and grammar used, the register and the actual information provided all interact with one another to produce a coherent text which successfully fulfils its purpose and reaches its target audience.

ACTIVITY 8.1

1 Read the text on hazel trees in Activity 9.2 of the following unit.

2 Divide it up into segments using a frame diagram like those above as a guide.

3 How are the different segments connected with each other?

Arguing a point

Another typical non-chronological type of writing is one which discusses or argues a particular point. One typical form of textual organisation will follow the pattern represented by the following diagram:

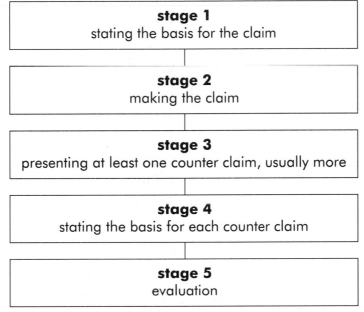

| **stage 1** |
| stating the basis for the claim |

| **stage 2** |
| making the claim |

| **stage 3** |
| presenting at least one counter claim, usually more |

| **stage 4** |
| stating the basis for each counter claim |

| **stage 5** |
| evaluation |

Within this pattern, other elements might also appear, which depart from the main frame but relate to material within it. For the text to make coherent sense, all the elements, however they are organised, will be contained within a frame. For example, if information is presented or referred to but then never mentioned again, this will probably leave a loose thread hanging, detracting from the overall coherence of the text and thereby confusing the reader.

The following activity looks at this second type of text frame in more detail.

ACTIVITY 8.2

1 Read the following extract, then draw a diagram dividing it up into segments using the frame given above to help you. There is no need to paraphrase or summarise the material: a short heading will do.

2 Do all the parts of the text fit the frame?

3 Have you had to alter or add to the frame shown in the diagram above? How?

'In only six days I lost four inches off my waist and seven pounds of weight.'
'In only five weeks I added two inches to my bust line.'
'Two full inches in the first three days!'
These are the kinds of testimonials used in magazines, newspaper, radio and television ads, promoting new shapes, new looks, and new happiness to those who buy the

preparation, the device, or the prescribed program of action. The promoters of such products claim they can develop the bust, shape the legs, wipe out double chins, build muscles, eradicate wrinkles, or in some other way enhance beauty or desirability.

Often such devices or treatments are nothing more than money making schemes for their promoters. The results they produce are questionable, and some are hazardous to health. To understand how these products can be legally promoted to the public, it is necessary to understand something of the laws covering their regulation. If the product is a drug, FDA (Food and Drug Administration) can require proof under the Food, Drug, and Cosmetic (FD&C) Act that it is safe and effective before it is put on the market.

But if the product is a device, FDA has no authority to require pre marketing proof of safety and effectiveness. If a product already on the market is a hazard to health, FDA can request the manufacturer or distributor to remove it from the market voluntarily, or the Agency can resort to legal actions, including seizure of the product. In such cases FDA must prove that the device is adulterated or dangerous to health when used in the dosage or manner or with the frequency or duration prescribed, recommended, or suggested in the labelling.

Obviously, most of the devices on the market have never been the subject of courtroom proceedings, and new devices appear on the scene continually. Before buying, it is up to the consumer to judge the safety or effectiveness of such items. It may be useful to consumers to know about some of the cases in which FDA has taken legal action.

One notable case a few years ago involved an electrical device called the Relaxacisor, which had been sold for reducing the waistline.

The Relaxacisor produced electrical shocks to the body through contact pads. FDA brought suit against the distributor in 1970 to halt the sale of the device on the grounds that it was dangerous to health and life. During the five-month trial, about 40 witnesses testified that they had suffered varying degrees of injury whilst using the machine, and U.S. District Court Judge William P. Gray issued a permanent injunction prohibiting the sale of the device to the general public. It is to be hoped that all owners of Relaxacisors have destroyed the device so there is no longer a possibility of harm to a user who might not be aware of the danger...

HEW No 76-40001, June 1975, © FDA Consumer, in Carter and McCarthy:
Language as Discourse

4 Now read the following advert. Taking the information given in both the article above and the advert, write an article of around 120 words to appear as part of a page devoted to health issues in a general interest magazine such as *Company* or *GQ*. The purpose of your article is to give your readers a balanced view on using mechanical aids to help shape the body.

Points for consideration:
  – Read a health issues page in *Company* or *GQ* to familiarise yourself with its style. For example, does it use the first, second or third person?
  – Fill in a text frame based on the one on page 135 or design and fill in your own text frame to illustrate the organisation of your text.
  – Highlight the facts you are going to include in your text. You don't have to use all of them, just the ones which will help you to make your points. You will *always* have more material than you need.
  – Be bold in your own writing and don't be afraid to take risks.
  – When you have finished your writing, make sure you include a title and an approximate word count.

FIRM UP IN HOURS
SHAPE UP IN DAYS
WHY SPEND WEEKS IN THE GYM?

Right from your very first session with Ultratone you'll notice a visible difference.

Curves begin to appear where you want them and disappear where you don't. You'll see and feel a new firmness in sagging muscles, goodbye to midriff bulge, flabby thighs and hippy hips, hello taut tummy, firm thighs, shapely hips.

All achieved faster than you dreamed possible. And with less effort, too, because Ultratone is the exercise machine that does the exercise for you, toning and firming slack muscles with concentrated spot on exercise, activating each muscle an amazing 450 times in 30 minutes.

And with Ultratone can you cover eight body areas in one go while you sit back and relax.

Secure in the knowledge that you've opted for the only system of its kind approved to the highest Medical Standards.

ULTRATONE™ The Ultimate Bodyshaper

8.3 Summary: a successful text

The success of your finished draft will probably depend on the degree to which you have managed to fulfil three important criteria.

Firstly, have you successfully created a new text? You will have been asked to produce a new text written for a specific purpose and of a specific type for a specified audience. Are you sure you have achieved this? What is the proportion of your own words to source material?

Have you organised it into a coherent whole, with the content clearly and unambiguously linked within the text? Have you used the material you were given to create a new and coherent text? In other words, is it clear where the text is going and what it wants to say? Is the information grouped in meaningful ways? Have you included an appropriate introduction and conclusion? Have you included headings and sub-headings?

Have you written it in an appropriate register and tone for your audience? Does your writing address its audience in a suitable tone? Is the information too simplistic or over complicated?

Getting the right tone is not an easy thing to achieve, and requires a fair degree of practice. Tone can be defined as the way in which a writer signals that he or she knows there is someone out there, an audience, and that what he or she has to say is of interest and worth saying. It is important that your writing is clear and focused, showing commitment without being overbearing or over earnest.

As you undertake practice activities to prepare you for an examination which asks you to re-represent source material to create a new text, it is important that you get used to sharing your writing with others. Other people are always in a better position to answer the questions posed above, since they will be reading your writing from a new perspective.

The following, final unit of this book gives further sample material and practice exercises for text transformation. Any of them can be done on your own or collaboratively in groups.

9 Practice activities

9.0 An overview
9.1 Evacuees
9.2 Hazel trees
9.3 Claude Monet
9.4 Aromatherapy

9.0 An overview

9.0.1 The activities

Activity 9.1 Evacuees
This activity asks you to write *either*:
i. part of a schools' programme aimed at fourteen- to sixteen-year-olds about life in Britain during the Second World War
or
ii. part of a history textbook on the Second World War for secondary pupils aged eleven to thirteen.

Activity 9.2 Hazel Trees
This activity asks you to write *either*:
i. a section in a textbook on woodland aimed at eight- to twelve-year-olds
or
ii. part of a page on nature in a general interest magazine aimed at eight- to twelve-year-olds.

Activity 9.3 Claude Monet
This activity asks you to write *either*:
i. an information booklet on the Impressionist artist Claude Monet to accompany an exhibition of his work
or
ii. an audio cassette to accompany visitors to the gallery as a guide.

Activity 9.4 Aromatherapy
This activity asks you to write *either*:
i. a prepared talk on aromatherapy as part of a planned programme of health and leisure activities
or
ii. a free-standing display board for an exhibition on alternative health and medicine as part of an open day at an alternative health clinic.

9.0.2 Completing the activities

The tasks can be written individually, or collaboratively in pairs in a workshop atmosphere. It is important that you get used to others reading your work and passing comment on it, just as you should learn to comment constructively on the writing of others. This can be difficult, but it is important that you get used to receiving feedback on your work, as it can help you put your ideas and information across more coherently and intelligibly. Other readers, for example, can point out where the writing is unclear, stilted or ambiguous.

There are certain points you need to consider that are common to any of the tasks given in this unit:

1 Familiarise yourself with the material you have been given. Section 8.1 above suggests strategies for doing this.

2 Be absolutely clear as to the exact nature of the task you have been set. Filling in an information table like the one below may help you to do this.

task summary	
text type	
audience	
purpose	
tone	
special instructions	
word limit	

3 Select the material you think will be appropriate to your task, by highlighting it or marking it in some way.

4 Design a text frame for your text, as described in Section 8.2.

5 From the material you have selected, pick out the actual parts you will use. Decide which particular section of your text frame each part will be appropriate for. Use the information given to write your own text, according to the conventions and style of the particular text type you are writing. Remember that you do not need to make your writing *look* like the text it will finally be: that is an editor's or publisher's task.

6 If you are unfamiliar with the particular text type you have been asked to write, then it would be to your advantage to read or listen to some examples of

it, find out how they are set out, what kinds of sentence pattern and vocabulary they use and any other stylistic considerations you may need to be aware of, or, in the case of an audio text, how it is presented.

7 Decide how you are going to present any notes to a publisher, editor or director to give them some idea of how you might wish your text to look when it is printed, or how you would wish it to sound, as appropriate.

8 Remember to give your text a title.

9.1 Evacuees

ACTIVITY 9.1

Choose either part 1 or part 2. The photocopiable source material is on pages 142–149.

1 As part of its schools' programmes schedule, the BBC is making a series of programmes called *Life in War-torn Britain.* This series of programmes is intended for pupils studying GCSE history.

Each programme in the series looks at a particular aspect of life in Britain during the Second World War. You have been asked to write a section of the programme dealing with the experiences of children during the war, specifically those who experienced evacuation. The producer has sent you some material on which to base your script.

Using this material, write your section of the programme, including the linking piece which introduces it. Each programme adopts a magazine-style format, incorporating sound effects and actors' voices as well as the presenter's voice. You are required to keep to this style in writing your script. Your contribution to the programme is planned to last three minutes and should be about 500 words long.

2 You have been commissioned to write part of a chapter on evacuees to be included in a textbook called *Life in War-torn Britain* designed for lower secondary pupils aged eleven to thirteen. The book aims to present its material in a lively and interesting way which it hopes will appeal to children of its target age group.

Your section forms part of a chapter called 'The Children's War', dealing with the experiences of children in Britain during the Second World War. You have been given the background material to use in producing the text.

Your text should include study tasks or questions. It would be helpful to the publisher if you could give some idea of how you would like your writing to be set out, including the use of illustrations. In total, your contribution should not exceed 500 words. You should also choose a title for your section of the book.

WISH ME LUCK AS YOU WAVE ME GOODBYE

From *No Time to Say Goodbye* by Ben Wicks, published by Bloomsbury.

During the summer of 1939, thousands of British children were moved from urban homes to escape the threat of German bombs. For some, the new rural life was idyllic; for others, a living hell.

The evacuation of thousands and thousands of youngsters from London when war broke out was a masterpiece of organisation. It was also an operation that was to have a profound effect in later life on the children, who were uprooted from their homes and, with their Mickey Mouse gas masks, despatched to live with strangers in what often amounted to a 'foreign land'.

I know how they felt because I was one of them, a six-year-old cockney more familiar with the smells and sounds of Billingsgate fish market than with manure and bird song. Certainly I came in for my share of rough treatment from the family who first took me in, but I went on to enjoy some halcyon days over the next six years growing up on a 200-acre farm in Norfolk, which changed me from a young 'city slicker' into the country-lover I am to this day.

The brief definition of 'evacuee' in the 'Everyday English Dictionary' – 'a person transferred from a vulnerable to a safe area on account of air raids' – may be accurate as a general description, but it gives no inkling of the thousands of stories, both sad and happy, behind that momentous evacuation in the last war.

MICHAEL CAINE

All you could hear was the feet of the children and a kind of murmour because the children were too afraid to talk. We had a big banner with our number in front. Ours was an 'H' something. Mothers weren't allowed with us but they came along behind. When we got in the station the train was ready, we hadn't the slightest idea where we were going and we put the children on the train and the gates closed behind us. The mothers pressed against the iron gates calling, 'Goodbye darling.'

I never see those gates at Waterloo that I don't get a lump in my throat.

L.A.M. BRECH, escort and teacher

the school in their aprons and overalls. I recall already sitting on this bus with my two sisters and my mother screaming, 'Let Maureen off. Let my baby off. She's too young, she's too young,' and they said, 'It's too late now, it's too late now,' and I can see her running behind the bus screaming, 'Betty, don't let them go, don't let them be billeted with anyone else, you've got to look after them, you've got to have them.'

BETTY WORLEY

I thought it was a Sunday-school outing down to the seaside, sort of thing. And I looked out of the bus window and I saw my mother crying outside and I said to my brother, 'What's Mummy crying for?' and my brother said, 'Shut up!'

ALAN BURRELL

Smut the cat, Joey the canary and a large tortoise we had had for 16 years... what were we to do with them? There was only one thing left and that was to have them put to sleep.

Word went around the street (you know what little slum streets are like with little houses) that the children were being evacuated and all the mothers ran up to

I bravely put Smut into a box, the tortoise in a bag on my back and the cage in the other hand. I walked along the Hastings seafront to a vet's. I can ▶

tell you how much I hated Hitler.

Putting my sad cargo down to have a rest and have a cry, I was aware of a soldier staring. He asked what was wrong and when I told him he offered to help.

Only the tortoise never did get to the vets – instead we put him into the local flowerbeds. But sadly we joined a large queue at the vet's. People were all forced to do the same. Sorrowfully we walked back empty-handed.

JOAN HARPER
(who met the soldier again years later, and married him)

The journey seemed to take for ever. It can't have done though, because as I found out later we were only about 85 miles from home. It's funny but I can remember that journey so well. We got tired of counting fields as we passed them – for many it was the first time they had seen fields. I was just a little more fortunate. I was once taken out to the country. I can remember though how we had to cross a viaduct, how frightened we all were in case the train should come off the rails and we should all fall into the water underneath. You should have heard the sighs of relief when we crossed safely.

MARGARET SCICLUNA

I thought, 'This is a nice holiday.' So then the welfare officer said, 'Come on, you're coming with me.' And I said, 'Well, where are we going then?' So she said, 'Home.' And I was a seven-year-old kid and I thought, 'Home? You mean I've come all this way and now I am going to turn around and go home?' She then took us to our billet.

HARRY WRIGHT

What happened was that my two sisters went to the toilet and this lady came up to me and said would I like to come and live with her. But I never told her I had two sisters so she took me, and about an hour later my two sisters were at the door, crying, with a lady who said these two children wanted to be with their sister. Anyway, we all ended up together... but we were soon split again.

TERESA DAY

If you were a child with glasses or with spots, you were always left till the end.

JOAN TOPP

The couple were quite old – maybe around 50, which seemed old then. She had greasy hair in a plait and used to ask me to braid it for her. I hated doing it. If we were sick we had to wait until money arrived from our parents before she would get medicine. We weren't allowed in the house till about 5pm and in the evenings had to sit in the scullery with its stone floor. She said the alternative to us was a couple of Irish labourers, otherwise she would never have consented to our living there. I think she was trying to save money on the allowance given her. We became very thin. From 7 to 9 at night we met two other girls, similarly treated, we would sit in the bushes, around a fire if we could steal matches, talking about when we got home...

PAM HOBBS

My sister and I devised a plan. We knew Mrs Hudson read our letters from home before she gave them to us to read, and she insisted on reading the letters we sent to our parents before she would give us a stamp to post them. We therefore wrote to our parents telling them how unhappy we were and left the sealed letter in our bedroom. We didn't have to wait long before our plan showed results. The same day we returned from afternoon school to find our belongings in the front garden and we had no reply to our banging on the front door.

We went to tell our story to the headmaster, who lived a short distance away. He returned with us and knocked on Mrs Hudson's front door but found no response. He picked up our bags and took us to the sea-front where he deposited my sister and me with our bags and told us he would try and get us accommodated for the night.

We must have looked an unhappy pair. A lady came along with a dog and she asked us what was wrong. We told her our tale and she sat beside us and promised that we could go home with her and stay with her as long as we wanted to. When the headmaster returned he was overjoyed as he had found it impossible to find any accommodation for us.

MARGARET ROWE

My brother became homesick, yet the little bugger wouldn't write home – he left it to me to do. I had unwittingly accepted responsibility for him. I can't remember feeling homesick myself, but I did miss our Saturday tea treat of a pint of winkles.

PETER ANTHONY WHYMAN

I was terribly unhappy there and I remember a day when it was raining hard and she sent me outside. She bolted the door and I crawled into the chicken-house full of straw, and I stayed there until she came out and brought me in. She didn't want me in the place, you see. This other little girl's daddy was a soldier and one day the lady said to me, 'You're to go upstairs and stay in the room and don't come down.' And she got Margaret Rose ready and made her pretty and she locked my door.

I could hear their talking in the kitchen below and I got a pencil and piece of paper and I wrote a little note: 'Please tell my mummy to come and ▲

Government evacuation scheme 1939–45

Based on local counts of evacuees taken generally at six-monthly intervals throughout the war.

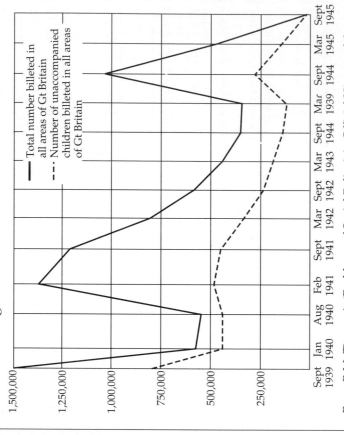

Total number billed in all areas of Gt Britain

Number of unaccompanied children billeted in all areas of Gt Britain

From R.M. Titmuss's 'Problems of Social Policy', in Official History of the Second World War, p. 356

get me.' I waited until I heard the back door open and as soon as I heard Margaret Rose's father's footsteps, which were heavy with his Army boots, I dropped my little piece of paper out of the window and dodged back quick. I was horrified he wouldn't see it and that the lady would find it and I would be in big trouble.

About a week after that I was on my way to school. There was a thick fog and I could hear footsteps coming towards me on the other side of the road. And I suddenly heard my mum saying, 'Is that you, Mary?' and I said, 'Oh, Mum,' and I went dashing across the road and she was quite horrified when she saw me. She took me back to the house and told the woman exactly what she thought of her and she said, 'How dare you send my daughter out on a morning like this. She's got holes in her shoes and no coat on,' and she said, 'What do you keep scratching your head for?' and she grabbed hold of me and I was absolutely full of lice, and with that my mum told the woman, 'I'll make sure you never get any more little kids to look after, after the way you treated her.'

MARY DOHERTY

At first everyone was very nice and then the woman that had taken us there left and we sat down to eat. The woman said, 'Here's your meal,' and she gave

us a tin of pilchards between the two of us and some bread and water. Now we had been in this rich woman's house so we said, 'Where the butter?' And we suddenly got a wallop on the head. From then on it started… not the husband, he was never there… just her. What we later found out was that the woman hated kids and was doing it for the extra money. So that food was the cheapest meal you could dish up… a tin of pilchards and dry bread.

MAURICE MICKLEWHITE
(now Michael Caine)

At the beginning of the war all parents in our town were asked if they would like their children to be evacuated to Canada or the USA. Everyone in the neighbourhood decided against it except one couple who had two sons aged about 12 and they felt it would be safer for the boys to go. Not long after they had left, their mother woke one night having had a nightmare in which she could hear her sons calling her. They had sailed on the City of Benares which was torpedoed…

Both of the boys died, but for the next 40 years, on the anniversary of their death, I always used to see a memorial notice in our local newspaper and always felt so touched by it.

J. DAVIS

Effects of Evacuation

From Children's War by Ruth Inglis, published by Collins.

Memory and repression can dovetail strangely and some former evacuees say that they have only recently begun to analyse what must have been a traumatic experience of uprooting. Sometimes the trauma manifests itself merely in a curious behavioural quirk, but, with hindsight, mature evacuees now realise it was originally forged in the heat of the evacuation experience itself.

Lallie Didham, for instance, the London evacuee who became the shy, precocious toast of Manhattan night-clubs at the age of fifteen, tells of one legacy of her abrupt transplanting as a child:

I'm a hoarder now, as I lost so many things when we left England. Today, I'm still afraid of losing things. We packed in such a hurry when we were evacuated and I was forced to leave many things which were precious to me so that it's turned me into a real magpie in middle age. I will never forget how we had to live on charity in America and I suppose I must have felt a bit put down by this as a teenager, particularly remembering what lovely possessions I had to leave behind.

As a character change created by an outside circumstance, Lallie's hoarding and 'magpie complex' is intriguing, but still a reasonably superficial effect. By contrast, one of the most disturbing effects of evacuation was to make a child find, upon return to his own home, that this home was somehow wanting. This happened when children were evacuated to grander residences than their own. It also, of course, occurred when their evacuation experience had been happy, or they had been a little spoiled while there. Naturally, this didn't always happen. Harry Salmon, the Leyton off-licence

manager, returned from a fine country manor to his 'two-up, two-down' terraced house in East Ham and was thrilled to be home, even though it was not only far more humble than the country mansion he'd left, but bomb-damaged, too. But sometimes the return home to a meaner life style put a child into near shock, causing him to find his own home despicable and then to feel a little ashamed of this emotion.

Stan Clater, fifty-four, a retired merchant-navy captain, resident in Hull and now a part-time teacher of nautical studies, was sent to a friend of his maternal grandmother's during the worst of the bombing in 1940-1. Hull was blitzed in May 1941, but had previously been relatively peaceful. The May raids made up for this, mirroring the savagery of Coventry. Out of a population of 330,000 people, 40,000 were rendered homeless and 1,000 were killed. How fortunate it was for eight-year-old Stan that his grandmother had privately taken it upon herself to send him away to a large farmhouse. He stayed with an elderly couple in a small Lincolnshire village just across the estuary from Hull. They were quite affluent and lived in a house filled with books. Under their tutelage he devoured the works of Jack London and Charles Dickens.

Stan enjoyed being with them, but found it odd that they wanted to appear to be his 'adoptive' parents and not his foster-parents. He was made to assume their surname. They were very attentive to him, coached him in his reading and, when he wasn't being a bookworm in their home, he cycled over to the nearby US Air Force base where American airmen showered him with chewing gum, sweets and Captain Marvell comics with what became known in wartime as the customary Yankee generosity. Stan had a good war, and wasn't prepared for the shock awaiting him when he returned.

My first feeling on coming home was claustrophobia. I was used to space – a large room of my own, stairs wide enough for two people to pass on with shallow steps and a landing half-way up big enough to hold a fair-sized table. I came back to a tiny terraced house and the first thing I saw when the front door was opened were the stairs. I had never imagined that such appalling, narrow, steep stairs could exist.

They were a continuation of the narrow, dark passageway from the front door. Two doors in this passage opened into the two rooms which made up the ground floor. The front room was the equivalent of the Victorian parlour and was never used. The back room – smaller than my previous personal room – had a fireplace and was kitchen, dining room, living room and somehow bathroom for two adults and five children. We were typical of the rest of the street. Our house was one of a block of four. These four dwellings housed a total of twenty-one children, eight parents and a couple of grandparents to boot.

It was hate at first sight. I let it be known loudly and persistently that I wanted to go back to my 'real home'.

Stan's parents seem to have handled his hurtful behaviour very understandingly. They let him go back to visit his foster-parents regularly and before long, the charms of Hull lured him back: 'going on board trawlers, riding on buses, swimming at the baths, pilfering from Woolworth's, having lots of kids to play with, exploring bombed buildings, and so on ....', as he puts it. Later he fell for the beautiful girl next door, Valerie, and his nostalgia for Lincolnshire all but disappeared from his mind.

That Stan didn't become totally alienated from his background was a tribute to his parents' delicate handling. The realisation that he lived in a 'mean street' and that his parents' lives were compressed and humble, materially speaking, hit him and threw him temporarily off balance. Fortunately, his experience as an evacuee didn't, however, make him 'look down' on his mother and father (he is a devoted son today, regularly visiting his ageing parents).

But many poor evacuees did acquire an abiding taste for the good life; once having encountered it they were loath to give it up on returning home. Two 'showbiz' personalities, Justin de Villeneuve and Michael Caine, both Cockney boys from working-class families, have spoken of the rich tastes they acquired in the manorial homes to which they were sent, as I mentioned in Chapter 2.

Justin de Villeneuve, who played Pygmalion to Twiggy's Galatea in the 1960s, was evacuated from London, age five, as the flying bombs spluttered overhead in 1944. Born Nigel Davies and living in the East End, he was taken with his adored mother, Kitty, to J.B. Priestley's glamorous, Shropshire country manor house, where he learned to enjoy 'posh' things, a taste he has never relinquished. His memories, both visual and olfactory, of his life at the home of the famous writer and wartime radio commentator are potent. He remembers eating with silver cutlery and inhaling the heady aroma of roses.

He lives, unsurprisingly, in Chelsea, where he runs a tailoring business. He is twice divorced and a father of three daughters – his youngest, age eight, is the breathy voice who has made the recorded message on his answering machine. He retains little of his origins, except perhaps a liking for slang (he is liable to sign-off a telephone conversation with 'hasta la pasta', for example). Talking with him is to find yourself trotting conversationally through 'designer' land. We spoke in April 1988, before he went to the Italian Grand Prix as a commissioned photographer (taking his Rolliflex); he was not sure what he was going to wear but it ▲

might be soft, casual jogger gear (Yamamoto)... Amiable, soft-voiced, busy and talented (he has written a witty autobiography, *An Affectionate Punch*), he confirms that his Shropshire days changed him for life.:

It did affect my taste for good things in life later on, no question. I learned to speak posh in Shropshire. I'm working on a musical film about the evacuation right now and one of the lead songs is called *I've Seen a Better Way*. I think that says it all.

J.B. Priestley was remote but kind. He would always dine with the evacuees he housed and he gave them lovely parties – Justin remembers a Hallowe'en celebration in particular. The author had a self-contained flat on the top floor of his manor and otherwise was not much present. 'But I remember one time when he appeared, he played a funny game pulling faces. He loved doing this. If you laughed you were out,' Justin relates.

Michael Caine admits he was marked forever by the enviable life style he enjoyed at the home of a country square during evacuation: he did not want to evict the squire, he told Ian Jack of the *Observer* magazine in a recent profile, but wanted to *become* the squire, metaphorically speaking. And he has, in a way. As he is quoted as saying: 'Today I have the squire's house in my village on the Thames. I mean, it isn't actually the squire's house, but if you look at the psychology of me, that's what I have.'

Returning to 'Edenholme', the ridiculously grand name for his family's modest bungalow in Southampton, writer Anthony Bailey was as bereft as Stan Clater in Hull. His home for several years, as an English evacuee in America had been a vast, luxurious, suburban edifice in Dayton, Ohio as I stated previously. Going home was like entering the wide end of a telescope and travelling in reverse.

The symmetry of the house was visible once one was through the gate, the front door smack in the middle between the windows and door giving the impression, as with a low forehead, of constrained development. The front door opened onto a narrow corridor: hemp doormat at one's feet; round brass casing of a clockwork-operated doorbell between the letter-box and a frosted glass panel in the top fifth of the door that cast a pale light like that coming from the similar panel in an interior door at the other end of the corridor. Passing along it, I could almost touch the wall on each side by sticking my elbows out.

Discomfiture with smaller houses; shock at tiny parents. Helen Cuthbert, who had such a glorious time as an evacuee in Australia (as recounted in Chapter 7) recalls her especially jarring discovery in *The Evacuees*: 'At Southampton we were met by our parents. It was a wonderful reunion, although I can remember thinking and remarking how "wee" my father was...'

Patriotic British parents and schoolchildren who came to greet the long-awaited evacuees thought they must be ecstatic to be back in 'England's green and pleasant land'. Well, this wasn't always the case as the then fifteen-year-old Helen Cuthbert goes on to reveal:

... people ... would ask ridiculous questions such as, 'You must be pleased to be home – but which country do you like best, the United Kingdom or Australia.' Of course I would say here, but I hoped to return there.

My parents, when we speak of this time, very generously say that they remember no difficulties, but I remember on one occasion when I had been unspeakably difficult, my Mother saying, 'Oh, well, we'll try it for a year, and if you are still unsettled, then you can return.' What it must have cost her to say that: having just got back a daughter after five years' absence!

The significant thing about Helen's answers to those who asked her which country she liked best, I believe, is that she felt she had to tell a lie and say 'England', though at first she didn't mean it. To be an evacuee was a contorted business: first learning to adjust to one strange place, then adjusting so well you come to loathe the place you left when you return to it. The evacuee was a veritable India rubber ball.

Learning to adapt to totally new circumstances is a sophisticated task and one which exerts its toll on a young child. One of the qualities which sometimes gets lost in the exercise is honesty or, at least, the child can acquire a creeping case of hypocrisy, a tendency to bend the truth in order to please. Helen told everyone she preferred England to Australia upon her return to Britain five years later because, though it was untrue, it was what she thought her family and friends expected her to say, and it made life easier to respond accordingly. The trouble about being forced into a chameleon-like existence is that a child can become almost too good at changing coloration and saying things to please:

Gloria Cigman, an eleven-year-old Jewish girl from Cardiff, found herself in a farming village called Gilmorton, in the Midlands, between Rugby and Leicester, and tried to roll with all the punches this experience meted out to her, even pretending she enjoyed seeing pigs slaughtered for very porcine repasts. As she writes in *The Evacuees*:

...I find that one aspect of it all emerges very powerfully. This is a kind of chameleonism that those of us who were successful evacuees cultivated. (By successful, I mean those of us who were happy and who felt accepted most of the time.) This faculty made it possible to sense what would please, what would make us acceptable, what would not alienate or offend, what would not violate the way of living into which we had been transplanted, or, by being different, imply criticism. We were tactful and appreciative. We ate what we were given and enjoyed it, we did not just pretend to enjoy it. I learned to eat with relish every single part of a pig, despite my upbringing which not only excluded all pig-derived food, but regarded the eating of it as a violation of a God-given law. My Gilmorton family would nurture a pig to gross proportions, then send it down the road for slaughter... then render every single part of that pig edible: pork, bacon, ham, trotters, head, tail. I loved it all.

Gloria Cigman ate the pig in an almost masochistic way, like a Christian missionary exulting in a cannibal feast in the bush.

Evacuees could almost taste the humility of *having* to adapt and come to enjoy it. But they doubtless lost something in the effort of refining their own hypocritical act. Tom Wolfe, the author, is fond of saying that 'a liberal is a conservative who has been arrested' (a phrase oft-repeated in his latest success, *The Bonfire of the Vanities*), and bearing the same kind of thinking in mind you could say that the well-adjusted evacuee child was the one who made evacuation work for him. For if a trauma is needed to reshape one's stance or alter one's convictions, then the evacuation process, like an unexpected arrest, did this admirably well. But for a child to have to remodel his or her beliefs or entire personality so drastically, for the sake of survival, must mean the loss of something else – innocence.

Jonathan Miller, who described watching his father talking to a Welsh farmer on a hazy but ominous summer's day (see pp. 102–103), says that all the travelling about he and his family did to evade bombs has probably left him with a lasting passion to stay in the same place. As he told me:

During the Phoney War of 1939, we went to South Wales and stayed at our nanny's house in Monmouthshire near Tintern Abbey. Later on, during the flying bombs episode, Mother picked us up again and took us to North Wales. The only real terror I can recall was in 1944 when I was ten with the so-called doodlebugs. We lived twenty miles north of London in Watford and so were more or less out of their over-fly space but I was terrified of the siren warnings. They were prolonged warnings, going on for six hours at a time. There was no off and on wailing as you had during the earlier blitzes. Also, there was that terrible phrase used by the War Office to tell us about them – 'pilotless planes'. It was as if someone told you 'Dracula's bats are here...'.

I suppose travelling from one place to another and having no stable home when I was seven and eight has had its lasting effect. My wife is sure that it has. I do tend to cleave to my home. I've been here in my Northwest London home for twenty years. I travel around a great deal but I've always liked the idea of returning to a familiar base.

But I don't think you could say that the iron entered my soul in any way. It was a comfortable evacuation. We followed our father around. It wasn't self-consciously an evacuation for us. It was more that my father and mother wanted to get the family beyond the reach of the bombs. Father was fortunate in being too old to be posted abroad so we saw him a lot. He was here with the War Office making a statistical analysis of war recruits. There was a lot of moving around for us, all the same.

9.2 Hazel trees

ACTIVITY 9.2

Choose either part 1 or part 2. The photocopiable source material is on pages 151–152.

1 You have been invited to contribute a section on hazel trees for a book forming part of the non-fiction section of a reading scheme aimed at the upper primary age range, eight to twelve. The chapter is called 'Magic Trees' and gives information about trees which have magical associations. The publishers are keen that you capture the interest of the age group with your writing, making it fun to read as well as interesting. The reading scheme has five levels to it, and the book for which you are writing is part of level 3.

You have been given the background material that you need, and your section should be no more than 250 words long. You should choose the title for your section.

2 A fortnightly magazine for children aged eight to twelve has decided to make its theme 'magic' to coincide with Hallowe'en. The magazine is based on a cartoon character, but also includes separate pages of puzzles and facts.

As part of the 'facts' page, you have been asked to write an article on hazel trees, drawing on the material you have been given. The editor hopes that you will make your writing both informative and entertaining for young readers.

Your contribution should be no more than 150 words long, including any source material you use, and should be given a title.

THE VIGOROUS HAZEL

From *The Living Countryside* Vol. 1 no. 4, published by Orbis.

The hazel may be one of our smallest native trees, but it has had an important role to play in the history of woodland management. Apart from its value as wood, it also has – according to Celtic folklore – magical properties.

The hazel grows as a small native tree in the shade of woods and in hedgerows. In old neglected coppices it throws straggling limbs from old stools and is rarely able to form the single trunk to give it the status of a tree.

Yet it is an important tree. In the fossilized pollen records preserved in peat which are our guide to the earliest native plants after the Ice Age, hazel predominates over much of the British Isles – appearing at much the same time as the initial spread of other wind-pollinated trees such as alder, willow and birch. Remains of hazel nut shells have been found at the foot of peat deposits, suggesting that the early Stone Age hunters were probably at least partly dependent on the nuts for food, in the absence of any sort of cereal.

Since hazel is associated with man's earliest ancestors, it is perhaps not surprising that in Celtic folklore it was known as the tree of knowledge, and was supposed to have many magic properties. Irish aches and pains caused by the damp climate or elfin malevolence were thought to be warded off by a hazel nut carried in the pocket. A double hazel nut was said to cure toothache in Devon, and defend against witches in Scotland. Hazel is one of the magic trees of May Day, like hawthorn in England and rowan in Scotland: these are the three trees of white magic that oppose the forces of evil which many people thought were present in the woods.

Looking closely at a hazel catkin

each male catkin has over 100 tiny flowers

bract

stamen

each flower has one bract and 8 stamens

The stamens will ripen when the temperature is over 0°C. The ripe stamens split open lengthways to release their yellow pollen.

In 1956 there were more than 16,000 acres of hazel coppice, little of which was used. Since then the coppiced areas have dwindled as foresters have gradually turned them over to conifer production. For truly wild hazel trees you must go to the Lake District, the Western Highlands or the Burren in County Clare, Ireland. You can see coppiced hazel in Hatfield Forest, the Sussex Weald and on the Wiltshire downs.

The hazel belongs to the same family as the hornbeam, which has more scaly catkins and winged nutlets. The hazel leaf is a dense, deep green colour which turns to brown then yellow-gold towards the end of the year. Hazel bark is shiny, brownish grey with horizontal pores (lenticels) which enable the tree to breathe.

Catkins and flowers The brownish-yellow male catkins begin to develop in autumn; early the following spring they open to a creamy yellow colour. The female catkins are small and brown with bright crimson styles and they generally ripen after the male catkins of the same tree, a mechanism which usually prevents self-pollination. Like all catkin-bearing trees, the hazel is wind-pollinated. At least two hazel trees growing close together are needed for fertilisation and the production of nuts.

Nuts There are between one and four, and occasionally five, hard-shelled nuts on each stalk. They are pale green in summer, but by autumn have turned to a warm, soft brown colour. Each nut is enclosed in a pair of downy husks or bracts with deep scallops. Many children's fairy stories show pixies wearing hats of a similar style.

Birds, especially pigeons and pheasants, and small mammals such as squirrels and mice, take the nuts for food and bury them. This is one way the trees become dispersed. You can grow the hazel in your garden either from a seed or from a sapling. For your own trees to produce nuts you will need at least two trees to ensure cross-pollination because the species is naturally self-sterile (i.e. the tree cannot fertilise itself). A hazel tree produces nuts in abundance from six years old. There are several varieties available, including *Pendula* which makes a standard tree with a trunk of at least 1.5m (5ft).

Selective breeding of the hazel in the 19th century produced the large Kentish cob nut which is redder and rounder than the wild nut. The more oval filbert nuts come from a different species, *Corylus maxima*. It is thought they originated in France and were named after Saint Philbert.

Today many English nuts in shops come from the Kentish nut plantations, although we import thousands of tons from the Mediterranean for use in confectionary. Richard Mabey in *Food for Free* recommends using the nuts in salads, chopped or grated, in muesli, blended into a milk drink, or as nut cutlets. Weight for weight, he says, hazel nuts have half as much protein as eggs, seven times more oil and fat and five times more carbohydrate.

Hazel nuts are rich in oil and the oil from a single nut rubbed over the surface of a stout hazel walking stick will give it a good polish.

Management The management of hazel woods dates back to the late Stone Age. The tough straight poles produced by coppicing the tree are still used today in fencing and as bean and pea sticks and small stakes. The rod used by a diviner to detect the source of water is often made of hazel.

In the days of open field farming, split green hazel poles were woven into hurdles to fence in pigs, cattle and sheep to stop them eating the crops on adjoining land. The tree also produced the wattles for wattle-and-daub building as well as the spurs used in thatching. The brushwood was bundled into faggots that were used for the weekly firing of bread ovens.

Hazel *(Corylus avellana)*, deciduous, native, grows to 6m (20ft). May live hundreds of years if coppiced regularly. Common throughout the British Isles. Flowers Jan-April; cob-nuts Sept-Oct.

9.3 Claude Monet

ACTIVITY 9.3

Choose either part 1 or part 2. The photocopiable source material is on pages 154–164.

1 The art gallery of a large town is mounting an exhibition of paintings by the French Impressionist painter, Claude Monet. The director of the gallery is expecting a large number of people to visit the exhibition, including schoolchildren, as well as local residents.

   You have been commissioned to write a leaflet about the painter that will be given to everyone visiting the exhibition. The director is anxious that the leaflet is written in such a way that people will want to read it and take it away with them. She also wants the leaflet to serve as an introductory guide to the painter, his life and his work.

   The text of the leaflet should be no more than 500 words long. It would be helpful if you could provide the publisher with some guidance as to how you wish the text to be set out.

2 The art gallery of a large town is mounting an exhibition of paintings by the French Impressionist painter, Claude Monet. The director of the gallery is expecting a large number of people to visit the exhibition, including schoolchildren, as well as local residents.

   You have been commissioned to write the text of an audio cassette, primarily to provide background information on the painter and information on a few selected paintings. The director is anxious that the cassette should not assume any previous knowledge about Impressionist art on the part of visitors, but that it should not patronise them either.

   The text of the audio tape should be no more than 800 words long, and should include a title.

Claude Monet (1840-1926)

From *Monet in the Nineties* – background material for teachers, published by the Royal Academy of Arts.

1840-1880

Claude Monet is often described as the archetypal Impressionist painter. A leading member of the Impressionist movement which emerged in Paris during the 1870s, Monet's work best exemplifies the group's aim to *'achieve even greater naturalism by the exact analysis of tone and colour and by trying to render the play of light on the surface of objects.'*

Born in Paris in 1840, Monet was the eldest son of a wholesale grocer and chandler who due to financial difficulties moved to Le Havre when Monet was five. Undisciplined by nature, Monet spent as little time as possible at school, preferring to roam the cliffs and seashore. He began to draw caricatures and soon acquired a reputation for his skill, selling them for 20 francs each.

At the age of seventeen Monet met Eugène Boudin (1824-98) who ran a stationery and picture-framing shop in Le Havre and had taken up painting in his spare time, encouraged by his customers who included Thomas Couture (1815-79), Jean-Francois Millet (1814-75) and Constant Troyon (1810-65).

It was Boudin (see fig. 1) who introduced Monet to landscape and seascape painting and who encouraged the young artist to paint en plein air in an effort to capture the fleeting qualities of light: *'Everything that is painted directly from nature and on the spot, has a force, a power, a vivacity of touch that is not to be found in studio work... Study actual daylight and express the changing aspects of the sky with utmost sincerity.'*

Partly through Boudin's encouragement, Monet went to Paris in 1859. There he chose to study at the Académie Suisse, an informal school which did not offer any specific tuition and was particularly popular with landscape painters. It was there that he met the painter Camille Pissarro (1831-1903). However, in 1860 his studies were cut short by military service; he returned to Paris after two years' service in Algeria. This time he attended the studio of the painter Charles Gleyre (1806-74) and soon became acquainted with artists such as Frédéric Bazille (1841-70), Alfred Sisley (1839-99), Pierre-Auguste Renoir (1841-1919) and Gustave Courbet (1819-77).

In 1862 Monet also met the Dutch painter Jongkind (1819-91) whose work proved to be very influential on the younger artist. Jongkind was interested in painting the same scene under different light conditions and at different times of the day or season. His paintings were made directly in front of the subject and the results were similar to the work of the early Impres-sionists. Monet continued to paint out-of-doors and, when Gleyre's studio closed in 1864, he worked alongside Renoir and Sisley at Chailly on the edge of the Forest of Fontainebleau outside Paris. This village was close to Barbizon, the home of the famous group of landscape painters that included Théodore Rousseau (1812-67), N.V. Diaz (1807-76), C.F. Daubigny (1817-79), Jean-Francois Millet and Jean-Baptiste Corot (1796-1875).

There was one other artist working in Paris who could not have failed to catch Monet's attention; his name was Edouard Manet (1832-1883). In 1863 Manet exhibited his notorious painting ***Le Déjeuner sur l'Herbe*** (Musée d'Orsay, Paris) at the Salon des Refusés which had been established as a place to exhibit paintings that had been rejected by the official Salon. Both the style and subject-matter of this painting were heavily criticised. Manet's spontaneous brushwork and his disregard of smooth modelling annoyed the critics almost as much as the presence of a naked woman with two clothed men. The full impact of this work upon the younger artist became apparent when Monet began a large figure composition in 1865 also called ***Le Déjeuner sur l'Herbe*** (large study, Pushkin Museum, Moscow). Monet's painting was an obvious tribute to the older artist although, unlike Manet, he was primarily interested in the effects of light upon a scene of fully clothed, elegant men and women having a picnic under the trees.

Between 1866 and 1867 Monet actually completed a large figure composition out of doors entitled ***Women in the Garden*** (Musée d'Orsay, Paris). It demonstrated a far greater degree of naturalism than his earlier work and in order to capture the spontaneous poses and the effects of light Monet used a special easel with pulleys that was lowered into a trench in the garden. Soon after this painting was rejected from the Salon of 1868, Monet decided to work almost exclusively on a smaller-scale. Although he had some success at the Salon in the 1860's exhibiting both landscape and figure com-positions, he chose to show mainly in group exhibitions and dealers' galleries after 1870.

Monet concentrated upon subjects of contemporary life drawn from the city and surrounding suburbs. In 1869 he painted with Renoir at the popular bathing resort of La Grenouillère at Chatou on the River Seine near Paris (fig. 2). Their paintings explored the effects of light on water and surrounding objects; they are characterised by rapid brushstrokes and daubs of pure, unmixed colour.

Apart from looking at the work of Manet and that of the Barbizon school, Monet was also influenced by Japanese prints and photography. By the late 1860s Japanese prints were well known in artistic circles in Paris. Monet admired them for their decorative qualities and compositional devices. Japanese prints (see figs. 14 and 22) are characterised by the strong use of line, flat areas of colour and distortions of scale and pers-pective. Often space is established by silhouetting objects in the foreground against a distant landscape. The development of the camera was likewise to influence artists interested in compositional devices. A photograph could capture an instant, a 'snapshot', without selection or hierarchy of composition; it could also cut off figures or forms abruptly. Monet began to use the devices of painting flat areas of colour or dramatically truncating a figure or object in his work. His painting **On the Beach at Trouville** (fig. 3) made during his honeymoon with Camille Doncieux in 1870, conveys the feeling of a 'snapshot' with its rapid brushstrokes and truncated, schematic forms.

Later that year Monet went to London to escape the Franco-Prussian War. There he met up and worked with Pissarro who had fled to London for the same reason. Monet also encountered the dealer Paul Durand-Ruel who was to become an important patron and supporter. In London he painted many pictures of the Thames including **The Thames below Westminster** (fig. 4); he loved the London light and the amorphous effects of fog, smoke and clouds. Monet and Pissarro visited the London museums together and, although Pissarro was later to deny it, they were both influenced by the work of John Constable (1776-1837) and J.M.W. Turner (1775-1851).

When Monet returned to Paris in 1872 his Impressionist style was fully developed. The landscapes painted while he lived at Argenteuil between 1872 and 1877 are now his most popular works (see fig. 6) and it was during those years that Impressionism most clearly approached a group style. Monet often worked beside Renoir, Sisley, Gustave Caillebotte (1848-94) or Manet, recording scenes of French river life from his studio boat. At the time, his work was ridiculed and he suffered extreme financial hardship, eventually moving to the cheaper neighbourhood of Vétheuil. When the Impressionists held their first exhibition in 1874 it was Monet's painting **Impression: Sunrise** (fig. 5) that was singled out by the critic Louis Leroy and described in a derogatory sense as a mere 'impression'. This comment was to give the movement its name. The public dismissed Impressionist paintings as ephemeral and trivial; they saw them as mere 'paint scrapings on a dirty canvas'.

In the 1870s Monet continued to explore the effects of light and colour falling upon objects. He had discovered that shadows were neither black nor brown, but related to the colours of their surroundings. Indeed, the Impressionists' concern to capture the scene in front of them as faithfully as possible led them to explore and discuss certain colour theories. Monet was probably aware of the scientists James Nicol or Hermann Helmholtz and he was familiar with Eugène Chevreul's **Principles of Harmony and the Contrast of Colour and their Application of the Arts** (1839). Monet discarded local colour in favour of bright complementary hues such as orange and blue. He would prepare his canvas with a light ground before applying his paints directly to the canvas without undercoating and used a variety of brushwork to build up an impasto. Monet used a great variety of paints and some of the more unexpected colours are a direct result of the development in the manufacture of chemical pigments which were packed in tubes at this time.

In 1877 Monet painted a number of views of the Gare St. Lazare (fig. 7). He was drawn to the station by the atmospheric effects produced by the steam and smoke; in the paintings he combined both this atmosphere and coloured light in a scene of modern life. After his St. Lazare works, Monet became increasingly obsessed with an attempt to capture the effects of light. This preoccupation eventually led him beyond the original aims of the Impressionists in the 1880s.

1880-1926

By 1880 Monet had begun to express dissatisfaction with Impressionism and he declined to exhibit in the group exhibitions in 1880, 1881 and 1886. He announced that: *'I am still and always intend to be an Impressionist – but I rarely see the men and women who are my colleagues. The little church has become a banal school which opens its doors to the first dauber.'* Monet was partly expressing what he saw as the decline of the original aims of the movement. The 1880s witnessed a general crisis within the movement and many of the founder members including Renoir and Pissarro, chose to explore new styles. They thought that Impressionism as a style was limited by its essentially ephemeral nature and they attempted to create more monumental, lasting effects. The group also faced new challenges from artists such as Georges Seurat (1859-91) and Paul Gauguin (1848-1903). Seurat extended the scientific basis of Impressionism analysing colour and light in his pointilliste technique, later known as Neo-Impressionism. Gauguin by contrast, took a more subjective approach to painting, believing that the artist should express ideas and emotions through his individualistic depiction of objects in the natural world.

Monet became increasingly successful in the 1880s. In 1880 he had a one-man show at the offices of a new newspaper called *La Vie Moderne*. Dealers began to compete for his work and he gradually gained a reputation in America through Durand-Ruel's exhibitions. By the 1890s he enjoyed a comfortable income.

After his departure from Argenteuil in 1878 Monet's subjects changed from scenes of modern suburban life to pure landscape. Increasingly he did not include people in his paintings. He frequently painted along the Seine at Giverny which became his home after 1883. He also began to travel incessantly working at Poissy, at Étretat and other locations along the Normandy coast, on the Italian and French Rivieras, in Holland, at Belle-Isle off Brittany and in the rugged valley of the Creuse River in the Massif Central.

Monet's paintings of the 1880s are of dramatic landscape and seascape subjects; they record stormy weather, strange geological formations, and often evoke different moods and atmospheres. He began to use a box with slots to hold several canvases of the same size. Each day, when he returned to a subject he would choose the canvas that best suited the light of the moment. His colours became brighter, and local colour was often ignored in favour of an overall colour scheme. His brushstrokes were directed in a way that differentiated the various planes of the composition, creating greater formal unity.

Creuse Valley

In the spring of 1889 Monet made a trip to the Creuse Valley in the Massif Central area of France. This trip was to be his last major excursion for more than five years and the twenty-four paintings that resulted were to have great significance for his subsequent work. The paintings indicated tendencies in his work that had developed with his views of Belle-Isle in 1886 and which were fully realised in the **Grainstacks** series. In their appearance and subsequent exhibition they could be considered the first real series.

Monet made the trip with his friend, the critic Gustave Geffroy, and they stayed in the small town of Fresselines which is situated high above the Creuse River overlooking the valley. At Fresselines the two rivers, the Petite and Grande Creuse, meet to form an even larger body of water that winds its way northwards. The remote landscape is characterised by rugged, rocky terrain and Monet was attracted by the *'awesome wildness of the place.'*

Monet chose several views along the valley and for twelve of his canvases he concentrated exclusively upon one vantage point. Under varied light and weather conditions he focused upon the hills that sweep down to where the rivers converge. The river seen in these pictures is the united Creuse, the Petite being out of the scene to the right and the Grande behind to the left. Monet therefore chose the most dramatic site – the place where the rivers joined and where the now larger body of water winds away between the rocky slopes. Monet was fairly faithful to the site, as a photograph taken around the turn of the century reveals (see fig. 10), but he evidently enjoyed and emphasised the primitive qualities of the scene. In another set of canvases he chose a sharp bend along the Petite Creuse, marked by an old twisted tree.

In **Valley of the Creuse, (Sunlight effect)** (fig. 9) Monet deliberately linked the compositional elements to emphasise the natural drama of the site. The triangular shape of the river becomes a wedge that drives into the hills forcing them apart. Shapes and colours are subtly interlinked; the furthest hill is as blue as the water in the foreground. The shapes of the trees echo the clouds above and the hillsides are animated by ribbon-like strokes of colour and strong contrasts of tone. The pink-red rocks and the thick dabs of yellow-white across the waves suggest the play of light across the scene. It is characterised, like the majority of the paintings in the series, by a vigorous technique. The paint has been applied with a variety of brushstrokes which build up a thick dry texture.

Soon after his return from the Creuse Valley Monet's joint exhibition with Rodin opened at the prestigious Galerie Georges Petit. This exhibition of over one hundred and forty-five paintings was the largest gathering of Monet's works to date. It was to prove both highly successful and deeply significant. Although the exhibition was meant to be a retrospective, more than half the works shown had been painted in the last three years. Monet clearly saw the exhibition as a way to prove his worth and reinforce his claims to the leadership of French painting. He asked his admirer, the novelist and cultural critic Octave Mirbeau, to write the catalogue and the show received a considerable amount of favourable critical attention.

Monet included at least fourteen of the **Creuse Valley** canvases in the show and, unlike any other views of a single locale, he chose to exhibit, hung altogether, at least five of the confluence and three of the bend in the Petite Creuse – a concentration that he did not repeat with any of the other groups in the show. As an ensemble they were evidently impressive: nearly every critic who mentioned these 'tragic landscapes' was struck by the range of natural effects that Monet had been able to capture and was impressed with the ruggedness of the motif that he had chosen to paint. By 1892 nine of the Creuse Valley paintings had been sold to dealers or private collectors. The artist himself obviously considered these works to be important since he gave them such a central part in his exhibition. He had even contemplated going back to the Creuse but by the time the show had closed he was already fully absorbed by his series of **Grainstack** paintings at Giverny.

Grainstacks

Between 1888 and 1891 Monet executed thirty paintings of grainstacks situated in a field to the west of his house at Giverny (see fig. 12). Although he had painted five of these pictures by 1889, the majority of them were painted during the autumn and winter of 1890-1. Monet became so involved in the project that he arranged with the farmer to have the stacks left so that he could paint them throughout the year. It soon became clear that the *Grainstacks* series was to play a crucial role in the development of his later work.

In the spring of 1891 fifteen of these paintings were exhibited at Durand-Ruel's gallery. They were hung together in a small room and viewers were dazzled; the exhibition was an enormous success. This show distinguished the series from earlier multiple treatments of a single subject. Monet had shown groups of works together before but they had always been seen within the context of other quite different subjects. In contrast, the *Grainstacks* were meant to be experienced as a separate group independent of any other works.

The *Grainstacks*, often described as *Haystacks*, actually represent stacks of wheat (meules de blé). Monet's choice of subject reflected a shift away from his extensive travels of the 1880s in favour of rural subjects close to home. Immediately before he became fully immersed in the series he painted a number of pictures that depict fields of oats and poppies around his home at Giverny (see Gallery 3). Grainstacks represent the fruits of the harvest; they symbolise the wealth of their owner or in more general terms the wealth of the nation. The theme was both a familiar and popular subject in nineteenth-century French painting. There are numerous paintings such as J.F. Millet's *Autumn, Grainstacks*, 1868-75 (Metropolitan Museum of Art, New York) or Jules Breton's *End of the Day*, 1867 (location unknown) which embody within the subject political and social references. Monet's series could be taken as another interpretation of the traditional allegory of the cycle of the seasons. His *Grainstacks* trace the effects of seasonal change from late summer to winter snow. They can also be seen as a deliberate attempt to focus upon a subject that was close to the heart of the nation. Paintings of rural France had become increasingly popular and by the 1890s landscape had become the dominant subject in the official annual salon. Monet's choice of subject reflects his ambitions to produce paintings which were both popular and marketable.

However, Monet's approach was primarily the result of a concern to record the subtle changes of light and the fugitive qualities of colour. Monet referred to his paintings as a *'series of effects'*, claiming that only the surroundings gave value to the subject. He stated that he was trying to achieve *'instantaneity, above all enveloping atmosphere'*. By choosing a subject that was so simple he was able to concentrate upon these effects. That the stacks were not the primary purpose of the painting was immediately spotted by the young Wassily Kandinsky (1866-1944) who saw examples of the

Grainstacks in an exhibition in Moscow in 1895: *'Previously I knew only realistic art... Suddenly for the first time, I saw a 'picture'. That it was a haystack, the catalogue informed me. I could not recognise it ... what was absolutely clear to me was the unsuspected power, previously hidden to me, of the palette, which surpassed all my dreams. Painting took on a fabulous strength and splendour. At the same time, unconsciously, the object was discredited as an indispensible element of the picture.'*

Although the paintings vary in dimensions they all have extremely simple compositions consisting of one or two stacks set in a field beyond which stretches an irregular line of trees and houses that are silhouetted against distant hills, with a strip of sky closing off the scene at the top. The compositions are strongly geometric − the fields, hills and sky being reduced to parallel bands that in most cases extend across the entire canvas, with fields occupying approximately half of the surface, and the hills and sky a quarter each.

Grainstacks, (Mid-day) (fig. 11) belongs to a group of six canvases begun in the late summer of 1890. The painting reveals Monet's concern to evoke atmospheric effects as the stacks seem to literally melt in the light that floods the field. The use of *contre-jour* lighting contributes to this effect and Monet has built up a careful colour harmony by focusing upon the contrasts between the warm pinks of the sunlit field and the blues of the shadows. Local colours have been completely ignored. The elaborate colour scheme and the densely worked surface contrast strongly with his paintings of the 1870s.

The technique used for the series was complex and certainly involved work in the studio. Monet always spoke of the importance of working in front of the motif and he held that the first real look at the motif was the most important. At this stage the painting should cover as much of the canvas as possible, no matter how rough this initial working was, to determine the tonality of the whole. However, a close look at the painting reveals evidence of much re-working and pentimenti. Monet would continue to work on the painting back in the studio building up a thick surface of paint layers. In *Grainstack, (mid-day)*, there is evidence that Monet altered the position of the small stack on the left. He also added at a later stage the small touches of orange-red near the top of a large stack as well as the orange flecks across the sky. The final effect was therefore not the creation of a pure instant before nature but rather a more general effect achieved over a period of time and partly away from the actual motif.

Poplars

During the 1890s Monet continued to develop the procedures he had used for the **Grainstacks** in a succession of series, each intended to be seen as an integrated whole. In the early summer of 1891 Monet began a new series of paintings of some poplar trees situated on the banks of the Epte, north of the village of Limetz and 2 km from Giverny. Monet had painted poplars prior to this. However, he had never before concentrated so extensively upon the theme as a single motif for a series. He became so involved in the series that when he discovered the trees were to be auctioned and felled in June he made a deal with the wood merchant to leave them standing a few months longer. He worked on the series until late in the autumn producing a total of twenty four canvases. When fifteen of the **Poplars** were exhibited in an exclusive show at Durand-Ruel's gallery in March 1892 the works had an immediate collective impact.

Monet painted the series from the boat he had often used in the past as his studio. He positioned it carefully at a point where the river twice bent back on itself before disappearing from view, and turning slightly to the left he studied the trees which rose and fell in front of him. From this viewpoint his compositions adhered to two basic arrangements; one involving an accentuated zig-zagging perspective, the other using the trunks of the trees as a dominant foreground grid. Although Monet did work on some square canvases, he primarily restricted the **Poplars** to a vertical format and stretched the trees and their reflections from the bottom of the canvas to the top.

Once again Monet had chosen a local rural subject which had immediate symbolic connotations. The poplar was a tree that was cultivated for the market; its straight tall trunk was ideal for the construction trade. Such trees were often placed at regular intervals along a river bank, where they absorbed water to maximise their growth. As with grainstacks, the poplar was another element of rural France that contributed to the country's economy and stability. Monet was making a picture out of a common and familiar subject to most Frenchmen.

Above all else though, Monet wanted to record the effects of the different seasons, from spring to autumn, and he subtitled most of the paintings he exhibited with an indication to what season they represented. In **Poplars (Banks of the Epte. Cloudy day)** (fig. 13), Monet captures the effects of impending rain along the river bank. The pinks and blues of the heavy sky are picked up in the trees and the water. He has attempted to capture the 'instant' while at the same time he seems to have enjoyed the abstract elements of the subject. He recorded the trees not so much for their topographical content but for their decorative beauty and elegance. This is reinforced by his simple grid-like composition which emphasises the linear qualities of the tall slender trees creating a rhythmic arrangement moving diagonally with their bushy heads and punctuated by the spaces between them. The critic Octave Mirbeau commented on the 'beauty, novelty and grandeur of the lines' of the trees.

Monet had realised that the scene before him had inherent decorative qualities and he had set about translating this natural 'pattern' into an artistic arrangement. Such an aim had become the concern of many painters at this time and included artists such as Pissarro, Gauguin and Pierre Puvis de Chavannes (1824-98). As artists moved away from the doctrines of Impressionism they attempted to assert a more subjective approach to describing the world. In 1890 the Nabis painter, Maurice Denis (1870-1943) claimed: 'that a picture – before being a battle horse, a nude woman, or some anecdote – is essentially a flat surface covered with colours assembled in a certain order'. This concern was paralleled by a general revival of the decorative arts in France together with an increasing interest in Japanese prints.

Monet had long been interested in Japanese art and in a sense, the **Poplars** series represents one of the culminations of this interest. His house at Giverny was full of Japanese prints he had collected, and his dining room had been transformed into a Japanese interior while outside he planted exotic flowers. Monet admired Japanese art for its schematic decorative qualities, particularly woodblock prints. Japanese printmakers had developed a tradition of decorative landscape painting unknown to the West. Monet's **Poplars**, with their patterned compositions recall prints such as Utagawa Hiroshige's **Numazu, Yellow Dusk** (fig. 14).

Rouen

During the late winter months of 1892 and 1893 and on return visits in 1894, Monet painted a series of views of Rouen Cathedral. This massive structure is the most famous building in upper Normandy. The Cathedral dominates the town and as a Gothic design it is one of the most varied, picturesque and original in details.

Monet's choice of motif was not particularly surprising. He knew the city well since his brother lived there and it was only 60 km from Giverny. When Pissarro had painted at Rouen, Monet had visited him, and as early as 1872 he had painted the cathedral from the river. At the same time the significance of the subject cannot be overlooked. By choosing to paint one of France's revered monuments Monet was suggesting his ties to the country's past. The Gothic style had long been recognised as a particularly French style, the emblem of Catholicism. Never before had Monet focused so exclusively on an architectural element nor had he spent so long on a single motif. He painted a total of thirty canvases based on this subject.

Monet initially rented a room directly across the square painting some head-on views of the Cathedral. Later he managed to secure the front rooms of a drapers shop situated across the square from the Cathedral. There he set up his studio and a large number of paintings in the series were begun from this location. This south-western vantage point allowed him a slightly angled view of the facade; the structure rising on his left with the shorter Tour d'Albane to the taller Tour de Beurre on his right. The position also afforded the best view of light.

Most artists who had painted the building before Monet had depicted it within a picturesque tradition, showing it as an awe-inspiring structure which dominated the surrounding buildings. They focused on the draughtsmanship required to describe the sculptural details. Monet took a different approach, tending to suggests its humbler, organic qualities. He focused exclusively upon the west side following the light from early morning until sunset; he saw the facade as a giant textured screen upon which an infinite range of light and atmosphere could play. It was these effects that were Monet's theme and led him to produce such a large number of canvases.

Monet struggled to create the illusion of light across the Cathedral facade; he often remarked to his wife that he found the project difficult. He made a number of preparatory sketches for these canvases and his close scrutiny and knowledge of the structure was clearly vital to the series. It enabled him to maintain control over the forms without letting them disappear into a sea of paint or dissolve in the light. Monet's control also stems from his extraordinary sense of colour, which he employs in these pictures to create intricate spacial relationships and the illusion of plasticity.

In **Rouen Cathedral, Facade** (fig. 15), the building is ablaze with the light of early afternoon. The warm blues and oranges combined with touches of pink penetrate the crevices and forms. Touches of white have been added to his pigments enabling him to disentangle the transparent film of light from the surface beneath. Monet's technique is particularly striking. The way he manipulates paint through scumbles and glazes is almost sculptural. His strokes vary from thick, heavy jabs to quick, thin strokes to create the rough, weather-beaten surface of the Cathedral, with its various protrusions and hollows.

Through colour and texture Monet animated the Cathedral. 'The stones themselves live' wrote Georges Clemenceau. Across the series the structure seems to fluctuate and change according to the intensity of light. To enhance this effect Monet emphasised the building's irregularities and subtly manipulated the dense shadows and sculptural forms. If one compares the paintings to the engraving seen in fig. 16, it is clear that Monet abbreviated or emphasised certain parts to create a range of effects.

The Rouen paintings extended the challenge of his earlier series such as the **Grainstacks** and the **Poplars**. More than any other series they can only be fully experienced when seen as a group. Monet had proved that even the most solid structure fluctuated and changed under different light conditions. Ultimately, the proper content of the Rouen series was the subjective experience of nature's sensations seen through a succession of separate 'instantaneities'. When the series was exhibited in May 1895, after Monet returned from a three-month trip to Norway (see gallery 3), they caused a sensation. Some critics were startled by the treatment of the facade. Georges Lecomte complained that there *'was not enough sky ... not enough ground'*. However the majority agreed that Monet had triumphed and the Cathedrals were admired by artists such as Pissarro, Edgar Degas (1834-1917) and Paul Cézanne (1839-1906).

Mornings on the Seine

During the summer months of 1896 and 1897 Monet worked on a series of paintings of the River Seine. The twenty-one canvases in the series chart the progression of early morning light on the water and its leafy bank. Monet lived near the banks of the Seine all his life and he painted it more frequently than any other subject. In the first half of the 1890s Monet had painted the river on a number of occasions between his major series (see, for example, *Ice Floe* series, 1893, in Gallery 3). However, it was only after his extensive painting trip to the Normandy coast (see Gallery 4) that he decided to concentrate intensively upon the Seine.

Monet rose at 3.30 a.m. every morning to capture the dawn light. He positioned his boat in a quiet backwater close to the Giverny bank looking across to one of the river's many islands. The canvases were all painted from the same viewpoint showing the bank on the left with the quiet waters stretching out and reflecting the foliage of the island on the right. The paintings vary according to weather and light. Some are very misty, some show background trees emerging a little more clearly, in some the forms of the trees can be seen while in others the trees are caught by early morning sun. The harmonious and meditative qualities which characterise the series contrast strongly to earlier treatments of the subject.

Morning on the Seine, near Giverny, (fig. 17) exemplifies how Monet built up the soft rhythms and contrasts of texture and tone in a very subtle way. In this painting, where the forms of the trees have just emerged, Monet achieves a muffled quality by applying the paint broadly with integrated brushstrokes. He deliberately avoided the rugged technique used for the Rouen series and the opaque surfaces are built up through a careful process of retouching. The colours are also very soft; the pink of the early sunlight creeps across the water blending with the blue-green foliage. Through the series Monet gradually heightened the colour to reflect the increase in light.

The simple composition reinforces the soft rhythmic qualities. The arching branches act like screens on either side of the water, while the reflections create a decorative symmetry. A number of the canvases in the series are almost square. With this format the branches and reflections cut the scene vertically and horizontally forming an almost perfect grid. Although the branches and reflections on the left and right act as contrasting curves, the general effect is to create a surface pattern. The backlighting also tends to flatten the forms and in the thick mist they virtually dematerialise

Monet clearly took a simple motif in order to concentrate upon the changing light, and more than any other series, *Mornings on the Seine* documents the progress of the sun over the river. In this sense the paintings are extremely faithful to nature and to the immediate effects. Yet Monet is still improvising, as the decorative composition and careful colour harmonies reveal. What he achieves is a careful combination of the real with artifice; nature is transformed into art.

When fifteen of the canvases, together with the *Falaises* series (see Gallery 4), were exhibited in 1898, they were a resounding success. The critics saw Monet as extending his previous efforts, recognising that they carried a serious intention. Monet had expanded the notion of the Impressionist landscape and was now associated with the tradition of Corot and the Barbizon school. This comparison was particularly appropriate since Monet had a longstanding interest in Corot; furthermore he had witnessed a large retrospective of the latter's work in Paris in 1895. Monet admired Corot's ability to create simple views of rural France by a subtle combination of the real with the ideal. The *Mornings on the Seine* series achieves a similar combination.

Views of London

When Monet fled to London in 1870-71 as a refugee of the Franco-Prussian war, he painted a few scenes of the river Thames in the fog (see fig. 4). He had always planned to return and this was finally realised when he visited his son who was living in the city in the Autumn of 1899 and again in the early months of 1900 and 1901. On each occasion he stayed at the Savoy Hotel taking a room on the sixth floor looking out across the river. The view looked south across Charing Cross Railway Bridge to Big Ben and the Houses of Parliament and east across the busy Waterloo Bridge to the smoking factories beyond. Monet made a long series of each of these views together with one of the Houses of Parliament seen from across the river at St. Thomas's Hospital. These paintings, thirty-seven of which where exhibited in 1904, made over one hundred in total; it was the largest series that Monet had yet produced.

It was typical of Monet to return to an earlier theme. However his decision to travel to London and embark upon a large series had wider implications. It marked a deliberate move away from his paintings of rural France that characterised the 1890s. Disillusioned with his own country, where he had just witnessed the eruption of the Dreyfus Affair, Monet looked elsewhere for inspiration. London was an obvious choice considering his previous refuge there; he saw it as a place where one could receive a little more justice and common sense. At the same time he hoped to make an entry into the English market and further expand his reputation.

England had a strong landscape tradition of its own and the Thames had been the favourite subject of a number of artists. Monet was well aware of this tradition when he embarked upon the series. Monet had met J.M.W. Whistler (1834-1903) in the mid-1880s and the two artists had become good friends. Monet admired the way Whistler could evoke the mystery of the early evening light on the Thames in his **Nocturne** paintings (see fig. 18). Likewise his familiarity and admiration for Turner was significant to his work. Like Monet, Turner had been primarily interested in the effects of light upon landscape. Monet even admitted to having closely studied Turner's **Rain, Steam and Speed – The Great Western Railroad**, 1844 (fig. 20) which hung in the National Gallery. The combination of atmospheric effects and the reference to the railroad in Turner's work could be compared to Monet's London series.

In the same way as Turner, Monet set about painting the modern surrounded by the timelessness of light and weather. Monet was fascinated by the London fog:

'I like London much more than the English countryside... but I only like it in winter. In summer it's fine with its parts, but that's nothing beside the winter with the fog, because, without fog, London wouldn't be a beautiful city. It's the fog that gives it its marvellous breadth. Its regular massive blocks become grandiose in this mysterious cloak.'

He was fascinated by the way the enveloping mists could transform the architectural masses to weightless forms. The London paintings are characterised by the same qualities of mystery and extreme simplification seen in the **Mornings on the Seine** series. When Georges Lecomte reviewed the exhibition in 1904 he praised Monet for achieving such *'vaporous subtlety, such power of abstraction and synthesis'.*

A close look at the **Waterloo Bridge** series reveals the variety Monet could achieve by painting a single subject, changing only slightly in format and angle of vision, in different weather and light conditions. Each painting in the series shows the view seen through mist. The varying density of the mist reduces or enhances the colour and tone in the paintings. The forms of the bridge and chimneys beyond are reduced to silhouettes, an effect which is enhanced by *contre-jour* lighting.

The effects created in **Waterloo Bridge. (Cloudy day)** (fig. 19) are clearer and less dramatic when compared to others in the series. However the colour and lighting work together to create the atmosphere of a stormy winter day. The clear reds added to the traffic on the dark bridge give the picture a sharp colour focus across the centre of the composition, around which soft pinks and oranges are set against the dull blues and greens. Evidently Monet emphasised the forms and added the accents of red by re-working the painting at a later stage. Indeed, the majority of the paintings were re-worked in his studio after he had returned to Giverny. Monet would often define a form or burst of sunlight later, using more distinct, sketchy brushmarks.

Japanese Bridge

In 1893 Monet began to construct a water garden on a strip of marshy land which he had recently bought below his house at Giverny. Monet constructed the pond by diverting a small stream from the river Epte. He filled the pond with water lillies and around it planted flowers, trees and bushes. He also constructed a wooden footbridge. This garden was the theme for a series of eighteen paintings in 1899, twelve of which were exhibited a year later at Durand-Ruel's gallery. This series became known as the *Japanese Bridge*.

At Giverny, Monet created a horticultural paradise collecting exotic plants from all over the world. Although he denied there was any direct reference to a Japanese garden, visitors often commented upon the particularly Eastern feel of the water garden. The bridge reminded them of those seen in Japanese prints (see fig. 22) and Monet had surrounded the pond with bamboo, ginko trees and Japanese fruit trees.

The majority of the paintings in the series have a square format. Monet took a low view-point, close to the water, looking directly towards the bridge. The water leads the viewer into the distance, while the bridge spans the pond, cutting across the canvas just above the central line. For some of the paintings he moved slightly to show the left bank, but in all of them he maintains this simple, essentially symmetrical composition.

In both format and composition the paintings seem to follow on from the *Mornings on the Seine* series. However, they do not evoke the same sensitivity to momentary qualities and atmospheric conditions seen in the earlier series. In contrast, Monet seems more interested in the description of textures that the garden offered. In the National Gallery painting (fig. 21) Monet used a variety of brushwork to describe the trees, shrubs, willows and iris beds. These textures are interrelated and unified by their reflections and the carefully coordinated colour scheme of blues and yellows. This balance between texture and colour characterises the series creating a highly decorative effect. In some of the canvases his colours are quite garish with heightened reds, yellows and blue-greens, while the brushwork is activated to resemble calligraphic strokes.

By 1900 Monet's reputation was secure. As an aging man, with failing eyesight, he could retreat to his self-made sanctuary to concentrate upon his great passion – the communion and description of the natural world: *'I have been able to identify myself with the created world and absorb myself within it.'* The 'Japanese Bridge' was the first series based upon a subject which was to preoccupy Monet for the rest of his life. Apart from his visits to London (1899, 1900 and 1901) and Venice (1908) he worked solely at Giverny producing over five hundred canvases. The pond was enlarged several times over the next decade and as he worked obsessively upon the theme he began to concentrate upon the surface of the water and the abundant lillies. These *Nymphéas* paintings, with their almost abstract use of colour and paint, were the extreme extension of the series concept.

Chronology

1840	Born in Paris, moves to Le Havre as a child.
1850's	Monet gains a reputation in Le Havre for his caricatures of local figures. Meets Boudin who persuades him to become a landscape painter.
1959-60	Travels to Paris, briefly attends the Académie Suisse, meets Pissarro.
1861-2	Military service; visits Algeria with the Chasseurs d'Afrique.
1862	Meets Jongkind on the Normandy coast; returns to Paris to study at the Atelier Gleyre, meets Bazille, Sisley and Renoir.
1863	Salon des Refusés – Manet's painting *Déjeuner sur l'Herbe* exhibited.
1864	Gleyre's studio closes. Monet, Bazille, Sisley and Renoir work at Chailly, near the Village of Barbizon.
1865	Meets Cézanne. Two of his seascapes accepted by the Salon.
1866	Meets Manet. Paints *Le Déjeuner sur l'Herbe*. Portrait of Camille exhibited at the Salon.
1867	*Woman in the Garden* refused by the Salon.
1869	Paints at La Grenouillère with Renoir.
1870	June: marries Camille Doncieux and takes her to Hôtel Tivoli in Trouville. July: travels to London to escape the Franco-Prussian war. Meets Pissarro and the dealer Durand-Ruel in London.
1871	Visits the National Gallery and the South Kensington Museum (Victoria and Albert Museum) with Pissarro, works rejected from the Royal Academy in London, returns to Paris via Holland, settles at Argenteuil, which is his main base until 1878.
1872	Visits Le Havre where he paints *Impression: Sunrise*.
1872-3	Durand-Ruel buys a number of paintings from Monet.
1874	First Impressionist exhibition, Monet's painting *Impression: Sunrise* is derisively quoted by the critic Leroy.
1876	Second Impressionist exhibition, Monet exhibits some of his La Grenouillère pictures.
1876-88	Monet and his family suffer extreme poverty, eventually moving to the cheaper neighbourhood of Vétheuil.
1877	Paints his series of Gare St Lazare. Exhibits at the third Impressionist exhibition.
1879	Exhibits in fourth Impressionist exhibition. Sept: death of Camille.
1880	Does not show at the fifth Impressionist exhibition. One-man show at the offices of the newspaper 'La Vie Moderne'. Working on Normandy coast at Petites-Dalles.
1881	Does not show at the sixth Impressionist exhibition. Dec: moves from Vétheuil to Poissy, with Alice Hoschedé and her children. Painting on the coast around Trouville.
1882	Exhibits at the seventh Impressionist exhibition. Painting at Pourville.
1883	Paints at Étretat on the Normandy coast. One-man show at Durand-Ruel's gallery. Moves from Poissy to Giverny.
1884	Paints on the Mediterranean coast, at Bordighera and Menton.
1885	Exhibits in Georges Petit's fourth *Exposition Internationale*. Paints at Étretat.
1886	Does not exhibit at the eighth (final) Impressionist exhibition. Paints at Étretat, Belle-Isle in Brittany and Holland. Exhibits at Petit's fifth *Exposition Internationale*.

1887	Makes first sales to Boussod and Valadon, through their branch manager, Theo Van Gogh.
1888	Paints at Antibes, Mediterranean coast. Ten Antibes seascapes exhibited at Boussod and Valadon. Refuses Légion d'Honneur.
1889	One-man show at Boussod and Valadon. Paints at Fresselines on River Creuse in Massif Central. June: major joint retrospective exhibition with Rodin at Georges Petit's gallery.
1890	Works on *Grainstacks* series. Purchases Giverny.
1891	One-man show at Durand-Ruel's gallery, includes fifteen of the *Grainstacks*. Summer-autumn: paints *Poplars* series.
1892	Exhibition of fifteen Poplars at Durand-Ruel's gallery. Feb-Apr: paints Rouen Cathedral. Marries Alice Hoschedé.
1893	Feb-April: paints Rouen Cathedral. Begins construction of water garden at Giverny.
1895	Jan-Apr: paints in Norway. Exhibition at Durand-Ruel's gallery includes twenty paintings from *Rouen* series.
1896	Feb-Apr: paints on Normandy coast at Pourville, Dieppe and Varengeville. Summer: begins series of *Mornings on the Seine*.
1897	Jan-Apr: paints on Normandy coast. Summer: continues *Mornings on the Seine* series.
1898	June: exhibition at Petit's gallery includes twenty-four *Falaises* paintings and fifteen *Mornings on the Seine* series.
1899	Summer: begins first series of his water garden. Sept-Oct: paints in London.
1900	Feb-Apr: paints in London; exhibition at Durand-Ruel's gallery includes twelve paintings of his water garden (*Japanese Bridge* series).
1901	Feb-Apr: paints in London.
1903	Begins second series of water garden which continues until 1908.
1904	May: exhibition of thirty-seven paintings from *London* series at Durand-Ruel's gallery.
1908	Sept-Dec: paints in Venice.
1909	May: exhibition of forty-eight paintings of the water garden at Durand-Ruel's gallery.
1911	May: death of Alice Monet.
1912	Exhibition of *Venice* paintings at Bernheim Jeune gallery. Cataracts in both eyes diagnosed: his eyesight deteriorates over the next decade.
1914	Begins construction of new studio (finished 1916) in his garden for execution of monumental Water Lily Decorations.
1922	Water Lilly Decorations presented to the State, for installation in the Orangerie.
1926	Dec: dies at Giverny.

9.4 Aromatherapy

ACTIVITY 9.4

Choose either part 1 or part 2. The photocopiable source material is on pages 166–174.

1 Your local library is planning to run a series of evening events for the general public, based on the theme of health and leisure and called 'Lifestyle'. One evening is going to be centred on alternative approaches to medicine and healthcare. As part of the programme for that evening, you have been asked to give a talk on one particular form of alternative healthcare, aromatherapy.

   Your talk will take place towards the middle of the evening's programme, following a demonstration and explanation of massage. The library has an overhead projector you can use, as well as a display stand for any other visual aids you may wish to bring.

   You have been asked by the programme coordinator to assume that most of your audience will be new to forms of alternative medicine. Your talk should last about ten minutes and be about 800 words long. You have also been asked to produce a fact sheet summarising the main points of your talk.

2 An alternative health clinic in a large town near you is planning to hold an open day to raise public awareness of the services it has to offer. As well as talks, demonstrations and a tour of the facilities, the centre is planning to mount an exhibition about the main areas of its activities, to be positioned in the entrance foyer of the centre.

   You have been asked to produce the text for the aromatherapy part of the exhibition. The material will be mounted on commercially available boards. It would be helpful to the organisers if you could provide notes on a suggested layout of your material, including suggestions for photographs to be used to illustrate your text. You have been told that your text should not exceed 750 words.

Your personal guide to Aromatherapy

From 'Personal Guide to Aromatherapy' by Penny Rich in *Good Housekeeping* Magazine, April 1994.

Although highly fashionable and much in the news, aromatherapy is not always fully understood. It is, in fact, the modern name for the ancient knowledge of healing and improving health using fragrant, natural ingredients. Called essential oils, these are found in herbs, plants, flowers, fruits and the bark, roots or resin of some trees. Essential oils give the aroma to the plant, but they also contain dozens of complex chemicals with the power to beautify skin or speed healing, or to put you to sleep or numb a headache.

Even if you think you have never come across these oils before, all of us are affected by them each day. Every time you peel an orange, the essential oil squirts out of tiny pockets in the peel and evaporates into the air, releasing its bitter-sweet, tangy, citrus smell. This can have a refreshing but relaxing effect on the way you feel.

When you take flowers to someone who is ill in hospital, you are using aromatherapy to help them feel better. The essential oils that give the smell to a bouquet of jasmine, roses, geranium and lavender, for instance, all contain chemicals that relax the nervous system and instantly improve spirits.

THE ULTIMATE HEALER

Pure essential oils have a greater effect on both the mind and body than any benefits you get from simply sniffing flowers. Although researchers can't isolate all of the hundreds of molecules in each plant oil, they do know that the oils can penetrate human skin and enter the bloodstream, that some have anti-inflammatory and antiseptic properties, that others trigger the body's natural relaxing or stimulating hormones, and that many have such potent effects on the mind that you can go from a bad mood to a good one within minutes.

Essential oils come from different parts of plants and offer many different benefits. In some, they accumulate in the petals, in others they are found in the roots, rinds, stalks, seeds, sap, nuts, leaves or bark. Sandalwood gathers in the heart wood of the trees but only once the tree is 40 years old. Jasmine is most concentrated in the petals on the night when the flowers are only one day old, so, to get the best oil, they need to be hand-picked before dawn.

Rose is the rarest (and most expensive) essential oil of them all, with two tons of fresh petals in full bloom yielding a mere two pounds of essential oil. The humble orange tree, on the other hand, produces three different oils – neroli from the blossoms, petit-grain from the leaves and orange oil from the fruit rind – all of which have different properties.

HOW TO USE OILS

Because essential oils are so potent, they need to be diluted before you apply them to the skin. If you are pregnant, or suffer from asthma or epilepsy, always consult a qualified practitioner before using essential oils. Here are some of the most beneficial ways of using them.

Massage: add 7-10 drops of your chosen essential oil (see below) to 30ml (2tbsp) of carrier oil for dilution (good carriers are sweet almond, sunflower, safflower and grapeseed oils).

Relaxing: 5 drops lavender, 4 drops sandalwood. **Invigorating:** 5 drops geranium, 3 drops peppermint. **Sensual:** 3 drops each jasmine and neroli, 2 drops sandalwood. **For sore muscles:** 6 drops lavender, 4 drops eucalyptus. **For a hangover:** 5 drops each of rose and lavender massaged into temples, eyes, scalp, neck and top of shoulders.

Baths: add 5 drops of the stronger smelling oils (eucalyptus, lemon, peppermint) or 10 drops of the more fragrant ones to the surface of bath water once the taps are turned off. Use just one oil or mix up to 3 oils per bath.

▶

Camomile has a light aroma that recalls apples and straw. It has a relaxing, calming effect and is good for sunburn or rashes.
Eucalyptus has a strong, refreshing camphor smell. A powerful antiseptic, it also clears the head, so is good for fever, colds and flu.
Geranium has a sweet, fresh, soothing aroma. It acts both as a tonic and a sedative, and is particularly good for relieving anxiety.
Jasmine has a romantic, sensual and exotic aroma. The oil acts as an aphrodisiac and gently changes your mood.
Lavender has a fresh, clean scent. Both soothing and stimulating, it is a good all-round skin healer.
Lemon has a unique, tangy, citrus smell. It is refreshing and stimulating.
Neroli soothes dry skin and is an hypnotic sedative and anti-depressant.
Peppermint has a 'peppery' smell. It invigorates, refreshes and clears the head.
Rose is romantic and sensual. It can boost your confidence, beat stress, and is great for mature skin.
Sandalwood is the base of most green or woody perfumes. It acts as a sedative and stimulant, so is good for insomnia, stress and loss of libido.
Ylang-Ylang has an exotic jasmine scent. It stimulates the senses and lifts negative moods.

Relaxing: 5 drops each of lavender and rose. **Energising:** 3 drops peppermint, 5 drops geranium. **For summer:** 3 drops each of jasmine, rose and neroli. **For winter:** 2 drops eucalyptus, 3 drops each of sandalwood and ylang-ylang. **For sleeplessness:** 3 drops each lavender, neroli and camomile.

Showers: add 10 drops of essential oil (lavender, lemon, neroli, orange and peppermint are the most invigorating) to 60ml (4tbsp) of carrier oil; dip a damp sponge in and rub over your body while under the shower.

BEAUTY TREATMENTS

Choose the most relevant essential oil to suit your skin type (see below) when following these recipes.
Face exfoliator: add 3 drops of essential oil to 30ml (2tbsp) of sweet almond oil; add finely ground oatmeal and desiccated coconut to make a paste, then rub in circles over face and rinse off.
Mature skin: neroli. **Dry skin:** 2 drops rose, 1 camomile. **Oily skin:** 2 drops geranium, 1 drop lavender.
Steam facial: add 5 drops of essential oil to 1 litre (1 3/4 pints) boiling water in a bowl; bend over with a towel over your head to trap the steam. Continue until the steam subsides.
Mature skin: 3 drops rose, 2 drops neroli. **Dry skin:** 3 drops jasmine, 2 drops camomile. **Oily skin:** 3 drops geranium, 2 drops lavender.
Cleansing face mask: 2 drops geranium, 3 drops lavender, 1 drop rose in 30ml (2tbsp) hot water and enough finely ground oatmeal to make a soft paste. Leave to dry then rinse off.
Moisturising face mask: 3 drops each neroli and rose in 30ml (2tbsp) apricot oil with 5ml (1tsp) warmed clear honey and enough finely

ground almonds to make a paste. Leave for 5 min then rinse off.
Face moisturiser: add 3 drops of essential oil to 30ml (2tbsp) of carrier oil; massage gently into skin. **Mature skin:** neroli. **Dry skin:** rose. **Oily skin:** lavender.
Body exfoliator: add 3 drops of essential oil to 5ml (1tsp) of carrier oil. Add to 75ml (5tbsp) of coarse sea salt; rub into skin and shower off.
Dry skin: rose. **Oily skin:** 2 drops lavender, 1 drop lemon. **Sensitive skin:** camomile.

AROUND THE HOME

As well as influencing your mood essential oils also have practical uses in the home.
As a room spray: add 10 drops of the relevant essential oil (see below) to 600ml (1 pint) of water in a pump-action bottle; spray into the air to freshen a room when needed.
Refreshing: lavender to kill airborne germs and to relieve tiredness and tension. **Purifying:** peppermint to remove the smell of stale cigarette smoke and improve mental alertness.
As a vaporiser: add 8 drops of the relevant essential oil (see below) to a saucer of hot water and place on top of a radiator; top up every few hours as needed.
Relaxing: sandalwood (romantic).
Uplifting: ylang-ylang (sensual) or jasmine (euphoria and confidence).
For sleeplessness: camomile (mellowing). **For coughs and colds:** eucalyptus (mental alertness).
To repel insects: sprinkle 5 drops of the relevant essential oil (see below) onto a damp cloth; wipe around wardrobes, shelves, draws, windows and door frames, or apply a few drops to pillows or hems of curtains.
For mosquitoes: citronella. **For flying insects:** lemongrass. **For ants, fleas and most insects:** tea tree.

USING ESSENTIAL OILS AT HOME

From Aromatherapy by Gill Martin, published by Vermilion.

The aromatherapist will often give you some essential oils to take away and use at home. These may be for you to use in the bath, to massage into your body or to use for inhalations. The essential oils will usually be given to you ready diluted with a label saying what they are and how to use them.

If you become interested in aromatherapy and the effects of the essential oils, you may want to begin experimenting on your own at home. This is fine as long as you use the oils with care, asking advice from your aromatherapist or by using a good book. Though essential oils are safe and free from side-effects when used by a qualified therapist, they are very concentrated substances and need to be used in the correct way. Below are some brief guidelines about using the essential oils and some suggestions about the ones that will be most useful to you at home.

Methods of application

Details of how essential oils are administered are given in Chapter 3, but here is an idea of dilutions of the oils suitable for home use. Some oils can cause irritation to sensitive skins (these are indicated below) so begin with half the normal dilution stated and increase to normal if no reaction is experienced. The same applies when using oils

for elderly people and children. It is possible to use essential oils for babies and very young children, though only in very weak dilutions – I would advise just using the mildest of oils, camomile and lavender, and not exceeding a dilution of one drop of essential oil to 1 teaspoon of carrier oil. If using the oils in a child's or elderly person's bath always dilute them in base oil first and agitate the water well to disperse the oil.

Baths – Add 4 to 8 drops of neat oil to the surface of the water just before getting into the bath and mix the water to spread the oil. Alternatively mix up a bottle of bath oil by using any vegetable-based carrier oil (see page 40) and adding up to 50 drops of one or more essential oils to 50ml of base oil. Always store this bath oil in a dark glass bottle and if you are going to keep it for more than a month add a teaspoon (5ml) of wheatgerm oil to stop it going rancid. Use 1 teaspoon for each bath and to get full benefit from the oils, soak in the bath for twenty minutes.

Massage oils – Make up as for bath oil, but only use 25 drops of essential oil per 50ml of base oil (see page 40). Store, as for bath oil, in a dark glass bottle. Alternatively make up as required, using 6 drops of essential oil to 1 tablespoon of carrier oil.

Vaporization – Place 5 to 8 drops of essential oil on a source of heat (see page 36, Chapter 3 for possibilities).

Compresses – Use 6 drops of essential oil to 1/2 pint of hot or cold water. Put a flannel or a piece of lint on top of the water, wring out and apply to the affected area. Leave until the compress has returned to body temperature (for cold water) or has cooled down (for hot water), then reapply as above. Repeat three to six times or until pain has eased.

Inhalations – Begin with 1 drop of essential oil to a drop of near boiling water. Increase the number of drops if necessary up to a maximum of 6 drops. If you don't have the facilities to do this, put a couple of drops of oil onto a handkerchief or inhale directly from the bottle.

Internal – Although some books on aromatherapy recommend taking essential oils on a spoon of honey, in honey water or on a sugar cube, I strongly advise against it. If you are interested in taking the oils as an internal medicine, then find an aromatherapist with a medical/clinical background who will make up the oils for you.

Ten essential oils for home use

Ask a group of aromatherapists to choose the ten essential oils they use most often and the lists might differ considerably. Each therapist has his or her own favourites, though I doubt if lavender would be missing from any of the lists. Below is my list of ten. I've tried to pick a variety of aromas from floral to exotic, citrus and herby and a combination of sedatives and stimulants. The list of further reading on pages 101–102 suggests some of the many books available at the moment, which deal with the oils in more depth.

Lavender – A great all-round oil with a familiar fragrance, it is often described as 'balancing' in its nature. It is good first aid oil, useful for burns and cuts, headaches, colds, flu and sinusitis, as well as for general aches and pains. It is helpful for cases of anxiety and depression and also for insomnia. A lavender bath is a perfect end to the day, easing a tired body and mind at once. Lavender also blends well with most other oils.

Rosemary – Having slept well after a lavender bath, get yourself going next morning with a stimulating rosemary one. Rosemary helps the memory and concentration and eases general debility and fatigue. It is a useful tonic for the heart, liver and gall bladder and makes a good inhalant for respiratory problems. As an oil which is useful to ease muscles after physical exertion, try combining it with lavender for an after sports rub. It is also warming when used for rheumatic pain and has a history of being a good hair tonic. It can cause irritation to sensitive skin and should be avoided by pregnant women and epileptics.

Bergamot – This refreshing citrus oil comes from the fruit of the bergamia tree which grows mainly in southern Italy.

Juniper – Juniper has been known since ancient times for its antiseptic properties. It is a great cleanser, useful for helping the body eliminate toxins and therefore indicated for the treatment of arthritis, gout and rheumatism, as well as conditions such as water retention and obesity and also some forms of eczema. It is also helpful for clearing the mind, especially if problems stem from contact with other people.

It is a wonderfully uplifting oil, useful for many forms of anxiety and depression. It is particularly useful for urinary infections such as cystitis and also for skin care, especially for oily skin and acne. If you like Earl Grey tea (which is China tea with added oil of bergamot) you are sure to like this essence. This oil makes the skin more sensitive to the sun's rays so don't use it before going out in strong sunlight.

Basil – I am including basil in the list, primarily for its use as a nerve tonic. It is used for clearing the head and is great when you need to use your intellectual faculties. It can help with indecisiveness and with certain cases of anxiety and depression. Though it is a stimulant, I find it useful mixed with lavender in cases of insomnia, where sleeplessness is caused by thoughts churning through the mind. It is good for respiratory problems and for sluggish or congested skin conditions. Use in weak dilution as it can cause irritation.

Geranium – There is some dispute between authorities on essential oils as to whether this light, floral oil is sedative or stimulating. It does have a pronounced effect on the nervous system, though different people tend to react to it in different ways. It is useful for skin conditions, being both antiseptic and anti-inflammatory and has a balancing effect on the hormonal system. It is good for poor elimination and conditions such as cellulitis.

Eucalyptus – Eucalyptus is probably best known for its affinity with the respiratory tract, where its antiseptic, expectorant and antispasmodic actions are helpful in relieving conditions from sinusitis to bronchitis. It has a cooling effect on the body, so is good for feverish conditions. It can also be used for muscular aches and pains and rheumatoid arthritis. As an antiviral agent, it can be used in epidemics of 'flu or measles to help stop the spread of infection.

Camomile – Camomile is a calming and soothing oil, which is useful for many children's ailments. It is a mild oil and in very weak dilutions (though never to be taken internally) it can be very helpful for treating teething pains and soothing fractious toddlers. It contains a powerful anti-inflammatory constituent and is also analgesic, so is useful for aches and pains, from backache, headaches and ear ache to stomach ache and period pains. On an emotional level, its action mirrors that on a physical plane, that is it is good for states of restlessness and nervous irritability.

Sandalwood – Sandalwood is my favourite choice from the exotics for its woody, sensuous smell and indeed it is renowned as a potent aphrodisiac. It is highly sedative and can be useful for depression of the tense, uptight kind. In skin care its action tends to be balancing and it has benefits for dry, dehydrated skin and oily skin alike. It also has an affinity with the respiratory tract. It is useful for bronchitis sufferers to use as a chest rub at night as it eases the congestion, while at the same time by helping with the anxiety caused by breathlessness, it helps promote sleep.

Rose – Though rose is extremely expensive, it is a beautiful floral oil which is seen as being particularly feminine. It is a useful antidepressant, especially when the depression is linked in some way to female sexuality. It is an aphrodisiac, useful for frigidity and impotence and is useful for coping with grief. For skin care, it is helpful for ageing and sensitive skins. Though costly it needs only to be used sparingly.

Carrier Oils

Any vegetable oil can be used as a base for massage. This does *not* include baby oil, which is mineral based and therefore will not penetrate the skin. The following are my favourites.

Grapeseed – This is a light, easily absorbed, inexpensive oil which is good for full body massage. It is completely odourless, making it an ideal base for essential oils.

Wheatgerm – This rich oil is high in vitamin E, which is good for any skin condition, from dry skin to healing scars and blemishes. Use up to 25 per cent combined with another base oil.

Aromatherapy and you

From *Practical Aromatherapy* by Shirley Price, published by HarperCollins.

In ancient times, in the East, people visited their 'physician' not when they were ill, but when they were *well*. If they became ill just after the visit and the physician hadn't foreseen the illness, they didn't pay the bill! Physicians then were mainly acupuncturists, and *kept* the bodily systems in health by regular treatment of all the pressure points on the body, thus ensuring good blood and lymph circulation.

This theory still holds good. If we could keep our blood circulating freely, and the lymph moving at its correct speed round the body, illness would be greatly reduced.

But how many of us have a perfect circulatory system? And why not?

Because, somehow, we all manage to produce tension of some sort in our bodies, either physical or emotional. Not only does modern living lessen the amount of exercise we give our muscles, but we sit with our spines bent, we walk incorrectly, and when we stand we let our weight go first on one leg and then the other.

The effect of this is that the muscles are working overtime to keep us in our 'slovenly' positions; tissues and organs are pushed into the wrong place, pressure is applied where it shouldn't be, and the result of all this is that the blood and lymph have greater difficulty in flowing round evenly, and the toxins and waste carried by the venous and lymphatic systems cannot be eliminated quickly enough by natural means, so therefore they escape into the tissues, causing disturbances in the bodily systems and organs.

The emotional tensions we suffer from bring much more serious consequences. Heart and blood pressure symptoms, sometimes due to incorrect diet, are more often brought about by tension due to such things as traffic (this affects us more than is realised if it is a daily double trip through a large city) or the pressure of work, or the day to day worries which some people cannot seem able to deal with in a relaxed manner.

The other effect on the blood circulation is simply the ageing process. In youth, while we are growing, the body cells are constantly dying and being renewed in every single part of the body; every cell of every bone, muscle, nerve and every drop of blood is continually being replaced, therefore all the organs, including the skin, go through this never ending process of renewal.

As we get older the dead skin cells take longer to be thrown off and longer then to be absorbed (or rejected – in the case of skin) and the new cells take longer to form and grow. This slowing down of the regeneration of cell tissue shows itself by a slowing down of all bodily functions, loss of energy, possible constipation, muscles without good tone, loose and often sallow skin.

It is now generally accepted that our state of mind can affect the state of our body, and many illnesses today have a psychosomatic origin. The mind is the most important part of us, yet it is the one thing we cannot touch or even X-ray. It is responsible for our feelings; love, hate, generosity, selfishness, anger, fear, embarrassment, frustration – what a long list of components there are that make up the mind.

Plant hormones, or essential oils, have much the same effect on us, except that they have first to be chosen to suit the emotional upset, and then be applied and hence absorbed into the bloodstream.

If the art of relaxation can be practised, whether by yoga, mind dynamics or by hypnotherapy, then the mind itself can be ▲

strengthened in positive application, and a better life can be lived by the owner of that mind, positively affecting both career and health.

Given belief in ourselves – practically anything is possible; it is known that *determination* to succeed is almost inevitably followed by success, in just the same way that determination not to succumb to the common cold will almost inevitably send it away with only the mildest of symptoms. It is no use trying to help someone who does not believe in the method of help used, because their mind has automatically put up a negative barrier.

People already convinced about natural products are more prepared to believe that brown bread is better for health than white bread, than someone who thinks health food eaters are just cranks; bread is just bread and white bread tastes better anyway!

By making a conscious effort at a quiet time in each day to relax, and train our minds to run only in *positive* channels leading to success and health, we can greatly minimize the negative channels, which only lead to physical and mental disease.

Finally, the other aspect of living which affects our bodily and mental health is our *diet*. Eating a lot of artificially prepared foods containing chemical additives is not conducive to good health or clear skin. The skin reflects the condition of the body, which in turn gives us an idea of the state of mind. No skin preparations, natural or otherwise, will improve the texture or appearance of a blemished skin so long as unsuitable foods are continually being eaten.

Unnatural (i.e. refined and artificially processed) foods are a contributory factory to ill-health, as much as physical and mental stress. With this type of diet we are putting the digestive system under tension, too many rich foods can lead to troubles in the gall bladder or stomach.

Too much sugar (white, refined) and animal fat is often said to contribute to heart disease. The organs of elimination become congested because too many refined starchy foods are eaten, with not enough roughage, and this in itself can cause malfunctions within our systems.

What a sad story!!

However, all these harmful effects can be considerably minimized if we can keep our blood circulation as healthy as possible. Unaided we can see that we eat only the correct foods and not too much of them! (The recent high-fibre diet is an excellent example of giving the roughage needed to keep the bodily systems in good order, and one can eat a lot yet lose weight with this diet, too!).

When the mind is at peace, we experience only positive feelings like love, contentment, selflessness, generosity, etc., and our body responds by being healthy. At other times anger, fear, jealousy, selfishness and depression dominate, and these adversely affect the state of the body. Hormones are released automatically to cope with these feelings and try to return them to a positive state as quickly as possible.

We can make sure that we not only get plenty of exercise, but also re-educate ourselves in the art of sitting, standing and moving correctly. The trouble is that these things need a conscious effort of will, and we have to be really keen and interested to persevere until it simply becomes a habit.

Nonetheless, there is another way to help ourselves, and this is by the use of essential oils.

We tend to wait these days until we showing symptoms of illness before going to be treated, whereas prevention is, and always will be, better than cure. Aromatherapy is a very good way of *keeping* healthy, and should be used as a preventative treatment ▲

in the same way as the Chinese used acupuncture centuries ago.

Methods of getting essential oils into the blood stream (other than by taking them internally) are by baths, inhalations, compresses and various types of massage, varying from simple effleurage through to more advanced forms such as lymph drainage, neuro-muscular technique and shiatsu (where the acupressure points on the meridian lines are used.)

Aromatherapy Body Massage

Regular aromatherapy treatments from a qualified person will bring about, and retain for much longer, a dramatic improvement in well-being and general health, increased vitality and a visible improvement in the texture and colour of the skin.

Every treatment is individual – no two people are exactly the same, and many factors must be taken into consideration when deciding on the form the treatment will take, and the oils that will be used.

Essential oils are extremely concentrated. One drop in 10 to 20 ml of carrier oil will give an identifying aroma, and in fact the true aroma of the plant is obtained by the correct dilution of the essence. Essential oils in their natural state give off too strong an aroma to be pleasant, and this is an important fact to consider. Each one gives off its own peculiar waves, affecting different people in various ways. From the nose a message is sent to the brain, and either pleasure or distaste results as the brain interprets the message.

Our olfactory nerves play a very big part in the success of the treatment so the oils chosen must, when blended in the carrier oil, have an aroma that is pleasing. If the person doesn't like the fragrance it is necessary to find other oils which have the same therapeutic effect but are more appealing aesthetically.

A good aromatherapist will blend oils taking into consideration the volatility, the effects on the bodily or mental conditions, and also the effect of the aroma on the person being treated. This last, as mentioned earlier, is of equal importance to the other two, when essential oils are being used in a specialized aromatherapy massage.

It is important, and interesting, to note that after an aromatherapy massage the oil should never be washed off, and a bath or shower should not be taken until six to eight hours after treatment, to ensure full absorption of the essential oils (even though they appear to have penetrated fully).

Should there not be an aromatherapist in your area it is possible to help yourself by using essential oils in various ways, all of which will be dealt with in detail in the following chapters.

Answers to selected practice activities

Answers are given to selected activities in Units 1–3 only, to give students confidence that they are answering questions accurately.

ACTIVITY 1.3

Extract 2:
To Hedli: poem by Louis MacNeice. Example of a poem; fiction, narrative, non-chronological. Features: broken lines; one long sentence; unusual use of words, etc.

Extract 3:
Handling ponies. Taken from *The Manual of Horsemanship*. Example of instructive writing; non-fiction, non-narrative, non-chronological. Features: prose printed left to right; specific vocabulary but non-technical; slightly old-fashioned use of language; 'A horse... *favours* the same thing being done in the same way each day', etc.

Extract 4:
A letter to the author about non-display of a tax disc. Example of a letter; non-fiction, non-narrative, non-chronological. Features: layout distinctive; vocabulary associated with letters: 'Thank you for your letter...'; legal language: reference to legal act; longer than average sentences, etc.

Extract 5:
A letter to John Hamilton Reynolds from John Keats. Example of a letter; non-fiction, narrative, non-chronological. Features: complex sentences; first person; esoteric subject matter, etc.

Extract 6:
Advert for computer program. Example of an advert; fiction, narrative, chronological. Features: parodies a poetic style: short sentences; laid out as a poem; specific vocabulary relating to computers, etc.

Extract 7:
From *Harnessing Peacocks* by Mary Wesley. Example of prose fiction; fiction, narrative, chronological. Features: direct speech; description of characters and action, etc.

ACTIVITY 2.2

1 The Garden of Love

> I went **to the** Garden **of** Love,
> And saw what I had never seen:
> **A** Chapel was built **in the** midst,
> Where I used to play **on the** green.
>
> And **the** gates **of this** Chapel were shut,
> And 'Thou shalt not' writ **over the** door;
> So I turned **to the** Garden **of** Love
> That so many sweet flowers bore;
>
> And I saw it was filled **with** graves,
> And tomb-stones **where** flowers should be;
> And Priests **in** black gowns were walking their rounds,
> And binding **with** briers my joys and desires.

2 Snowdrop

> Now is the globe **shrunk** tight
> round the mouse's **dulled** wintering heart.
> Weasel and crow, as if **moulded** in brass,
> **move** through an outer darkness
> Not in their right minds,
> With the other deaths. She, too, **pursues** her ends,
> brutal as the stars of this month,
> Her pale head heavy as metal.

ACTIVITY 2.5

b I (*noun phrase*) could hear (*verb phrase*) the piano (*noun phrase*).

c It (*noun phrase*) was (*verb phrase*) the smell (*noun phrase*) of innocence (*adverbial: prepositional phrase*).

d The little girl (*noun phrase*) performed (*verb phrase*) her journey (*noun phrase*) in safety (*adverbial: prepositional phrase*).

All three sentences follow a similar pattern of noun phrase/verb phrase/noun phrase, followed by an adverbial in both **c** and **d**.

e The first event (*noun phrase*) of any importance (*adverbial: prepositional*) in the family (*adverbial: prepositional*) was (*verb phrase*) the death (*noun phrase*) of Mr. Norris (*adverbial: prepositional*).

f The Mis Bertrams (*noun phrase*) were now fully established (*verb phrase*) among the belles (*prepositional phrase*) of the neighbourhood (*adverbial: place*).

g Fanny (*noun phrase*) had no share (*verb phrase*) in the festivities (*adverbial: prepositional*) of the season (*adverbial: time*).

The phrase pattern in these sentences is more varied, with more use of adverbials, two of which separate the noun and verb phrase in **e**.

ACTIVITY 2.6

2   He had often come up here (*main clause*) without stating his purpose to his mother (*subordinate: noun clause*).

The fact that his coming 'up here' is mentioned first, in the main clause, sets his action up as one of defiance.

3   Mushrooms and toadstools are names given to a large group of gill-bearing, fleshy fungi (*main clause*) which are collectively given the scientific name of 'agarics' (*relative clause*).

The main classification is established and given first in the main clause, followed by additional information in the relative clause.

4   When going for country walks, (*adverbial clause*) one often comes across a railway line (*coordinate clause*) and (*conjunction*) it is tempting to walk along either beside the rails or stepping on the sleepers between the rails (*coordinate clause*).

Locating the event described in the second coordinate clause by mentioning time and then place gives the effect of 'zooming in' like a camera.

5   Stella Artois Dry has linked up with one of the UK's top street fashion labels, Dr. Martens, (*coordinate clause*) and (*conjunction*) will be bringing their gear direct to your local watering-hole (*coordinate clause*).

As in sentence 1, the two clauses in this sentence are syntactically balanced as coordinate, but the information given in the second depends upon that given in the first.

ACTIVITY 2.9

a   The year (*subject*) began (*verb*) with lunch (*object*).

The sentence follows a standard SVO pattern. The use of an inanimate object such as a year as a subject, though, makes the focus of the sentence a state rather than a person. Its juxtaposition with 'lunch', an activity associated with people, personifies the year, making food of prime concern not only to people but also to time.

b   The proprietor of the restaurant (*subject*) was dressed (*verb*) for the day (*adverbial*) in a velvet smoking jacket and bow tie (*object*).

The sentence follows an SVO pattern with an adverbial clause embedded within it (SaVO). This added clause provides information about the subject's dress, which has the effect of making us aware that there are other ways to be dressed. Although the gender of the proprietor is not stated, the description of the dress leads us to believe that it is a male rather than a female.

c   He (*subject*) beamed (*verb*).

Although the verb *to beam* is usually associated with a facial expression, generally that of smiling, by using it on its own the effect is to convey an expansiveness and happiness which extends beyond the face to the whole body.

d Henriette (*subject*) was (*verb*) a brown, pretty woman (*complement*) with a permanent smile and a spinster's enthusiasm for reaching the finishing line of each sentence in record time (*adverbial*).

The verb in this sentence takes a complement instead of an object, with the long adverbial adding to the description it provides.

e The cold weather cuisine of Provence (*subject*) is (*verb*) peasant food (*complement*).

This sentence has the same SVC pattern as the previous one, but the absence of any description through adverbials makes it into a simple factual statement.

f Over the next four or five days (*adverbial*), we (*subject*) came to know (*verb*) the chemist (*object*) well (*adverbial*).

This sentence has a less uniform pattern to it; the adverbial by coming first highlights the time it took to get to know the chemist, thus implying that they saw a lot of him or her.

ACTIVITY 3.3

a active
b passive; passive
c active; passive; active
d active
e active
f passive
g passive
h active; active

Additional material for Activity 6.4

Scene on the Kawa Dol

Miss Quested: It's almost a mirage.

Dr. Aziz,
May I ask you something rather
personal?

You were married, weren't you?

Doctor Aziz: Yes, indeed.

Miss Quested: Did you love your wife when
you married her?

Doctor Aziz: We never set eyes on each other
till the day we were married. It
was all arranged by our families.
I only saw her face in a photograph.

Miss Quested: What about love?

Doctor Aziz: We were man and woman. And
we were young.

Miss Quested: Dr. Aziz.
Did you have more than one
wife?

Doctor Aziz: One.
One in my case.

I'll be back in a moment.

Specimen NEAB examination questions, answers and comments

This section is based on the Examiner's Report for the 1994 NEAB GCSE Advanced English paper. It provides you with sample examination questions for stylistics, followed by answers which have been written in exam conditions and an examiner's general comments on the answers. These are *not* presented as ideal or 'model' answers, but are intended to give you some idea of the kinds of answers that have been written in examinations. Following each question, answer and comment are some questions for you to consider about the strengths and weaknesses of each one.

The second part of the section gives a summary of an examiner's comments on transformation exercises. Again, these are general, but very important, points to be borne in mind when undertaking this kind of activity.

Section A: Stylistics

Question 1

Poem A, *The Kiss,* was written by Siegfried Sassoon and published in 1916. Poem B, *Arms and the Boy,* was written by Wilfred Owen and published in 1918. Siegfried Sassoon and Wilfred Owen were both officers in the trenches during the First World War.

Comment on how the poems use language.

In your answer you may comment on vocabulary, figurative language, overall structure, grammar, phonology and any other linguistic matters you think are relevant to the meaning and tone of the poems.

Poem A

The Kiss

To these I turn, in these I trust –
Brother Lead and Sister Steel.
To his blind power I make appeal,
I guard her beauty clean from rust.

5   *He spins and burns and loves the air,*
And splits a skull to win my praise;
But up the nobly marching days
She glitters naked, cold and fair.

Sweet sister, grant your soldier this:
10   *That in good fury he may feel*
The body where he sets his heel
Quail from your downward darting kiss.

Poem B

Arms and the Boy

Let the boy try along this bayonet-blade
How cold steel is, and keen with hunger of blood;
Blue, with all malice, like a madman's flash;
And thinly drawn with famishing for flesh.

5   *Lend him to stroke these blind, blunt bullet-leads,*
Which long to nuzzle in the hearts of lads;
Or give him cartridges whose fine zinc teeth
Are sharp with sharpness of grief and death.

For his teeth seem for laughing round an apple.
10   *There lurk no claws behind his fingers supple;*
And God will grow no talons at his heel,
Nor antlers through the thickness of his curls.

Examiner's comments

Many of the strongest answers to this question moved from subjective interpretation of the poems to an awareness of how language contributes to their overall meanings. Good answers recognised that the poems explored attitudes to weapons of war in different ways, and the use and effects of imagery, and especially personification, were generally appreciated, though few candidates were aware of eroticism as well as the violence in *The Kiss*. The explicit violence and the characterisation of the soldier as 'innocent' in *Arms and the Boy* were widely discussed in stronger answers, with some answers showing sensitivity to the tenderness/violence contrasts, though the imagery in the last stanza was often seen as relating to the devil rather than to animals. Some answers also identified the supplicatory tone in *The Kiss*.

In some answers a promising discussion of how the developing thought of the poems is embodied in the language may have been because candidates imposed expectations about 'war poetry', possible derived from study at GCSE. Some candidates found *Arms and the Boy* more difficult, leading to imbalanced answers.

The following answer makes explicit comparisons between the poems.

Candidate's answer to Question 1

Both poems begin with interesting titles which make an impact. Poem A is called *The Kiss*, which can immediately be juxtaposed with the context of the poem – war. A kiss is something of affection and love whilst war is the exact opposite of such qualities. Sassoon emphasises this even more with the definite article before the noun, giving the kiss even more importance. Poem B also uses the definite article for emphasis in the title – 'the Boy'. Again this is highlighting a collocation of the words 'Arms' and 'Boy', with 'Arms' producing an image of war and combat contrasted with the innocence of childhood.

The contrasts continue in both poems. In the second stanza of Poem A, 'loves the air' is follows by 'splits a skull' in the next line, foregrounding the violence of the latter phrase. In the next line, 'nobly marching' is followed by 'glitters naked'. This contrast of nobility and nakedness is particularly useful in the context of a war poem, as the poet is revealing the lack of nobility in the subject – 'a gun'. In

Poem B, the use of verbs provides an interesting contrast, as in 'stroke... bullet-leads' and '[bullets] long to *nuzzle* in the hearts of lads'. These 'gentle' verbs are being used to great effect, making the violent actions which they are describing seem even more so.

Personification is the main tool of figurative language in Poem A. 'Brother Lead' and 'Sister Steel' not only produce gender images of what are obviously a bullet and a gun, but also give them religious qualities through the use of 'Brother' and 'Sister'. This could be trying to strike out against religion, or maybe just trying to shock the reader. Whichever, the personification succeeds in slotting the bullet and gun neatly into gender roles – the 'power' of the bullet, and the 'beauty' of the gun. With the latter we see yet more contrasting imagery – beauty representing what can only be described as killing devices. Personification is fully used to great effect in line 9 – 'Sweet Sister, grant your soldier this'. The possessive pronoun 'your' creates the impression that the gun is owning the soldier and not the other way round. Sassoon here is illustrating the power of the gun over any human.

Animation is used in Poem B and is also connected with guns – 'fine zinc teeth', 'nuzzle in the hearts of lads'. 'Nuzzle' has already been discussed, yet when combined with 'teeth' creates a very animal-like impression, maybe in an attempt to make the weapon seem wild, almost out of control. The repetition of 'sharp' in the next line emphasises the danger and impact of the cartridges for which the teeth were a metaphor. The use of 'famishing' in line 4 can also be related to the animal imagery.

The lexis of the two poems is quite similar at times. Both the adjectives 'blind' and 'cold' are repeated in each poem. 'Blind' refers to bullets both times and illustrates the misguidedness of war, i.e. a blind bullet cannot see where it is going and will kill regardless. The use of 'cold' is, once again, creating a certain kind of imagery. Steel is cold but in this context it is meant more in the sense of 'a cold killing' or 'a cold-blooded murder' – 'cold' as in evil.

The last stanza of Poem B is very powerful: 'claws', 'talons' and 'antlers' are referring to the devil. Saying his teeth are 'for laughing round an apple' is to increase the boy's innocence. 'There lurk no claws', 'God will grow no talons' and 'nor antlers through thickness of his curls' is basically deflecting any evil imagery (i.e. Beelzebub) from the soldier, contrasting it with his innocence – 'curls', 'laughing round an apple' – so as to shift the blame of war and killing away from him.

The alliteration in Poem A of 'Sweet Sister' (first line, last stanza) creates a more emphatic plea from the poet which ends the way it started – with the contrasting imagery of a 'kiss'.

Points to consider
How effectively does the candidate discuss particular words, phrases, images and contrasts?

Question 2

The following passage is from *Dombey and Son* by Charles Dickens, first published in 1848.

Florence Dombey and her maid, Susan Nipper, accompanied by a close friend, Captain Cuttle, have gone to ask advice from Captain Bunsby about the likely fate of Walter Gills, who has embarked on a long sea voyage. The passage begins as they approach Captain Bunsby's residence, a boat named the *Cautious Clara*.

How does the language in this passage convey impressions of Captain Bunsby?

In your answer you may comment on vocabulary, figurative language, grammar, dialogue, overall structure and any other linguistic matters you think relevant to meaning and tone.

'Clara a-hoy!' cried the Captain, putting a hand to each side of his mouth.

'A-hoy!' cried a boy, like the Captain's echo, tumbling up from below.

'Bunsby aboard?' cried the Captain, hailing the boy in a stentorian voice, as if he were half-a-mile off instead of two yards.

'Ay, ay!' cried the boy, in the same tone.

The boy then shoved out a plank to Captain Cuttle, who adjusted it carefully, and led Florence across: returning presently for Miss Nipper. So they stood upon the deck of the Cautious Clara, in whose standing rigging, divers fluttering articles of dress were curing, in company with a few tongues and some mackerel.

Immediately there appeared, coming slowly up above the bulk-head of the cabin, another bulk-head – human, and very large – with one stationary eye in the mahogany face, and one revolving one, on the principle of some lighthouses. This head was decorated with shaggy hair, like oakum, which had no governing inclination towards the north, east, west or south, but inclined to all four quarters of the compass, and to every point upon it. The head was followed by a perfect desert of chin, and by a shirt-collar and neckerchief, and by a dreadnought pilot-coat, and by a pair of dreadnought waistcoats: being ornamented near the wearer's breastbone with some massive wooden buttons, like backgammon men. As the lower portions of these pantaloons became revealed, Bunsby stood confessed: his hands in their pockets, which were of vast size, and his gaze directed, not to Captain Cuttle or the ladies, but the mast-head.

The profound appearance of this philosopher, who was bulky and strong, and on whose extremely red face an expression of taciturnity sat enthroned, not inconsistent with his character, in which that quality was proudly conspicuous, almost daunted Captain Cuttle, though on familiar terms with him. Whispering to Florence that Bunsby had never in his life expressed surprise, and was considered not to know what it meant, the Captain watched him as he eyed his mast-head, and afterwards swept the horizon; and when the revolving eye seemed to be coming round in his direction, said:

'Bunsby, my lad, how fares it?'

A deep, gruff, husky utterance, which seemed to have no connection with Bunsby, and certainly had not the least effect upon his face, replied, 'Ay, ay, shipmet, how goes it?' At the same time Bunsby's right hand and arm, emerging from a pocket, shook the Captain's, and went back again.

'Bunsby,' said the Captain, striking home at once, 'here you are; a man of mind, and a man as can give an opinion. Bunsby, will you wear, to oblige me, and come along with us?'

The great commander, who seemed by the expression of his visage to be always on the look-out for something in the extremest distance, and to have no ocular knowledge of anything within ten miles, made no reply whatever.

'Here is a man,' said the Captain, addressing himself to his fair auditors, and indicating the commander with his outstretched hook, 'that has fell down, more than any man alive; that has had more accidents happen to his own self than the Seamen's Hospital to all hands; that took as many spars and bars and bolts about the outside of his head when he

*was young, as you'd want a order for on Chatham-yard to build a pleasure-yacht with;
and yet that his opinions in that way, it's my belief, for there ain't nothing like 'em afloat
or ashore.'*

*The stolid commander appeared, by a very slight vibration in his elbows, to express some
satisfaction in this encomium; but his face had been as distant as his gaze was, it could
hardly have enlightened the beholders less in reference to anything that was passing in his
thoughts.*

*'Shipmet,' said Bunsby, all of a sudden, and stooping down to look out under some
interposing spar, 'what'll the ladies drink?'*

*Captain Cuttle, whose delicacy was shocked by such an inquiry in connexion with
Florence, drew the sage aside, and seeming to explain in his ear, accompanied him below;
where, that he might not take offence, the Captain drank a dram himself, which Florence
and Susan, glancing down the open skylight, saw the sage, with difficulty finding room
for himself between his berth and a very little brass fireplace, serve out for self and friend.
They soon reappeared on deck, and Captain Cuttle, triumphing in the success of his
enterprise, conducted Florence back to the coach, while Bunsby followed, escorting Miss
Nipper, whom he hugged upon the way (much to that young lady's indignation) with his
pilot-coated arm, like a blue bear.*

*The Captain put his oracle inside, and gloried so much in having secured him, and having
got that mind into a hackney-coach, that he could not refrain from often peeping in at
Florence through the little window behind the driver, and testifying his delight in smiles,
and also in taps upon his forehead, to hint to her that the brain of Bunsby was hard at it.*

Examiner's comments

Most of the stronger answers to this question noted the semantic field of sailing,
and particularly its realisation in imagery and lexis, concentrated on the physical
appearance and behaviour of Bunsby, often linking these to characterisation, and
identified the narrator's use of humour and irony. Some recognised the sources of
impressions of Bunsby, including direct narrator comment, narrator irony, direct
speech and imagery. Only a few answers commented on the contradiction
between the descriptions of Bunsby's behaviour and his characterisation as a
'philosopher' and 'oracle', though most noted the respect shown to him by
Captain Cuttle.

Some more limited answers offered inferences from the passage's content about
Bunsby's character, with limited reference to the part played by language. Some
answers used paraphrase of the text as a basis for comment. Some candidates
limited their own scope for comment by taking all aspects of the passage at face
value. Some answers described the content, language and style of the passage as a
whole, with limited focus on impressions of Bunsby. Some answers concentrated
on the physical descriptions of Bunsby early in the extract, and paid little or no
attention to the later interaction between characters.

The following answer contains detailed inferences about the appearance and
character of Captain Bunsby.

Candidate's answer to Question 2

The language used in the passage to convey impressions of Captain Bunsby is
extremely elaborate and laced with figurative language.

The description of Captain Bunsby begins in line 10 and the tone of the piece seems to change somewhat at this point from a quite calm narrative to an awesome tone which builds up an atmosphere and a sense of anticipation of Captain Bunsby's appearance. This change in tone leads the readers to believe that they are about to witness something great, or out of the ordinary. The writer obviously wants Bunsby's character to make an impression on the reader.

The writer uses a subordinate clause to intensify this sense of anticipation, i.e. 'coming slowly up above the bulk-head of the cabin' and this also provides the writer with a simile, 'another bulk-head', which accurately conveys a sense of awesomeness.

Throughout the whole description of Bunsby's appearance, the writer uses a large amount of figurative language, all of which is related to his seafaring qualities. An extended metaphor describes one of Bunsby's eyes and this is followed up in line 26 where the eye is described as if 'coming round in his direction', just like the action of a lighthouse. His hair is described with a simile referring to the points of the compass and it is first stated that Bunsby's hair is inclined to 'all four quarters of the compass' and 'every point on it'. This seafaring figurative language reinforces Bunsby's sailing roots in the eyes of the reader.

The sense of greatness which the writer immediately establishes in line 10 is made even greater by the way in which Bunsby is described as different parts, not as a whole person. Bunsby's head and hands are treated as completely separate entities, with the deliberate omission of any pronouns by the writer. Bunsby's head is not described as his head but 'This head', and Bunsby's hands are not in 'his' pockets, but 'in their pockets'. The omission of pronouns gives Bunsby an air of mystery and anonymity, as though he is quite a secretive man who seldom reveals himself to others on a physical or mental level. This is reinforced in line 18 where it is stated that 'Bunsby stood confessed' as though he had allowed himself to be looked upon on this occasion.

There is an extensive use of descriptive vocabulary with no head-word left unmodified. Adjectives are used exhaustively and wherever possible to continually enhance the description further. Bunsby's hair is described as 'shaggy', his chin a 'perfect desert', his face 'red'. This contributes to the extremely elaborate syntax. There is frequent use of the conjunction 'and' to link descriptive clauses, as though the writer is not satisfied until he has given a more thorough description.

When Bunsby talks, the writer again attempts to build up a sense of anticipation in the reader, with the three modifying adjectives 'deep', 'gruff' and 'husky' and the two subordinate clauses before the speech is submitted.

The writer continues to describe Bunsby even when the bulk of the description seems to be over and dialogue predominates. Captain Cuttle speaks to Bunsby and we are informed in the main clause of sentence 33 that 'the great commander ... made no reply whatever', and this should be sufficient, but instead the writer takes this opportunity to add two more descriptive subordinate clauses which reinforce Bunsby's seafaring quality. Bunsby is described as 'commander' and the writer modifies this more pretentious title with the adjectives 'great' and 'stolid'.

Bunsby's solid and unbroken profile is described with his almost humorous reaction to Captain Cuttle's exhaustive admiring comments, which is only 'a very slight vibration in his elbows', as though even the narrator himself cannot be sure of Bunsby's reaction.

Bunsby's solid seafaring profile is softened slightly towards the end of the passage with his actions towards the two female characters. Bunsby is described as testifying his delight in smiles and the passage concludes with a burst of humorous irony with the alliterated statement 'brain of Bunsby was hard at it'.

Throughout the passage, the narrator conveys a sense of admiration and adopts an awestruck tone in some places. This sense of mystery is kept quite constant throughout the passage so as to ensure the reader's curiosity about Bunsby's mysterious character.

Points to consider

1 How accurate are the candidate's inferences about Bunsby's appearance and character in this answer?
2 On the evidence of this answer, is the candidate's framework for describing language, in terms of lexis, grammar and figurative language, an adequate basis for commenting on this text?
3 How effective is the candidate's response to the tone of the passage?

Question 3

The following extracts are from *Roots* by Arnold Wesker, first performed in 1959. The first extract takes place near the beginning of the play and the second extract occurs near the end. Beatie Bryant, who lives and works in London, is visiting her family in Norfolk and her boyfriend, Ronnie, has arranged to visit, though he never appears in the play. Jenny is Beatie's sister, Frank is her brother, and Mr and Mrs Bryant are her parents. Jenny is married to Jimmy and Frank is married to Pearl.

How is language used in these extracts to convey ideas and relations between characters and to affect the audience?

In your answer you might comment on phonology, vocabulary, grammar, dialogue, overall structure and any other matters relating to meaning and tone.

---

1 JENNY.   *Look at her. No sooner she's in than she's at them ole comics. You still read them ole things?*

JIMMY.   *She don't change much do she?*

BEATIE.   *Funny that! Soon ever I'm home again I'm like I always was – it don't even seem I bin away. I do the same lazy things an' I talk the same. Funny that!*

JENNY.   *What do Ronnie say to it?*

BEATIE.   *He don't mind. He don't even know though. He ent never bin here. Not in the three years I known him. But I'll tell you* (she jumps up and moves around as she talks) *I used to read the comics he bought for his nephew and he used to get riled –* (Now BEATIE begins to quote Ronnie, and when she does she imitates him so well in both manner and intonation that in fact as the play progresses we see a picture of him through her.)
'Christ, woman, what can they give you that you can be so absorbed?' So you know what I used to do? I used to get a copy of the Manchester Guardian *and sit with that wide open – and a comic behind!*

JIMMY.   Manchester Guardian? *Blimey Joe – he don't believe in hevin' much fun then?*

BEATIE.   *That's what I used to tell him. 'Fun?' he say, 'fun? Playing an instrument is fun, painting is fun, reading a book is fun, talking with friends is fun – but a comic?*

A comic? for a young woman of twenty-two?'
JENNY.   (handing out meal and sitting down herself) *He sound a queer bor to me. Sit you down and eat gal.*
BEATIE.   (enthusiastically) *He's alive though.*
JIMMY.   *Alive? Alive you say? What's alive about someone who can't read a comic? What's alive about a person that reads books and looks at paintings and listens to classical music?*
There is a silence at this, as though the question answers itself – reluctantly.
JIMMY.   *Well it's all right for some I suppose.*
BEATIE.   *And then he'd sneak the comic away from me and read it his-self!*
JENNY.   *Oh, he didn't really mind then?*
BEATIE.   *No – cos sometimes I read books as well. 'There's nothing wrong with comics,' he'd cry – he stand up on a chair when he wants to preach but don't wanna sound too dramatic.*
JIMMY.   *Eh?*
BEATIE.   *Like this, look.* (Stands on a chair.) *'There's nothing wrong with comics only there's something wrong with comics all the time. There's nothing wrong with football, only there's something wrong with only football. There's nothing wrong with rock 'n' rolling, only God preserve me from the girl that can do nothing else!'* (She sits down and then stands again, remembering something else.) *Oh, yes, 'and there's nothing wrong with talking about the weather, only don't talk to me about it!'*

---

2   (There is a knock on the front door.)
BEATIE.   (Jumping down joyously) *He's here, he's here!* (But at the door it is the POSTMAN, from whom she takes a letter and a parcel.) *Oh, the silly fool, the fool. Trust him to write a letter on the day he's coming. Parcel for you Mother.*
PEARL.   *Oh, that'll be your dress from the club.*
MRS BRYANT.   *What dress is this then? I didn't ask for no dress from the club.*
PEARL.   *Yes you did, you did ask me, didn't she ask me Frank? Why, we were looking through the book together Mother.*
MRS BRYANT.   *No matters what we was doin' together I aren't hevin it.*
PEARL.   *But Mother you distinctly –*
MRS BRYANT.   *I aren't hevin' it so there now!*
(BEATIE has read the letter – the contents stun her. She cannot move. She stares around speechlessly at everyone.)
MRS BRYANT.   *Well, what's the matter wi' you gal? Let's have a read.* (Takes the letter and reads contents in a dead flat but loud voice – as though it were a proclamation.) *'My dear Beatie. It wouldn't really work would it? My ideas about handing on a new kind of life are quite useless and romantic if I'm really honest. If I were a healthy human being it might have been all right but most of us intellectuals are pretty sick and neurotic – as you have often observed – and we couldn't build a world even if we were given the reins of government – not yet any-rate. I don't blame you for being stubborn, I don't blame you for ignoring every suggestion I ever made – I only blame myself for encouraging you to believe we could make a go of it and now two weeks of your not being here has given me the cowardly chance to think about it and decide and I –'*
BEATIE.   (snatching letter) *Shut up!*
MRS BRYANT.   *Oh – so we know now do we?*
MR BRYANT.   *What's this then – ent he comin?*

MRS BRYANT.   Yes, we know now.

MR BRYANT.   Ent he comin' I ask?

BEATIE.   No he ent comin'.

(An awful silence ensues. Everyone looks uncomfortable.)

JENNY.   (softly) *Well blust gal, didn't you know this was going to happen?*

(BEATIE shakes her head.)

MRS BRYANT.   So we're *stubborn are we?*

JENNY.   *Shut you up Mother, the girl's upset.*

MRS BRYANT.   *Well I can see that, I can see that, he ent coming, I can see that, and we're here like bloody fools, I can see that.*

PEARL.   *Well did you quarrel all that much Beatie?*

BEATIE.   (as if discovering this for the first time) *He always wanted me to help him but I never could. Once he tried to teach me to type but soon ever I made a mistake I'd give up. I'd give up every time! I couldn't bear making mistakes. I don't know why, but I couldn't bear making mistakes.*

MRS BRYANT.   *Oh – so we're hearin' the other side o' the story now are we?*

BEATIE.   *He used to suggest I start to copy real objects on to my paintings instead of only abstracts and I never took heed.*

MRS BRYANT.   *Oh, so you never took heed.*

JENNY.   *Shut you up I say.*

BEATIE.   *He gimme a book sometimes and I never bothered to read it.*

FRANK.   (not maliciously) *What about all this discussion we heard of?*

BEATIE.   *I never discussed things. He used to beg me to discuss things but I never saw the point of it.*

PEARL.   *And he got riled because o' that?*

BEATIE.   (trying to understand) *I didn't have any patience.*

MRS BRYANT.   *Now it's coming out.*

BEATIE.   *I couldn't help him – I never knew patience. Once he looked at me with terrifying eyes and said, 'We've been together three years but you don't know who I am or what I'm trying to say – and you don't care do you?'*

MRS BRYANT.   *And there she was tellin' me.*

BEATIE.   *I never knew what he wanted – I didn't think it mattered.*

MR BRYANT.   *And there she were gettin' us to solve the moral problem and now we know she didn't even do it herself. That's a rum 'un, ent it?*

MRS BRYANT.   *The apple don't fall far from the tree – that it don't.*

Examiner's comments

Stronger answers examined dramatic impact and the relationships between Beatie and Ronnie and Beatie and her family, though sometimes at the level of inference from content. The best answers considered the contrasting values and cultures of the Bryant family and Ronnie, in some cases referring to differences between Ronnie's and Jimmy's ideas about 'fun'. Most answers made some comment on the use of non-standard dialect forms, and stronger answers contrasted this with the more standard forms used in Beatie's quotations from Ronnie, in some cases linking these to the contrasting values of Ronnie and the Bryant family.

Though some answers showed awareness that the extracts were part of a script written for performance, for example by referring to stage directions and authorial comment, many treated the text as natural conversation, often commenting in detail on features of regional dialect and accent and identifying characteristics of spoken language, but often without relating these to relations between characters, dramatic effect or the expression of ideas.

The following answer focuses directly on relationships between characters and dramatic effects throughout the answer.

Candidate's answer to Question 3

The first passage is used to build a picture, an idea of Beatie and the life she leads.

The first linguistic feature is the accent of the characters (the phonology of the words). It is evident from the spelling that there is an accent present and this is backed up by the fact that the characters are meant to live in Norfolk. Beatie speaks with the same accent; however, she explains that she only slips back into her accent when she returns home to Norfolk. (She could possibly use hypercorrection whilst in London?) The vocabulary that Beatie uses to create a picture of Ronnie, for example in line 11 of the text, 'Christ, woman, what can they give you that you can be so absorbed?' shows he is a serious person, who doesn't agree with all that Beatie does. This will affect the audience because as Beatie imitates Ronnie they will be able to create a picture of the striking differences between Beatie and Ronnie and imagine the relationship they have. Beatie's description of what Ronnie thinks and believes surprises her sister, who declares in line 17, 'He sounds a queer bor to me.'

With the responses that come from Jenny and Jimmy it is clear to see that their relationship is quite different from that of Beatie and Ronnie. Jenny and Jimmy come from the same area (shown by their accents) and are very similar, having the same ideas of what fun is. The use of vocabulary also helps to establish these images of the relationships. As Beatie impersonates Ronnie, she uses the vocabulary that he would use. It is quite different from the simple vocabulary and simple sentences that she and her sister and Jimmy have been using. This will again reinforce the idea to the audience that Ronnie is well educated and would not easily fit into the country life in Norfolk. The structure of the dialogue consists mainly of Jenny and Jimmy questioning Beatie about life with Ronnie: it always seems to be Jimmy or Jenny who gives the initiating utterance.

In the second passage, the rest of the family are present and the inter-relations within the family can be studied. Beatie shows the audience her excitement that Ronnie has arrived, using repetition to stress this – on discovering it is not Ronnie, the focus moves to Mrs Bryant (Beatie's mother). The vocabulary shows how stubborn and set in her ways Mrs Bryant is when insisting she is not keeping the dress. The way in which she says this to Pearl, her daughter-in-law, shows assertiveness and authority, as if she is used to being in charge and usually is in that relationship.

The audience are affected by the way Beatie is shocked by her letter. This demonstrates to the audience that it is bad news, and however much Beatie has mocked Ronnie she does really love him. The response Beatie receives from her mother stresses exactly what type of relationship they have. No sympathy is offered, or time to offer an explanation. Her mother takes the letter and reads it aloud. At this point the tone is extremely important to the effect on the audience. Mrs Bryant shows no emotion or compassion, she simply reads Beatie's business to the whole family. This demonstrates that these people are not very emotional or open with their feelings. Beatie does not have a close relationship with her mother. Mrs Bryant continues (after Beatie has retrieved the letter) with a series of terse sentences, repeating herself – for example, in line 24, 'Oh – so we know now do we?' and in line 26, 'Yes, we know now'.

At this point the dialogue includes many of the characters, all giving their opinion of the situation. Beatie is offered some sympathy by Jenny, who uses a strong tone to tell her mother to keep out of the situation. The vocabulary again is kept very simple throughout, as Beatie's mother continues in a very impersonal tone about Beatie being 'dumped' by Ronnie, as if to be saying 'I told you so'.

This piece is generally informal and colloquial, as dialogue would be expected to be within the family.

Points to consider

1 What evidence is there in the answer that the candidate has read the passages closely?
2 Is the framework used by the candidate for describing the language of the passages adequate for answering the question?
3 What strategies does the candidate use to ensure that her answer stays relevant to the question throughout?

Question 4

The passage which follows is from *A Paper House,* a book which describes the personal opinions of a journalist, Mark Thompson, on the conflicts in the former Yugoslavian Republic, based on his travels in the region during an intense period of conflict between Serbian and Croatian people in 1991. The passage describes Mark Thompson's journey from the resort of Budva to a town called Bar, and from there towards Belgrade, the capital of former Yugoslavia.

Identify the main effects of the passage, and discuss how language is used to achieve those effects.

In your answer you might comment on vocabulary, figurative language, dialogue, grammar, overall structure and any other linguistic matters you think relevant to meaning and reader response.

I had come to Serbia from Budva, on the Montenegrin coast. The streets there were lined with Belgrade-registered cars; the coast was packed with Serb holidaymakers whose favourite resorts in Croatia were out of bounds, and soon under fire.

The beaches were grubby and the mood was jovial. A teak-tanned beach bum in flowery bermudas sat beside my friend Sasa and smirked: 'Hey, shall we go to Knin to protect the Serbs, what about it?' On Montenegro's coast the war was a chat-up line.

July collapsed in vast electric storms. Under a graphite sky I bussed south, past the old royal resort of Milocer, where Serbia's political leaders were recreating themselves and their families: Democrats and Socialists and Renewalists savouring the seafood while Croatia burned.

The graffiti in Bar ranted 'THIS IS SERBIA'. At Bar I entrained for Belgrade.

The Bar–Belgrade line is an epic railway. From the coast the train climbs to Lake Skadar, pauses in Titograd, then embarks on a spectacular route through the Montenegrin hinterland, or rather above it. The line follows the Moraca gorge for a way, breaks across country to Kolasin, and dips into the Tara valley. After Mojkovac it switches to the valley of the Lim and exits to Serbia.

Railways in the Andes must look like this, pinned to the mountain like a curtain-rail, and feel like it too, clanking slowly over the points. Below the carriage windows, crags and scree cascade to tiny meadows and torrents. Montenegro appears a landscape of giant stone dunes, unfarmed, unhomed.

My status on the train from Bar changed from passenger to guest. Serb largesse enveloped me. My seat was only reserved as far as Prijepolje, but the new occupant wouldn't hear of me standing; he and his wife wedged up and insisted I make myself comfortable again. Opposite us a strapping widow poured coffee for everyone from an urn-sized flask. Beside her, a sleeping girl nestled in her boyfriend's arms.

The window seats were taken by a couple of engineers riding home to Valjevo. We talked about football for a bit; then I said how confused we were in Britain about the war in Croatia. They frowned unhappily and nodded that, yes, it was complicated for outsiders, but the thing was, the Croat fascists had to be stopped. The Serbs in Croatia were suffering genocide, as under the ustase *in the Second World War.*

But the ustase *killed hundreds of thousands of people, I said. In 1991 a few dozen Serbs and Croats were killed before the war began for real, in August. Now the war was killing far more Croats than Serbs. How could they say the situation was like 1941?*

They frowned again, and looked more unhappy. As usual at this point of a discussion, I was downcast by a sense of futility, but it was too late now to go back to football. I tried to look disarming, and their good nature overcame their bristling distrust, like a hedgehog uncurling after a false alarm. They began to talk about Serbs' sacrifices for the Croats and Slovenes since 1914, and how they were paid back with separatism. About the Albanians, separatists too. About the Macedonians, who were freed from the Turks by the Serbs in the Balkan Wars, and now wanted to separate.

So it continued. You would think these young engineers had lost the battle of Kosovo in 1389, rebelled with Karadjordje in 1804, beaten the Austrians in 1914, risen against the Axis in 1941, been terrorised in Kosovo in the 1980s. In Serbs' speech the people are conjured as one person, who is also Serbia; every generation becomes one generation, which is Serbia too. 'Serbia has had enough,' they warn you, like a lawyer whose client's Jobish patience is finally drained.

This speech compacts all Serbs into a 'we' that creates 'they', who are forever doing all manner of evil things to Serbia: bad-mouthing and subverting it, hating it, sapping its strength, killing its children.

Homogenising rhetoric was not exclusive to Serbs, of course; Croats and Albanians bind themselves just as passionately to their ancestors. What was unique to Serbs, as Yugoslavia died on its feet, was the stunning contrast between their self-image as projected in this piteous narrative, and the facts that were there for everyone else to see. There is no understanding Serbia without fathoming its wounded self-righteousness, its perception of itself as more sinned against than sinning.

Examiner's comments

The variety and serious purposes of the extract were well appreciated by candidates who attempted this question, and most answers engaged with the meaning and content of the text, and understood the author's interpretation of the situation. In some cases this may have compromised candidates' detachment, though most attempted at least a degree of comment, particularly of the political aspects.

The stronger answers showed response to the complex mixture of styles and purposes in the text, identifying features of travel writing, reporting and personal response. Many of these answers also identified the narrative form of the passage and commented effectively on the use of anecdotes, narrative and dialogue and the direct authorial statements of opinion. The vivid visual imagery was appreciated in many answers, and some candidates commented effectively on the contrasts drawn between the beauty of the landscape and the horrors of the war.

Weaker answers tended to paraphrase, though even here some responses emerged, together with understanding expressed through selection of key words and phrases for comment.

The following answer shows response to the text's content as well as to its use of language.

Candidate's answer to Question 4

The passage is an emotive and factual account of life in Serbia. The effect it has on the reader is one of disturbing sobriety. The first paragraph is ironic, talking of holiday-makers on the Montenegrin Coast. When one thinks of war, one does not think of holiday, and the sentence 'whose favourite resorts in Croatia were out of bounds, and soon to be under fire' shows the war as a plain fact, the inevitability of 'soon to be under fire' and the hopelessness of the situation.

Again the second paragraph highlights all we do not know about the war, and the use of 'A teak-tanned beach bum in flowery bermudas' gives the reader the image of every beach bum they have seen on holiday, 'beach bum' showing carefree attitudes towards the war. This imagery only reinforces the seriousness of the war and the plight of the population. '"Hey, shall we go to Knin to protect the Serbs, what about it?" On Montenegro's coast the war was a chat-up line.' This dialogue shows that the Croats and Serbs have accepted war as a way of life, and sarcastically and ironically joke about it. The factual tone, with no empathy, reinforces the seriousness and sobering effect that the paragraph has.

'July collapsed in vast electric storms', shows comparison with the collapse of the state and the collapse of life. 'Democrats and Socialists and Renewalists savouring the seafood while Croatia burned' again is a comparison, the life of the ordinary people to the life of those inflicting war on them. No opinion is offered here by the writer; the statement says it all. The description of the journey to Serbia on the train shows the beauty of the land in torment. 'My status on the train from Bar changed from passenger to guest. Serb largesse enveloped me. My seat was only reserved as far as Prijepolje, but the new occupant wouldn't hear of me standing'. This short paragraph includes language that gives the reader a powerful image, as happens throughout the passage.

The short paragraphs, rarely offering opinion, have great impact on the reader, by just offering fact and plain dialogue: no explanation is needed, the choice of dialogue and recollection of stories say all that is needed to be said. The writer notices everyday occurrences that could happen anywhere, and contrasts them with war stories or observation.

When the author asks about the situation of war he is given replies of unhappiness, and fact, and he relays this to the reader simply, like a story, using all the names of the different opposing groups to show how big the war is. They speak as a collective: 'Serbia has had enough,' they warn the author. The author battles against himself to understand what is going on, and finishes, 'There is no understanding Serbia without fathoming its wounded self-righteousness, its perception of itself as more sinned against than sinning.' The writer tries to understand but can only see what is facing him, wounded men, women and children. 'Self-image as projected in this piteous narrative' shows he does not think he can do the Serbs any justice by writing about them, and no-one can begin to put into words what is happening. 'They frowned again, and looked more unhappy. As usual as this point of a discussion, I was downcast by a sense of futility, but it was too late to go back to football.' This comparison of the war to football shows desperate attempts to understand, and the futility of comparing war to football, but the lack of knowledge to compare it to anything he knows.

Throughout the passage there are short sentences, short paragraphs, and statements with no explanation: 'The graffiti in Bar ranted "This is Serbia". At Bar I entrained for Belgrade.'

All these devices add up to give a powerful passage, the descriptive language giving the reader an image to work on, and the chance to form an opinion for themselves if they need to. There is a sense of desperation throughout, but a stronger sense of unreality – can this really be happening? The whole piece is emotive and strong.

Points to consider
1 What evidence is there in this answer of the candidate's response to the text?
2 How much of the answer consists of comment on the text's content and how much relates to its use of language? How far is it possible or desirable to separate these aspects of the text?

Section B: Transformation exercises

You are writing a new, cohesive text: as such, any text you produce will be a *combination* of selected passages from the source material interwoven with your own writing to form a new, coherent text which fulfils the task set. Examiners' reports for one examination board constantly stress the following points:

- There is no need to copy long sections from source material: cut and paste if you need to.
- Referring to specific sections of the source material makes it difficult to get an overview during construction of the text you are writing, and makes the examiner a corroborator rather than an appreciative reader of a new, cohesive text.
- Editing the source material needs to be carefully done to avoid things such as: illogical change of tense; abrupt inter-sentence connections; mystifying exophoric and anaphoric references; extreme stylistic incompatibility; not supplying a sub-heading where one is needed; an excerpt beginning or ending in mid-sentence. You can write over and change any part of the cut and paste material to help the coherence of the overall text. For example, you may want to change pronouns from third person to first or vice versa; change the tense from past to present or vice versa; add your own beginning or ending to a sentence. You can treat the source material as part of the draft itself, and indeed it will help the overall coherence of the finished text if you make sure that syntactic elements such as pronouns and tense agree where they should in both your own writing and that of the source material.

- There is no hard or fast rule as to how much of the final text should consist of source material; the range is somewhere in the region between ten and seventy per cent. It is clear then, that you need to include *some* source material, but by the same token you also need to provide some text yourself and not to construct a new text by using *all* source material. Such a practice will almost inevitably lead to the things mentioned above.

You are constructing a new text in a *draft* form. Therefore:
- There is no need to use non-standard stationery – the stationery provided by the examination board is probably adequate.
- Using coloured pens can be useful in the draft, but some examination boards do not allow the use of red ink or correcting fluid, which should be avoided.
- The draft should be legible; have competently cut and pasted any source material used, and generally be physically well-presented. This does *not* mean that there cannot be any crossings out, additions etc., all of which are perfectly legitimate features of drafts. But your text is going to be read by someone else, and it makes their task easier if your text does not literally fall apart in their hands or become stuck together.
- Even though you are writing a draft, examiners will expect you, as students of English language, to spell accurately key words used in source material and examination questions.
- The easiest source material does not necessarily give rise to an easier task. There is no correlation between the perceived complexity of some source material and the kind of question asked.
- As a writer, you are in control of the tone and register of your text and the ways into which you weave it into a coherent narrative or exposition.

The following points look at ways in which effective communication can be achieved between writers and readers:
- It is not a good move to pass on to the reader instructions given in the task (e.g. 'The aim of this display is both to interest you and to enhance your understanding and enjoyment of Music Hall' or 'We hope to present this information in a lively and interesting way...'). Statements like these have an oddly contrary, contrived, even alienating effect. It is the writer's business to achieve these effects unobtrusively.
- Telling the editor what you hope to achieve is not a good idea; it suggests uncertainty on the writer's part (e.g. 'It is hoped that the reader will get a better idea if...'). Editors want positive intentions, though an occasional (i.e. *very* occasional) request for advice is acceptable (e.g. Is this too long? If so, cut at line 10).
- It does not take too much to damage a reader's or listener's confidence in the author or presenter. Beware dangerous moments such as the opening sentences or the links you are making between sections of text. In radio scripts, the worst pitfall is that moment when a contributor has finished a reading and the presenter carries on. If all you can think of is 'Wasn't that a good attitude to have, listeners?', better to say nothing and move on to the next bit.
- Neither readers nor listeners take kindly to being addressed as 'You out there...'. Nor are they impressed by one-word directives such as 'enjoy' in a text which, however entertainingly written, is expected to be reliably informative and fundamentally serious.

- By and large, Radio 1 models of communication work best on Radio 1.
- Handling subject matter with respect does not mean writing pompously, a style most candidates try to avoid at all costs, but it does mean avoiding occasional flippancies (e.g. 'Good stuff, this, isn't it?') that are hardly likely to impress the original writers of the source material or to assure the reader that you can be taken seriously. Worse still are jokes at the expense of the subject matter (e.g. Vera the Volcano; Freddy the mad scientist) or dubious familiarities, such as 'Thank you Tony' (to Anthony Burgess).
- Record and observe how documentary topics are handled on Radio 2. How do they compare with samples from Radio 4?
- As an exercise in stretching your writing potential, complete for homework a task you would not normally have chosen, featuring texts you would most likely not have used.
- Compare a transformation text that someone else has already done with the source material, judging for yourself how far the transformation fulfils the task it had been set.

The following three points are ones which you would do well to bear in mind as you progress through any examination course which requires you to transform source material into new text:

- Examine a wide variety of text types in order to identify features of text organisation and to begin to detect genre clues in the language used. Classifying texts and looking for tell-tale signs of register not only helps prepare you for this examination, it will also contribute to your proficiency in stylistic analysis.
- Do concentrated, detailed exercises transforming short texts to meet the needs of different audiences and purposes, of the kind given in Unit 9 of this book.
- Record and study programmes from Radio 2 and 4 and learn to 'read' the shape and tone of the programme as well as its content. The important thing here is not learning how to write for the BBC, but using a sound medium in order to discover something about 'voice' in writing and about the unintended signals and effects that can be written into a text. A similar exercise would be the 'writing out' of effects, signals and messages in other people's text.

Above all, you need to notice some of the things that happen when source material is converted into a piece of partly original writing. It is in this process that style, register, organisation, imagination and communicativeness begin to show themselves. These are the indicators that earn the marks.

Finally, in the time you have to read the source material before the examination, your main task is to become familiar with the content of the material. It is clear from examination scripts that good candidates know their way around the source material and are alert not just to the information contained, but also to the provenance of the original text. It is likely that if you can infer meanings in source texts, you will be able to imply meanings in your own texts. Similarly, it is likely that your ability to evaluate what *kinds* of texts are in the source material will result in you being able to make better judgements about what is appropriate in the texts you are constructing yourself.

Glossary

adjectival clause a clause that functions like an adjective to modify a noun, e.g. a relative clause.

adjective a class of words used to modify nouns e.g. *large, square, beautiful.*

adverb a class of words used to specify the circumstances of an action or event, e.g. the manner *(slowly)*, the time *(soon)*, the place *(here)*; it also includes conjunctive adverbs *(however)* and adverb particles *(up, out).*

adverbial a type of element in sentence structure, referring to the circumstances of the sentence rather than to a place or person, often expressed by an adverb, prepositional phrase or adverbial clause. Sometimes called an adjunct.

adverbial clause a clause, often introduced by a preposition or a subordinating conjunction *(if, because, although)* that functions as an adverbial in sentence structure.

alliteration a sound pattern in which the first sound of two or more words is the same. e.g. Peter Piper picked a pickled pepper.

archaism a linguistic feature which has become outdated and is no longer in current usage. It is generally found in particular varieties of language, such as liturgical or legal language or in regional **dialects.**

assonance like alliteration, assonance refers to a particular sound patterning in words using repetition, but it is applied to the repetition of a vowel sound within a word, e.g. 'Break, Break, Break/On thy cold, grey, stones' (Break and grey; cold and stone).

authorial voice the extent to which an author intrudes into the story he or she is telling, and whether the author knows everything about characters and events (authorial omniscience) or simply reports what he or she might have seen and heard (authorial reportage).

auxiliary verb a small set of verbs, including the modal verbs, *be, have* and *do,* which accompany lexical verbs and indicate modality, progressive and perfect aspects, and the passive voice.

clause a syntactic unit having the structure of a sentence but embedded in (functioning as part of) a sentence or sentence element.

coherence the sense that a text is a meaningful whole; the semantic counterpart of **cohesion.**

cohesion the grammatical and lexical devices that serve to make a text hold together, e.g. pronouns, conjunctive adverbs, lexical repetition.

collocation a lexical feature relating to the mutual attraction of words; if two words collocate, there is a greater likelihood of them occurring together, e.g. dark and night, sour and milk.

complement   an element of sentence structure, usually an adjective or noun phrase, which describes a subject (in SVC structures), typically after the verb *be*, or an object (in SVOC structures), typically after verbs such as *consider, regard*.

compound   a word made up of the combination of two independent words, e.g. *rainfall, see-through*.

conjunction   a class of words used for joining sentences or clauses; coordinating conjunctions *(and, but, or)* provide coordination, subordinating conjunctions (e.g. *because, if, when, although)* join subordinate adverbial clauses to a sentence.

consonant   in writing, every letter of the alphabet which is not a vowel. The vowel 'u' sometimes acts as a consonant at the start of words (e.g. a unicorn).

coordination   the joining together of sentences, clauses, phrases or words by means of *and, but, or*.

deictics   features of language which are not referred to directly, but are heavily dependent on context for their meaning, e.g. *here, there, now, then*, etc.

demonstrative   a subclass of determiners and pronouns, comprising the words *this/these, that/those*.

determiner   a class of words that accompany nouns in noun phrases, including identifiers and quantifiers.

dialect   the regional and social variations of a language, especially in respect of grammar and vocabulary.

ellipsis   leaving out part of a sentence which can be readily understood, to avoid unnecessary repetition, e.g. *Two pints (of beer) please.*

grammar   the study of the written forms of language, particularly in relation to words and sentences and, in modern grammar, texts.

graphology   the writing system of a language, handwritten or typed, and related features such as punctuation, paragraphing, spacing, size of print, etc.

imagery   a term commonly used in literary criticism to describe the way language creates visual images or pictures with words; e.g. the use of **metaphor** and **simile**.

intransitive   a type of verb that is not followed by an object in sentence structure, also used of such a sentence; compare **transitive**.

kenning   a compound word used poetically in Old English.

lexical items   items drawn from the stock of words belonging to the language as a whole.

lexis   the term used to describe the total stock of words of a language.

metaphor   a term from rhetoric, meaning the substitution of a word or phrase for a non-synonymous word or phrase, so that attributes of the new word are taken as referring to the original.

modality   those features of a text (including modal verbs, evaluative adjectives and adverbs and so on) which seem to encode the author's attitude to the content.

morpheme   a unit of word structure, e.g. a **prefix** or **suffix.**

morphology   the study of the forms of words, including inflections, derivations and compounds.

narrative   a story, happening or events, real or imaginary, which a **narrator** considers interesting or important.

narrator   a person who narrates, tells a story, either factual or fictional.

noun   the largest class of words, referring to objects, people, places, etc.

noun phrase   a group of words consisting of a noun as head, with accompanying modifiers such as determiners, adjectives, prepositional phrases.

object   an element of sentence structure, usually a noun phrase or clause, occurring with a transitive verb and representing the thing affected by the action of a verb.

participle   one of two forms of a verb: either present participle, with -*ing* suffix (e.g. *laughing*), or past participle, usually with -*ed* suffix (e.g. *laughed*).

part of speech   see **word class.**

passive voice   the counterpart to the active voice, where an active sentence is rearranged by making the verb passive (with *be* + past participle) bringing the object of the active sentence to subject position in the passive sentence, and (optionally) putting the subject of the active sentence into an adverbial phrase starting with *by*; e.g. active *The judge sentenced the prisoner to life imprisonment;* passive *The prisoner was sentenced to life imprisonment (by the judge).*

phonology   the study of speech sounds.

phrase   a group of words that form a unit in the structure of sentences, clauses or other phrases, usually having a head word and accompanying modifying words, e.g. noun phrase, verb phrase.

point of view   the angle of vision or perception by which the events of a narrative are narrated and presented.

possessive   adjectives and pronouns indicating possession, e.g. *my/mine, you/yours*, etc.

prefix   a morpheme that is attached to the front of a word to make a new word, e.g. *re-apply, anti-nuclear.*

preposition   a small class of words, including *along, from, in, of, on,* used for joining noun phrases to other elements of sentence structure.

pronoun   a class of words that function in place of nouns, including the personal pronouns *I, you, he, she,* etc.

punctuation   the system of marks in writing used to indicate the structure of sentences, including comma, semi-colon, full stop, question mark.

reflexive   a type of pronoun, including *myself, yourself, themselves,* used for emphasis *(She did it herself),* or for self-reference *(She has cut herself).*

register   the different kinds of tone and degrees of formality used in different situations of everyday life, e.g. a telephone conversation; a business letter; a sports commentary.

relative   used of relative pronouns (e.g. *who, which, whose)* which introduce relative clauses.

rhyme   where two phonemes in different words are matched for sound, e.g. end rhyme, where the last words of two consecutive lines rhyme.

rhythm   the pattern of stressed and unstressed syllables in a language. Regular patterns of stress produce different metrical patterns.

semantics   the study of meaning in all its aspects, especially in relation to words and sentences.

sentence   a syntactic structure, consisting of at least a subject and a verb, but also possibly containing a complement, object and adverbial(s).

simile   comparing a word or phrase with a non-synonymous word or phrase, usually by using *like* or *as,* e.g. *as white as snow; my love is like a red, red rose.*

standard English   the dialect of English that has been most codified and which is promoted as a national variety of English.

stress   the relative prominence given to syllables in speech, e.g. in *certain* the first syllable is stressed and the second unstressed.

stylistics   a sub-discipline of linguistics concerned with examining patterns of style (e.g. lexical choice, agency, modality, etc.) in texts.

subject   an obligatory element of sentence structure, which precedes the verb in the neutral form of declarative sentences.

subordination   when a clause is introduced by a subordinating conjunction (e.g. *because, if, since, when),* usually an adverbial clause, but also used of all other kinds of embedded clause.

substitution   the replacement of one expression for another e.g. I bought a new shirt but I don't like *it.*

suffix   a morpheme that is added to the end of a word, either to create a new word (e.g. *like-able, fair-ness)* or as an inflection (e.g. *paper-s, wait-ing).*

syllable   a phonological structure consisting of a **vowel** as nucleus and **consonants** as peripheral sounds; words may consist of one or more syllables, e.g. *can, canteen.*

synonyms   words which are orthographically different but mean the same thing, e.g. *gift* and *present; horse* and *steed.*

syntax   (the study of) the structures of sentences.

tense   the way in which verbs change to show the position of events in time; in English only past and present tenses are marked by inflections.

text   a sequence of written sentences marked by cohesion and coherence.

text type   texts classified according to purpose and structural features, e.g. narrative, descriptive, expository.

transitive   a type of verb that takes an object in sentence structure, also used of the sentence structure itself; compare **intransitive.**

verb   a class of words that refer to actions, events and states; subdivided into **auxiliary verbs** (see above) and lexical or main verbs.

verb phrase   a group of words with a lexical verb as head, which may be preceded by auxiliary verbs and the negative *not*.

vowel   a type of speech sound, articulated without any restriction to the airflow in the mouth and formed by the shape of the mouth; in writing, associated with the letters 'a', 'e', 'i', 'o', 'u'; compare **consonant.**

word   a basic unit of syntax, entering into the structure of phrases and sentences, composed of morphemes.

word class   a grouping of words according to shared features of reference, morphology and syntax, such as nouns, verbs, adjectives and prepositions.

Suggestions for further reading

Stylistics has gained in popularity over recent years, and more books are being published every year on the subject. The books listed below are not intended to be an exhaustive list, but give an indication of the growing range of books available.

Cameron, D. (ed): *The Feminist Critique of Language*, Routledge, 1990.

Carter, R. (ed): *Language and Literature: An Introductory Reader in Stylistics*, Allen & Unwin, 1982.

Carter, R. and McCarthy: *Language as Discourse*, Longman, 1995.

Carter, R. and Nash, W.: *Seeing Through Language*, Blackwell, 1990.

Fowler, R.: *Linguistic Criticism*, Oxford University Press, 1986.

Haynes, J.: *Introducing Stylistics*, Routledge, 1989.

Leech, G. and Short, M.: *Style in Fiction*, Longman, 1981.

Montgomery M., Durant A., Fabb N., Furniss T. and Mills, S.: *Ways of Reading: Advanced Reading Skills for Students of English Literature*, Routledge, 1992.

Nash, W.: *The Language of Popular Fiction*, Routledge, 1992.

Rimmon-Kenan, Shlomith: *Narrative Fiction: Contemporary Poetics*, Methuen, 1983.

Simpson, P. *Language, Text and Context*, Routledge, 1994.

Toolan, M. *Narrative: A Critical Linguistic Introduction*, Routledge, 1988.

Van Pcer, W. (ed): *The Taming of the Text*, Routledge, 1989.

Wales, K.: *A Dictionary of Stylistics*, Longman, 1989.

INDEX